Horizons in Theory and American Culture
BAINARD COWAN AND JOSEPH G. KRONICK, EDITORS

Going the Distance

Dissident Subjectivity
in Modernist
American Literature

Going the Distance

DAVID R. JARRAWAY

Louisiana State University Press
Baton Rouge

cloth 12 11 10 09 08 07 06 05 04 03
5 4 3 2 1
paper 12 11 10 09 08 07 06 05 04 03
5 4 3 2 1

Designer: Amanda McDonald Scallan
Typeface: Adobe Caston
Typesetter: Coghill Composition Co. Inc.
Printer and binder: Thomson-Shore, Inc.

The author is grateful to the following publishers for permission to quote from the works noted: Excerpts from *The Complete Poems 1927–1979* by Elizabeth Bishop. Copyright © 1979, 1983 by Alice Helen Methfessel. Reprinted by permission of Farrar, Straus and Giroux, LLS.

Excerpts from *The Collected Poems of Langston Hughes* by Langston Hughes, copyright © 1994 by The Estate of Langston Hughes. Used by permission of Alfred A. Knopf, a division of Random House, Inc.

Excerpts from *Collected Poems* by Frank O'Hara, copyright © 1971 by Maureen Granville-Smith, Administratrix of the Estate of Frank O'Hara. Used by permission of Alfred A. Knopf, a division of Random House, Inc.

Excerpts from *Selected Writings of Gertrude Stein* by Gertrude Stein, edited by Carl Van Vechten copyright 1946 by Random House, Inc. Used by permission of Random House, Inc.

Excerpts from *The Collected Poems of Wallace Stevens* by Wallace Stevens, copyright 1954 by Wallace Stevens and renewed 1982 by Holly Stevens. Used by permission of Alfred A. Knopf, a division of Random House, Inc.

Excerpts from poems by William Carlos Williams, from *Collected Poems: 1909–1939, Volume I,* copyright © 1938 by New Directions Publishing Corp. Reprinted by permission of New Directions Publishing Corp.

Library of Congress Cataloging-in-Publication Data

Jarraway, David R.
    Going the distance : dissident subjectivity in modernist American literature / David R. Jarraway.
        p.   cm.—(Horizons in theory and American culture)
    Includes bibliographical references (p.) and index.
    ISBN 0-8071-2802-3 (cloth : alk. paper)—ISBN 0-8071-2839-2 (pbk. : alk. paper)
        1. American literature—20th century—History and criticism.   2. Modernism
(Literature)—United States.   3. Subjectivity in literature.   4. Dissenters in literature.
I. Title.   II. Series.

PS228.M63 J37   2003
811'.509353—dc21   2002034042

The paper in this book meets the guidelines for permanence and durability of the Committee on Production Guidelines for Book Longevity of the Council on Library Resources. ⊗

For Ian,
actio in distans

Life is a train of moods like a string of beads, and as we pass through them they prove to be many-colored lenses which paint the world their own hue. . . . Of what use is genius, if the organ is too convex or too concave and cannot find a focal distance within the actual horizon of human life?
  —RALPH WALDO EMERSON, "EXPERIENCE"

We define the aura of [natural objects] as the unique phenomenon of a distance, however close it may be. If, while resting on a summer afternoon, you follow with your eyes a mountain range on the horizon or a branch which casts its shadow over you, you experience the aura. . . . This image makes it easy to comprehend the social bases of the contemporary decay of the aura. . . . Namely, the desire of contemporary masses to bring things "closer" spatially and humanly, which is just as ardent as their bent toward overcoming the uniqueness of every reality by accepting its reproduction.
  —WALTER BENJAMIN, *Illuminations*

There is not, nor has there ever been[,] any presence-to-self that would not call into question the distance *from self that this presence demands. "To deconstruct," here, comes down to showing this distance at the very heart of presence, and, in so doing, prevents us from simply separating an outdated "metaphysics of the subject" from another thinking that would be, suddenly, elsewhere.*
  —JACQUES DERRIDA, *Points . . . : Interviews, 1974–1994*

First of all and above all—distance.
  —FRIEDRICH NIETZSCHE, *The Gay Science*

Contents

Acknowledgments

I would very much like to thank all the editors and the several anonymous readers of the very distinguished journals in which some of the work gathered here has appeared previously in a somewhat different form, as follows: "'Absence of More': The Struggle for Queer Self-Authorization in Gertrude Stein," in *time-sense: an electronic quarterly on the art of Gertrude Stein* <*http://www.tenderbuttons.com/review.html*>, 1.1 (March 1998), 1–20 (Chapter 1); "Montage of an Otherness Deferred: Dreaming Subjectivity in Langston Hughes," in *American Literature* (Duke University Press), vol. 68 (December 1996), 819–47 (Chapter 3); "'Vanilla Hemorrhages': The Queer Perversities of Frank O'Hara," in *GLQ: A Journal of Lesbian and Gay Studies* (Duke University Press), vol. 4 (December 1997, 67–108 (Chapter 4); and, "'O Canada!': The Spectral Lesbian Poetics of Elizabeth Bishop," in *PMLA*, vol. 113 (March 1998), 243–57 (Chapter 5). I am also grateful to the Office of Research and Publications at Ottawa under the deanship of Jean-Louis Major, and subsequently Robert Major, for the very generous support it has lent over the past few years to the presentation of my work both in Canada and abroad. My gratitude is further extended to the Research and Publications Committee of the University of Ottawa for its generous assistance on the permissions. David Staines, Dean of the Faculty of Arts, has also afforded tremendous support of a more personal kind; and in like vein, Joseph Kronick, co-editor of the Horizons in Theory and American Culture series, and John Easterly, Executive Editor, both at Louisiana State University Press, have been encouraging and sustaining to a fault. Thanks also to LSU Press for providing me the singular pleasure of working with the eagle-eyed Eivind Boe on all the copyediting and the scrupulous Linda Webster on all the indexing.

I am also grateful for the several insightful exchanges among colleagues and friends that have helped me to think (and then rethink) threads of argument in this book on more occasions than I am now able to remember, and so a heartfelt thanks to Eric Savoy (University of Calgary), Robert K. Martin (Université de Montréal), Don Childs (University of Ottawa), and especially to the indefatigable members of the gay men's reading circle at Ottawa's After Stonewall bookstore: John Barton, Al Galashan, Blaine Marchand, David Rimmer, and Gary Sealey. Finally, warmest of all tributes to Ian McDonald, partnership with whom goes the distance of a dedication, and the exciting promise of what lies beyond.

Abbreviations

A William Carlos Williams. *The Autobiography of William Carlos Williams.* New York, 1967.

AC Frank O'Hara. *Art Chronicles: 1954–1966.* New York, 1975.

BCP Elizabeth Bishop. *The Complete Poems: 1927–1979.* New York, 1986.

BCPr Elizabeth Bishop. *The Collected Prose.* Ed. and intro. Robert Giroux. New York, 1991.

EK William Carlos Williams. *The Embodiment of Knowledge.* Ed. Ron Loewinsohn. New York, 1974.

EN John Dewey. *Experience and Nature.* La Salle, Il., 1989.

G&P Gertrude Stein. *Geography and Plays.* Ed. and intro. Cyrena N. Pondrom. Madison, 1993.

HCP Langston Hughes. *The Collected Poems of Langston Hughes.* Ed. Arnold Rampersad. New York, 1994.

HPP Gerard Manley Hopkins. *The Poems and Prose of Gerard Manley Hopkins.* Ed. W. H. Gardner. New York, 1990.

HsCP A. E. Housman. *The Collected Poems.* London, 1971.

MM Theodor Adorno. *Minima Moralia: Reflections from Damaged Life.* Trans. E. F. N. Jephcott. London, 1978.

OA   Elizabeth Bishop. *One Art: Selected Letters*. Ed. Robert Giroux. New York, 1994.

OCP   Frank O'Hara. *The Collected Poems of Frank O'Hara*. Ed. Donald Allen. Intro. John Ashbery. New York, 1972.

P   William James. *Pragmatism, and Four Essays from the Meaning of Truth*. New York, 1974.

PSP   Ezra Pound. *Selected Poems*. Ed. T. S. Eliot. London, 1973.

SCP   Wallace Stevens. *The Collected Poems of Wallace Stevens*. New York, 1954.

SS   Frank O'Hara. *Standing Still and Walking in New York*. Ed. Donald Allen. San Francisco, 1983.

SSW   Gertrude Stein. *Selected Writings of Gertrude Stein*. Ed. and Intro. Carl Van Vechten. New York, 1972.

WCP   William Carlos Williams. *The Collected Poems of William Carlos Williams, vol. 1: 1909–1939*. Ed. A. Walton Litz and Christopher MacGowan. New York, 1986.

Going the Distance

Introduction

Spices fly / In the receipt—It was the Distance— / Was Savory—
—EMILY DICKINSON, #439

"I embrace ALL," says Whitman. "I weave all things into myself." Do you really! There can't be much left of you when you've done. When you've cooked the awful pudding of One Identity.
—D. H. LAWRENCE, *Studies in Classic American Literature*

Ships at a distance have every man's wish on board. For some they come in with the tide. For others they sail forever on the horizon, never out of sight, never landing. . . . That is the life of men.
—ZORA NEALE HURSTON, *Their Eyes Were Watching God*

THERE is a brief anecdote near the beginning of Zora Neale Hurston's *Their Eyes Were Watching God* (1937) that I would like to use in order to say a number of things about the representation of dissident subjectivity in American Modernism throughout this study, and about a certain "distance" that I perceive historically to be at the center of its poetical articulations. In this anecdote, the narrator, Janie, talks about being raised by her grandma in West Florida among several children from another family—"quality white folks," she calls them—and of how a photograph taken of her and her young friends, one day, gave Janie her very first real experience of having an identity. As Janie recollects the experience,

When we looked at de picture and everybody got pointed out there wasn't nobody left except a real dark little girl with long hair standing by Eleanor. Dat's where Ah wuz s'posed to be, but Ah couldn't recognize dat dark chile as me. So Ah ast,

"where's is me? I don't see me." Everybody laughed. . . . Miss Nellie, de Mama of
de chillun . . . pointed to de dark one and said, "Dat's you, Alphabet, don't you
know yo ownself?" . . . Ah looked at de picture a long time and seen it was mah
dress and mah hair so Ah said: "Aw, aw! Ah'm colored!" Den day all laughed real
hard. But before Ah seen de picture Ah thought Ah wuz just like de rest.[1]

Now several aspects of this short account of Janie's incipient self-awareness happen to coincide with the way Modernism, in various contexts, has taught us to
think about human subjectivity—a subjectivity that, only until American Modernism comes into its own last century, we may have been inclined to assume was
merely a given or "objective condition."[2]

In the first place, we're struck by the fact that Janie seems almost unaware she
even *has* an identity until it is pointed out to her. Perturbed to think that identity
is something that she might unthinkingly presume to possess as fixed and stable—"Ah thought Ah wuz just like de rest"—Janie at the same time seems almost
ponderous in constructing, and perhaps even beginning, a whole new life for herself, starting with the words, "Ah'm colored!" Secondly, then, we notice that
Janie's "renewed" sense of self is not something that we can easily say emanates
deeply from within some essential core of her being. Rather, it manifests itself as
a constitutive effect of her interaction with those she finds immediately around
her, in a quite material and locatable sense. "Without you," Janie conceivably
might be saying to these others—this Other—surrounding her, "I'm nothing."[3]
And although that something, that nascent awareness of negritude, may impart
to Janie a sense of what seems, finally, to be authentic or legitimate or true about
herself, such a realization we should understand is retroactive—a cause for her
being in the world that turns out to be a misrecognition of what is more accurately termed one of that world's socially induced effects. I say effects, of course,
to remark, in the third place, on the myriad ways, foregrounded in American
Modernism, in which, pendant upon time and place, identities *do* get constructed, in all the gendered and classed and nationed inflections with which we
are by now familiar. But the socially induced effects of subjectivity's cultural construction, I hasten to point out, ought to be as apparent to us within the context

1. Zora Neale Hurston, *Their Eyes Were Watching God* (New York, 1990), 8–9.
2. Michael Omi and Howard Winant, "On the Theoretical Concept of Race," in *Race, Identity,
and Representation in Education*, ed. Cameron McCarthy and Warren Crichlow (New York, 1993),
5–6.
3. See Elspeth Probyn, *Sexing the Self: Gendered Positions in Cultural Studies* (New York, 1993),
Chapter 6.

of a *single* identity as well, especially when viewed in its evolution through time, about which we only begin to be made aware in Janie's case. "What we've learned about the structure of the way in which we identify," as Stuart Hall rightly points out, "suggests that identification is not one thing, one moment. We have now to reconceptualize identity as a *process of identification,* and that is a different matter. It is something that happens over time, that is never absolutely stable, that is subject to the play of history and the play of difference."[4]

Hall's important insight into the thoroughly fluid and processual character of identity construction—"subject-ivity [as] an ongoing practice," in Trinh Minh-Ha's coordinate formulation[5]—brings me to a final and somewhat ironic aspect in the anecdote from Hurston. I refer here to the photographic presentation, to Janie, of her newfound sense of selfhood. The realism of the photograph in this situation, in marrying self and image so seamlessly together, can appear to have the effect of vastly foreshortening the *process* of identification, turning a potentially active subject of production into merely a passive object of reflection. In realism's cunning elision of what linguists would call the subject of the enounced (Janie's image) and the subject of enunciation (Janie herself), experience is seductively given to us as something entirely free standing, and seemingly beyond human control or contrivance.[6] Indeed, one might even conceive a whole history of American literature inscribed in the irony of little Janie's photograph. For is it not true that American letters, to a certain extent, is constituted by a kind of dialectical interchange between constructivist and essentialist views of experience: between the great Romances of the American Renaissance and the Realism of the Gilded Age, between High Modernism earlier last century and the literature of social protest during the Depression, and between the post-Modern skirmishes of Minimalism and Magical Realism in fictional work closer to our own time?

4. Stuart Hall, "Ethnicity: Identity and Difference," *Radical America* 23 (fall 1989): 15, emphasis retained.

5. Cited in Maria Damon, *The Dark End of the Street: Margins in American Vanguard Poetry* (Minneapolis, 1993), 28. As Damon herself remarks, "There can be no 'final' self-identification; we understand ourselves differently every day. Deleuze and Guattari's useful prefix 'becoming-' evokes such a non-static notion of identity, as does Michael Fischer's term 'the reinvention of ethnicity'" (12). Cf. Damon's later notion of "'floating' subjects," and subsequent remarks on "manhood" as "a work in progress, constantly subject to re-vision," and allowing "fluidity into the concept of 'I'" on 60, 152, and 124; 190 and 240 are related.

6. See Antony Easthope, *Poetry as Discourse* (New York, 1983), 40–44. Cf. Elizabeth Bishop's "Poem": "Our visions coincided—'visions' is / too serious a word—our looks, two looks: / art 'copying from life' and life itself, / life and the memory of it so compressed / they've turned into each other. Which is which?" (*BCP*, 177).

In what follows in this study of Modernist poetic subjects and texts, I want to argue that American literature has been historically constituted by and around and through what almost seems effaced in the photographically foundational experience of subjectivity so ready to assign Janie her gender and race and class early in Hurston's novel: namely, a constitutive space, at once dark, mysterious, unspeakable, that Janie initially can only gesture toward as a place "where I wuz s'posed to be." In a literature as self-referential as America's, I view this lettered space as a radical locus of misrecognition—"Dat's you, Alphabet, don't you know yo ownself?"—a space inveterately and omnivorously and indefatigably about the cultural work of *distancing* texts as various as photographs, novels, even people themselves, from essences, origins, ends, and ultimate truths. Janie's own reassignment of identity in subsequent relationships with Logan Killicks, Jody Starks, and "Tea-Cake" Woods, in "her great journey to the horizons in search of people," provides one example of the distance Zora Neale Hurston is attending to— "the horizon," as she puts it, "[that] is still way beyond you." But the instance is legion. In response to the age-old demand to describe what is life and what is death, the ancient female sage in Toni Morrison's Nobel Prize address, we notice, is guardedly silent: "she does not [answer]; she keeps her secret; her good opinion of herself; her gnomic pronouncements; her art without commitment. She *keeps her distance*, enforces it and retreats into the singularity of isolation, in sophisticated, privileged space."[7]

Let me suggest even further that the "sophisticated privileged space," in Morrison's own words here, that opens up between the self and the perennial social demands placed upon that self—the "distance" picked up by Morrison once again in my title—is a space that has been kept and guarded in American literature for a very long time. "Of what use is genius," Emerson for instance remarks in his essay entitled "Experience" (1847), "if the organ is too convex or too concave and cannot find a focal distance within the actual horizon of human life?" Cultural pundits in America, however, are not always of the opinion that such distance has been perennially maintained. Ilene Philipson, for example, recently argues: "A belief that each individual carried within him or her a self that could not be fully apprehended, socially contained, and subsumed—that self-knowledge and acceptance were more important than conformity to ideals, roles, and standards originating outside the self—served [America, in "the social movements of the 1960s,"] only as a way out of the gray flannel straitjacket of the postwar period."[8]

7. Hurston, *Their Eyes Were Watching God*, 85; Toni Morrison, *Nobel Lecture: 1993* (Ottawa, 1993), 5, emphasis added.

8. Ralph Waldo Emerson, *Essays and Lectures*, ed. Joel Porte (New York, 1983), 474; Ilene Philipson, "What's the Big I.D.? The Politics of the Authentic Self," *Tikkun* 6 (1991): 53. "During the 1960s and early 1970s," Philipson goes on to explain, "the form of political discourse that promoted

To the contrary, therefore, if there is a resistant and ultimately uncontainable sense of self in America today that has become endeared to the heart of its Modernist literary practitioners, I propose to locate its burgeoning on the scene in American literature much before the social protest of the 1960s. In fact, in the canonical writing of the poet to whom I shall turn in a moment, namely Wallace Stevens, I shall endeavor to make plain that, following in the wake of Emerson, it is perhaps a quite substantial tradition of pragmatist thought that has historically provided a happy berth for both Hurston's and Morrison's distanciated subjects in the evolution of American letters. And I might start by pointing out that it is a tradition that only goes the distance of a fully regenerate identity when the Cartesian project of a totally humanist and totally self-regarding subjectivity may be said to have ended in America in the early nineteenth century. In its place, consciousness accedes to self-consciousness only through the recognition of a certain distance within (and from) itself, "an other," as Warren Montag refers to it, "through which alone [the subject] may be permitted to know itself"[9]—the very point that my opening anecdote from a Modernist text in the twentieth century, I hope, will have served only to recapitulate, rather than newly proclaim.

The chief impediment for American writers desirous of opening up a new space for subjectivity, beyond its foundational Cartesian lineaments, is logic, pure and simple, the very cornerstone of European Enlightenment, and of the tradition of rational thought in the Western world. In the American counter-tradition that provides the historical context within which to locate my exemplary poet in this introduction, it is the pragmatist, William James, who, in *A Pluralistic Universe*, declares: "For my part, I have finally found myself compelled to *give up the logic*, fairly, squarely, and irrevocably." James' complete aversion to logic lies in its severe curtailment of reality, parceling it out, as logic does, first into "the essences of things" rather than their "appearances," and then matching these to "concepts," and later, to "definitions," so that ultimately, "inasmuch as the thing *is* whatever the definition expresses, are we sure of apprehending the real essence of it or the full truth about it." Such a tyrannous methodology could only "defeat . . . the end it was used for"—that end, of course, being to come to terms with "Reality, life,

---

the authentic self coexisted along with the antiwar movement, a movement that [itself] could unify all the authentic selves within its compass while recognizing their uniqueness." But with the end of the Vietnam War, even "the unifying issue that held together all the groupings of authentic selves on the Left" became removed. Still later, there was some thought that the "new social movements" might bind American Identity together "into some unspecified, latter-day united front." But as Philipson concludes, "nothing took" (53).

9. Warren Montag, "The Emptiness of a Distance Taken: Freud, Althusser, Lacan," *Rethinking MARXISM* 4 (spring 1991): 37.

6 GOING THE DISTANCE

experience, concreteness, immediacy" that we should always find "exceeds our logic, overflows, and surrounds it." Theodor Adorno, the great cultural critic and Frankfurt School theoretician, and himself a sworn enemy to rationalism, concurs with James here on reality's potential to exceed every conceivable form of human thought. Because experience is so overwhelmingly rich and varied, "thought loses not only its autonomy in face of reality, but with it the power to penetrate reality," and can thus serve only as "a mere provisional abbreviation for the factual matter" lying beneath it (*MM*, 126).[10]

Adorno sets these ideas down in the form of a Nietzschean aphorism entitled, interestingly enough, "Keeping one's distance." In this aphoristic fragment, the distance that opens up between thought and experience, or otherwise between mind and world, or words and things, is valued for two reasons. First, it sustains the complexity and the variability of experience, knowledge about which becomes mediated by what Adorno elsewhere describes as a vast "network of prejudices, opinions, innervations, self-corrections, presuppositions and exaggerations" (*MM*, 80). But secondly, and more important, keeping one's distance builds into thinking the very necessary guarantee of political autonomy. For in withholding (and thereby protecting) the ultimate intelligibility of experience, it assures that there will always be in thinking "an element of exaggeration, of over-shooting the object, of self-detachment from the weight of the factual, so that instead of merely reproducing being[,] [thought] can, at once rigorous and free, determine it" (*MM*, 126–27).[11]

The crucial distinction here between thought merely passively reproduced and thought more actively determined thus averts the dangerous slippage between the

10. William James, cited in Ronald E. Martin, *American Literature and the Destruction of Knowledge: Innovative Writing in the Age of Epistemology* (Durham, 1991), 86. Cf. Hall, "Ethnicity": "When that installation of Western rationality begins to go and to be seen not as absolute, disinterested, objective, neutral, scientific, nonpowerful truth, but dirty truth—truth implicated in the hard game of power—that is the fourth [force] that destabilizes the old logic of identity" (12). Anent Adorno, see William James, *Pragmatism, and Four Essays from "The Meaning of Truth"* (New York, 1974): "Your typical ultra-abstractionist fairly shudders at concreteness: other things equal, he positively prefers the pale and spectral . . . the skinny outline rather than the rich thicket of reality. It is so much purer, clearer, nobler" (55).

11. Joan Copjec casts a more personally political light on Adorno's point here when, in her Lacanian meditation on American democracy, she writes: "If one's difference is, by definition, that which escapes recognition, then any recognition of it will always seem to miss the mark, to leave something unremarked. The subject of democracy is thus constantly hystericized, divided between the signifiers that seek to name it and the enigma that refuses to be named." Joan Copjec, "The Unvermögender Other: Hysteria and Democracy in America," *New Formations* 14 (1991): 33.

subjects and objects of mimetic realism scanned previously. In Adorno's (and
James') formulation, the excess of distance maintained between thought and reality ought, in fact, to make objects flow in the direction of subjects. Why? We
sense this might be true when we realize that when we refer to a reality that must
exceed thought, our sense of reality ideally ought to exist *prior to* our thought. And
yet, as Judith Butler shrewdly observes in a related context, inasmuch as reality is
"delimited" by thought, it can only come into existence through the very thing
which reality had been posited as being prior to, and in some sense, free from.[12]
In sum, therefore, distance holds out the promise of politicizing thinking in the
very act of defamiliarizing it. "For the value of a thought," Adorno writes in another fragment, called "Gaps," "is measured by its distance from the continuity
of the familiar [and] is objectively devalued as this distance is reduced; the more
it approximates to the preexisting standard, the further its antithetical function is
diminished" (*MM*, 80). On this account, then, contrary to received wisdom, great
minds are likely to be "great" not because they think alike, but because they don't.
Ultimately, their going the distance allows for the fashioning of perspectives for
experience—those that can "displace and estrange the world, reveal it to be, with
its rifts and crevices, as indigent and distorted as it will appear one day in the
messianic light" (*MM*, 247).

   The fact, however, that subjects do often tend to become elided with (and as)
objects in discursive representation points to the importance, as Adorno notes, of
distinguishing between *two* kinds of distance. On the one hand, distance can
function as a "safety-zone," a sort of self-protective mechanism that would stave
off the alterity of experience by foundationalizing truth, viewing truth in the
terms that James had complained of, as so many embedded essences and sedimented concepts. On the other hand, distance is delimited by Adorno as "a field
of tension," that is to say, as a type of optative psychic space that manifests itself
"not in relaxing the claim of ideas to truth," but nevertheless as a kind of "delicacy
and fragility of thinking" that would honor "the impossibility of a coincidence
between the idea and what fulfills it" (*MM*, 127). In short, Adorno's two senses
of distance articulate the boundaries of the *process* of identification, noted earlier,
that I shall be outlining for Modernist (i.e., post-Cartesian) subjectivity in the
American poetic text. Now both of these impulses, and Adorno's formulation of
them, are to be found in the poetry of Wallace Stevens. First, there is the subjectivity given to us from the safety-zone of logical speculation, the kind of subjectivity predisposed to hold off otherness—"the abyss of relativity," as Adorno calls

12. Judith Butler, *Bodies That Matter: On the Discursive Limits of "Sex"* (New York, 1993), 11.

it (*MM*, 127)—in order to make its own truth entirely self-coincident. That would be the kind of indulgent self-representation that greets us in "Wild Ducks, People, and Distances" (1945), for instance, where "the final fatal distances" of Stevens' villagers only serve to show just how resistant they are to "the weather of *other* lives" (*SCP*, 329).

Secondly, however, in the process of identification that I view characteristically deployed in Modernist American poetry, we are more likely to encounter the representation overshooting its object, and as a proto-Modernist poet like Emily Dickinson seems to anticipate, find ourselves well beyond "the Distance / On the look of Death," and closer to her more daring space of "internal difference, / Where the Meanings, are—".[13] Let me just elaborate a bit more here the alternative representation of subjectivity in Stevens by further connecting it to the sense of distance that Adorno calls "purposeless activity." More precisely, the "purposeless activity" of children is what Adorno has in mind in this second kind of distance. For in play, the child "deprives the things with which he plays of their mediated usefulness . . . that equally deforms men and things. The little trucks travel nowhere and the tiny barrels on them are empty; yet they remain true to their destiny by not performing, not participating in the process of abstraction that levels down that destiny . . . [i.e.,] the vital process between men and things. . . . [Hence,] [T]he unreality of games gives notice that reality is not yet real. Unconsciously, [children] rehearse the right life" (*MM*, 228). The perfectly use-less space here that Adorno imagines the playful mind of the child opens up in its "unreal" negotiation—"the vital process"—between mind and world forms a vital link to the later writing of Stevens.

In "The Ultimate Poem Is Abstract" (1947), for instance, whose title parodies "the process of abstraction" just mentioned, Stevens alludes to a "placid space" very much in terms of the mental waywardness Adorno would ascribe to the young child:

> It is an intellect
> Of windings round and dodges to and fro,
>
> Writhings in wrong obliques and distances,
> Not an intellect in which we are fleet: present
> Everywhere in space at once, cloud-pole
>
> Of communication.
>
> (*SCP*, 429–30)

13. Emily Dickinson, *The Complete Poems of Emily Dickinson*, ed. Thomas H. Johnson (Boston, 1960), 118.

The "obliques and distances" in this passage severely cloud or curtail ready access to transparent communication, and what is more, fixing some definitive conception of "This Beautiful World of Ours" "at the middle" of that discursive transmission. As a result, we are left, in the poet's words, rather "Helplessly at the edge" of intellectual certainty, much as we are in Stevens' more baffling "Chocorua to Its Neighbor" (1943), whose opening lines at least have the virtue of vaguely reminding us of some of the ideas I have just been touching upon:

> To speak quietly at such a distance, to speak
> And to be heard is to be large in space,
> That, like your own, is large, hence, to be part
> Of sky, of sea, large earth, large air. It is
> To perceive men without reference to their form.
>
> (*SCP*, 296)

In a few other poems by Stevens, I would like to map out a little more of the distance surrounding those men perceived "without reference to their form." For it does seem to me that within that distanciated formlessness we are permitted the recovery of dissident subjectivity in modern American poetry in its fullest cultural context.

Earlier, I spoke of a lettered space in American literature within which we are invited to view the identity of individuals as produced rather than given. Michel Foucault does not identify such a space in the writing of Baudelaire, but he well might have. For it is Baudelaire, according to Foucault, who gives us the clearest conception of our current modernity, as the poet imagines "not the man who goes off to discover himself, his secrets and his hidden truth," but rather "the man who tries to invent himself," since modernity, in its truest sense, "compels him to face the task of producing himself," that is to say, of "constitut[ing] . . . the self as an autonomous subject." If in such terms a transition may be marked from a premodern, reflecting subject to a more modern, inventing and producing one, or to give this transition a more precise American context, from the individuality of rational Cartesianism to the identity of posthumanist Pragmatism, is it not possible to imagine this historical shift as occurring between the two kinds of distances previously rehearsed in Adorno: a shift, shall we say, from an ontological distance to one more relativist in character?[14] If this development helps to account for the

14. Michel Foucault, "What Is Enlightenment?" in *The Foucault Reader*, ed. Paul Rabinow (New York, 1984), 42. "What makes this attitude typical of modernity," remarks Mladen Dolar, "is the constant reconstruction and reinvention of the present which goes along with the reconstruction and

generally posthumanist treatment of the subject in Modernist American literature, it comes as no surprise that a poet such as Wallace Stevens would be predisposed to remark such a discursive alteration in much of his earlier writing.
"Academic Discourse at Havana" is perhaps exemplary in this regard.

In this majestic text from 1923, Stevens attaches the notion of an ontological
distance, which we have come to understand in terms of a beleaguered rhetoric of
transcendence and steadfastness, to the passing of an "urgent, competent, serener
myth," overblown and outworn in its excess of superlatives: "perfect plenitude,"
"ripest summer," "hottest bloom," "longest resonance," and so forth (*SCP*, 143).
More specifically, the protective distance is imaged in terms of "an old casino in
a park," an excrescent structure that has clearly seen better days:

> Life is an old casino in a park.
> The bills of the swans are flat upon the ground.
> A most desolate wind has chilled Rouge-Fatima
> And a grand decadence settles down like cold.
> (*SCP*, 142)

Not even the Yeatsian "indolent progressions of the swans" that once warded the
waters entailed to the casino can make the age of classicism that it represents
"come right," so that its boarded windows and leaf-encrusted fountains are there
clearly to mark the end of an era.

When Foucault talks about the "attitude" of modernity, he speaks of how the
new era is "indissociable from a desperate eagerness to imagine it, to imagine

reinvention of the self. Both elements—the subject and the present it belongs to—have no 'objective'
status; they have to be perpetually (re)constructed, and their status is purely 'ethical.' So modernity
essentially results in an ethics of self-construction." Mladen Dolar, "The Legacy of the Enlightenment: Foucault and Lacan," *New Formations* 14 (1987): 46. In terms not entirely different from mine,
Dolar further argues that "Aesthetic modernism as a whole can be seen as a counterpoint to the self-
transparent and unitary subject implied in the Enlightenment: a fragmented and mutilated subjectivity which has lost its unity and transparence as the result of the progress of the universality of reason"
(54 n. 3). In addition, Judith Butler also shadows my argument here, alluding to an "ontological
distance" in the context of a discussion of the writing of Nietzsche and Lacan in much the same terms
that I deploy. Butler, *Bodies That Matter*, 247 n. 12 (*sic*). Finally, "relativist distance" may be elided
by Foucault in Baudelaire, but very recent commentators on Foucault himself have been especially
sensitive to a corresponding "space" in the philosopher's work. "For Foucault," writes Geoffrey Galt
Harpham, "the essence of freedom lay in 'a space of individual autonomy—created in the margins or
interstices of an otherwise ubiquitous will-to-power whose watchwords are "reason," "enlightenment," and "truth."'" Geoffrey Galt Harpham, "So . . . What Is Enlightenment? An Inquisition into
Modernity," *Critical Inquiry* 20 (summer 1994): 537.

to imagine reality otherwise than it is, and to transform it — Foucault 11

it otherwise than it is, and to transform it." Imagination is powerfully signal to *on* modernity. In the decline that Stevens recounts, however, it is a "politic man" *modernity.* who looks down from the towers of the casino fearfully to pronounce "Imagination as the fateful sin" (*SCP*, 143). The pronouncement, nevertheless, cannot go unchallenged any longer. Choosing his thoughts carefully—"dark, pacific words" for an "infinite repetition" (*SCP*, 144), the poet finally rises to *his* balcony, and commences to intone a new myth, by the end of the poem:

> This may be benediction, sepulcher,
> And epitaph. It may, however, be
> An incantation that the moon defines
> By mere example opulently clear.
> And the old casino likewise may define
> An infinite incantation of our selves
> In the grand decadence of the perished swans.
>   (*SCP*, 145)

If the poet's concluding dark words are spiriting us to a new age off in the moon-like distance, what is perhaps most important to note is that an incantation of plural selves will be at the center of it. The plurality here prevents Stevens from having to say anything categorical about the subjectivity that the poet's new myth will foreground, a myth specifically allergic to the "world" and to the "word" that might "import a universal pith / To Cuba" (*SCP*, 144). Stevens himself, according to Thomas Grey, repeatedly remarked that "the poet must stay open to the flux of experience and unfinished, hence never quite himself," and in this connection, Grey cites the remark from a letter in Stevens' final year stating that "once one is strongly defined, no other definition is possible, in spite of daily change."[15] Accordingly, in Stevens' "Holiday in Reality" (1944), "a common man [does] not exist" (*SCP*, 312). And undoubtedly, "The Motive for Metaphor" (1943) is driven by the fact that "you yourself were never quite yourself / And did not want nor have to be, / Desiring the exhilarations of changes" (*SCP*, 288). What seems to be of overriding importance at the close of the much earlier "Academic Discourse," therefore, is that the incantation of selves is made "infinite." Therein lies the demise of the ontology of distance, its benediction and sepulcher and epitaph all rolled up into one. *incantation of the blue, is made infinite*

"Man and Bottle" (1940), a poem from Stevens' middle-period, gives us a

15. Foucault, "What Is Enlightenment?" 41; Thomas Grey, *The Wallace Stevens Case: Law and the Practice of Poetry* (Cambridge, Mass., 1991), 136–37 n. 36.

clearer idea of what we are mourning in the previous text. A tradition of Romanticism which removes a hieratic and theologically ordained conception of humankind, and offers in its place a more egalitarian and humanistically maintained sense of individuality represents, both intellectually and politically, a social and cultural advance in its way. But romantic individualism ceases to be of interest to the new kind of myth the poet might be constructing if it ultimately is merely bent upon reinstalling another absolutist regime of truth, founded now upon a rational rather than a spiritual Logos. Such a rationalist conception thus becomes the recycling of ontological distance in its romance-form—the "bottle" imprisoning the "man" in this later poem's title—that Stevens' poet must continue to write *beyond,* by destroying the "romantic tenements" (literally, holdings or containments) of rose and ice (*SCP,* 238).[16]

Hence, whereas the "old affair with the sun" here may represent the Classicism of "Academic Discourse at Havana," the "impossible aberration with the moon" becomes the suspect Romanticism of the present work. Both seen as imperializing epistemes that are, in fact, mirror-images of each other, they come together as the "grossness of peace", that must be strenuously "averted," each in its separate form (*SCP,* 239). Modernism, which rightly should come *after* both Classicism and Romanticism, but in terms of the relativist distance it gestures towards, ought more theoretically to be imagined as intervening in *between*[17]— such Modernism promises to set human subjectivity on a new footing:

> More than the man, it is
> A man with the fury of a race of men,
> A light at the centre of many lights,
> A man at the centre of men.
>
> (*SCP,* 239)

16. John D'Emilio, *Sexual Politics, Sexual Communities: The Making of a Homosexual Minority in the United States, 1940–1970* (Chicago, 1983), 109. We might look back five years to "Re-statement of Romance" and "Sailing after Lunch," both from 1935, for anticipations of the present text, a line concerning which from the latter poem, reads: "But the romantic must never remain, / Mon Dieu, and must never again return" (*SCP,* 120). See also David R. Jarraway, *Wallace Stevens and the Question of Belief: "Metaphysician in the Dark"* (Baton Rouge, 1993), esp. Chapter 1.

17. I attempt, accordingly, to remove "Modernism" from its conventionally chronological conceptualization, in the Whig view of history, and in this culturally distanciated spatialization, endeavor to approximate Homi Bhabha's notion in "The Commitment to Theory," *New Formations* 5 (1988), of a "contradictory and ambivalent split-space of enunciation [that] may open the way to conceptualizing an *inter*national culture" (21). "[W]e should remember," Bhabha further notes, "that it is the 'inter'—the cutting edge of translation and negotiation, the *in-between,* the space of the *entre* that

The pluralism of the representation—"race," "lights," "men" as opposed to "man"—picks up on the infinity of selves closing out the last poem. What *is* new, however, is the "manner of thinking," the kind of mode or style wherein to account for such a mammoth proliferation of identities.

Force or violence appears central to the notion of style Stevens has in mind here, a force or power that he images in terms of war, and the fierce lashings of the wind (*SCP*, 239). When we couple this force to the insistent repetitions supervening the passage just cited, we might perhaps be invited to think of it in connection with the "phonetic repetition" that Michel Foucault links to a "great plastic power," and equally, to "a whirlwind of frantic savage, or exultant scenes"—a power that does not usher us into the total "liberation of language" *beyond* "things, thoughts, and bodies," as we might think. Rather, the power of Foucault's repetition drives us back even more relentlessly *into* the body—"back in[to] the mouth and around the sexual organs," says Foucault—that is to say, back into life-experience and back into concrete reality that all the while, as we have seen, will always be opaquely withheld from the rational cogitations and the logical impositions of the omnivorously colonizing mind. "That every act is in some sense a repetition of what is *irrecoverable*," Judith Butler notes, is made plain also in the writing of Jacques Lacan, from whom she cites: "An act, a true act, always has an element of structure, by the fact of concerning a real that is not self-evidently caught up in it."[18] Joining this repetition and this real, more generally in Lacan, to the undermining of a master-ego in its effort to regain some "fantasized place," Butler thus helps us to understand "Man and Bottle" as a further approximation of a "distance" Stevens' discourse will have (under)gone from his earlier writing, in order to shift its rhetoric into a less metaphysical and logocentric, and ultimately, into a more worldly and more pragmatic register.

With that shift, we arrive at texts like "The Sense of the *Sleight*-of-Hand Man" (1939), and the "unhandsomeness" of what Stanley Cavell refers to as a more evanescent (i.e., Pragmatist) approach to human experience. In this later text, life is imaged by Stevens as a "sensual pearly spouse," and as a paradigmatic emblem for human identity constructed within and throughout that life, she re-

---

Derrida has opened up in writing itself—that carries the burden of the meaning of culture," and further, that "[i]t is in this space that we will find those words with which we can speak of Ourselves and Others . . . [,] elude the politics of polarity[,] and emerge as the others of ourselves" (22, emphases retained).

18. Michel Foucault, quoted in Steven Shaviro, *Passion and Excess: Blanchot, Bataille, and Literary Theory* (Tallahassee, 1990), 86–87; Lacan, quoted in Butler, *Bodies That Matter*, 249 n. 19.

mains "fluent in even the wintriest bronze" (*SCP*, 222).[19] Like the sun—"The fire in the clouds"—that has continued to remain impervious to, and so survive, an entire wheel of explanatory myths rayed around it through history, so this pearly spouse promises to outlive all the forms of identity she has been (and will be) conceived to signify. The key, however, is "man" himself continuing to remain "ignorant," that is to say, non-peremptory, non-categorical, non-prescriptive, in his "sleight-ly" unhandsome approach to her. For only then will he gain "any chance to mate his life with life" (*SCP*, 222), and thereby prolong and extend it in a variety of articulations, into the future.

Stevens' "anti-master-man," in the final "Landscape with Boat" (1940), can also approach this unhandsome condition of blissful ignorance described in the last text. But he won't succeed if his object is "to arrive / At the neutral centre" of experience, anticipating truth to be some "single-colored, colorless, primitive," rather than "a phantom, in an uncreated night" (*SCP*, 242). "Schopenhauer," Adorno likewise remarks, "recognized [the real self] to be . . . a phantom," and therefore "null and void," when he understood that "the individual is only appearance, not the Thing-in-Itself" as an "original entity" or "monad" (*MM*, 154, 153). Its place "had to be supposed," to recur to Stevens' own text, "Itself had to be supposed, a thing supposed / In a place supposed . . . parts, and all these things together, / Parts, and more things, parts" (*SCP*, 242). Now exactly why the anti-master-man must move beyond such a floribund exfoliation of parts, to arrive at "A truth-beyond all truths" (*SCP*, 242), is perhaps best explained, I think, as a weakness of nerve. "To be projected by one void into / Another" (*SCP*, 242)— precisely the dialectical standoff between reality and selfhood in the Modernist American context—is an extraordinarily radical moment in the history of theorizing about the evolution of modern subjectivity, particularly in view of the fact that:

> if nothing
> Was divine then all things were, the world itself,
> And that if nothing was the truth, then all
> Things were the truth, the world itself was the truth.
> (*SCP*, 242)

19. Raising the problematic of Reality, once again, we are perhaps invited to view this "pearly spouse" as making a strategic intervention somewhere between Mrs. Alfred Uruguay, who first "approached the real" "in order to get at [her]self," and later finds that self "Rushing from what was real" ("Mrs. Alfred Uruguay" [1940, *SCP*, 249]), and Lady Lowzen, "For whom what is was other things," and who therefore "Skims the real for its unreal" ("Oak Leaves Are Hands" [1942, *SCP*, 272]).

Only Wallace Stevens, after his "Academic Discourse at Havana" we realize, could be so daring.

In wrapping up this overview of American subjectivity in its Modernist historical context, I want to finesse two additional points with respect to the construction of identity just developed, and finally, entertain a more general speculation about where that rather protean identity was—and in the dissident climate of a more latter-day sexual politics (as we shall see) *continues* to be—headed.

D. H. Lawrence, alarmed at the fact that Walt Whitman could ventriloquize so *many* others, draws attention, potentially, to a kind of elephantiasis of Identity that, in the end, settles politely into Lawrence's slightly more respectful "awful pudding" (174). Still, the tendency to view the self as a multiple conglomeration or hodgepodge, as the alternative to some more moderately coherent and unitary conception, continues to labor within a kind of rationalism or exclusionary logic that can only register choices in either/or, right/wrong, hierarchical dualisms. In the dialectical process of identification we have been examining, however, we turn the verticality of peremptory, non-contradictory logic on its ear, and open it out to a more horizontal kind of discrimination. Conceived in these terms, we view subjectivity not so much as a static conglomeration, but rather, as an ongoing alternation of options—a discriminating experiment that makes the subject's continuous and relative negotiation with its other(s), in the words of Emily Dickinson, a "profounder site" of self-invention, and in a word, a "Finite Infinity." In such terms, the subject thus remains inaccessible not so much due to it structural but instead its temporal incompleteness—a temporal project, that is to say, that finds itself always already deferred.[20]

My second point, therefore, would be to remark upon the several important queer theorists writing today who would seem to have taken their lead from a model of deferred subjectivity arguably anticipated by Stevens. I am thinking in particular of those dissident theorists who invite us to think of subjectivity not as a discrete and self-contained state or category, but as a constantly shifting phenomenon over what Adrienne Rich, Eve Sedgwick, and Gayle Rubin, among others, have been pleased to articulate as a broad "range" or "continuum" of gendered agreements, positions, or assignments.[21]

Marjorie Garber, unpacking her own notion of a sexual "spectrum" in cross-

20. D. H. Lawrence, *Studies in Classic American Literature* (Harmondsworth, Eng., 1971), 174; Hurston, *Their Eyes Were Watching God*, 1; Dickinson, *The Complete Poems*, 691.

21. Adrienne Rich, "Compulsory Heterosexuality and Lesbian Existence," in *The Lesbian and Gay Studies Reader*, eds. Henry Abelove, Michèle Aina Barale, and David M. Halperin (New York, 1993), 227–54; Eve Kosofsky Sedgwick, *Epistemology of the Closet* (Los Angeles, 1990); Gayle Rubin,

Stevens as fren? of Queer theory

dressing, cites a passage from an exhibition catalogue of the photographs of Robert Mapplethorpe, which explains this particular horizon of subjectivity precisely:

Glut — identity as sum of poses

> The message that Mapplethorpe delivers is that the experience of any masculine or feminine identity is the sensation of an unstable, constantly readjusted succession of poses. In his work, the crossing of boundaries . . . is not simplistically developed as an opposition between masculinity and femininity, it is experienced as a drama that takes place within the entire range of sexual identities—in man and woman, and in homosexual and heterosexual alike.[22]

The constant and successive readjusting of identities or poses in this citation perhaps suggests how theoretically resonant a Modernist poetical project like that of Stevens might be with such a dissident conception of sexual identity.

My final point, then—a point which constitutes the theoretical burden of all of the chapters which follow—is a speculation about the radical *democratic*, rather than autocratic, context within which we are induced by Modernist projects like that of Stevens to position American subjectivity, constituted by a relativist as against an absolutist distance. Conceived *across* rather than above or below an open-ended range of formulations and figurations, identity-formation transcends the logic of finite representation, and resituates itself in the more equitable space of alterity, and speculative production. Relocated in such a vast distance as identity-formation is, for some, this more equitable space might suggest that an overwhelmingly intractable reality has paralyzed all thought—the ongoing controversy between constructionists and essentialists comes to mind[23]—and that the outcome has really been the *death* of the subject. Subjectivity in the Modernist American poetic context, as I hope to show in what follows, should offer us much more reason to feel sanguine.

The gay poet Mark Doty captures much of this optimism in the querying/queering of relativist distance when he recently observes:

> we all need forms of distance in order to be able to approach our experience and our emotions, in order to see them more clearly. . . . I think when you're a young poetry student, distance sounds like a dirty word: it sounds cold. Why would I want

---

"Thinking Sex: Notes for a Radical Theory of the Politics of Sexuality," in *Pleasure and Danger: Exploring Female Sexuality*, ed. Carole S. Vance (London, 1989), 267–319; see also Damon, *The Dark End of the Street*, 151, and Robert Schwartzwald, "'Symbolic' Homosexuality, 'False Feminine,' and the Problematics of Identity in Quebec," in *Fear of a Queer Planet: Queer Politics and Social Theory*, ed. Michael Warner (Minneapolis, 1993), 290.

22. Marjorie Garber, *Vested Interests: Cross-dressing and Cultural Anxiety* (New York, 1993), 161.

23. See Edward Stein, ed., *Forms of Desire: Sexual Orientation and the Social Constructionist Controversy* (New York, 1992).

D:tole a wy of Ceer

something so remote and clinical as that? Whereas, in fact, distance, the distance of art, is a great gift to us because it is a way of standing back and seeing who we are, what we have found. We are turning experience around in our hands so we can look at it, see its facets and its possibilities . . . shifting point of view, shifting tense, shifting the order of things, to encourage that kind of standing back in order to see that this impulse to write could take many different forms. . . . [Hence,] we can train ourselves to see over time that each impulse has in fact multiple possibilities . . . in order to make better intuitive decisions later on.

Doty's optimism leads me further to think that querying/queering the distance of subjectivity, historically as well as politically in American social life, stresses what Fredric Jameson, in parallel terms, describes as "the gap between the local positioning of the individual subject and the totality of class structures in which he or she is situated, a gap between phenomenological perception and a reality that transcends all thinking experience." The implication of both Doty's and Jameson's insights, as I read them, is to suggest the relocation of democracy itself, as a totality of structures, *in the distance,* and in such terms, to view its ideal of prolific self-invention, *beyond* what we can presently imagine, as a "future horizon, one in which the violence of exclusion is perpetually in the process of being overcome."[24] In sum, then, if going the distance in the Modernist American poet is coterminous with a radical democratic politics, it's only because the "Absence in reality" in such a one as Stevens subtends that distance (*SCP,* 176), and makes going there, again and again, an infinitely perdurable discursive encounter.

24. Mark Doty, "Ice and Salt: An Interview with Mark Doty," *Poetry Flash* 270 (November 1966): 1–6; Fredric Jameson, "Cognitive Mapping," in *Marxism and the Interpretation of Culture,* ed. Cary Nelson and Lawrence Grossberg (Urbana, 1988), 353; Butler, *Bodies That Matter,* 53. Peter Euben puts the case succinctly, by hypothesizing that "We steadily move toward [democracy] while recognizing that there is no finality to the goal that nonetheless guides us. . . . [Hence,] the distance between it and ourselves mandates that we treat every means as an end and every end as a means . . . that we add depth to the central terms of our political discourse: democracy, power, freedom, and politics . . . by taking seriously Lincoln's belief that government is rightly of, by, and for the people." Euben, quoted in Henry A. Giroux, *Living Dangerously: Multiculturalism and the Politics of Difference* (New York, 1993), 10. Chantal Mouffe is likewise persuaded that a political community is considerably advantaged to view "democratic principles" as absent though nonetheless worthy ideals, since "The common good can never be actualized. There will always be debate over the exact nature of citizenship. . . . Politics in a modern democracy must accept division and conflict as unavoidable. [Thus,] The reconciliation of rival claims and conflicting interests can only be partial and provisional." Chantal Mouffe, "The Civics Lesson," *New Statesman and Society* 7 (1988): 30. Accordingly, in Homi Bhabha's "split-space of enunciation," democracy's provisionally (un)representable nature "in itself" will ensure "that the meaning and symbols of culture have no primordial unity or fixity; [and] that even the same signs can be appropriated, translated, and read anew." Bhabha, "The Commitment to Theory," 21.

Chapter 1

"Absence of More":
The Struggle for Unique Self-Authorization in Gertrude Stein

> *William James was well within the bounds of moderation when he said that looking forward instead of backward, looking to what the world and life might become instead of to what they have been, is an alteration in the "seat of authority."*
>
> —JOHN DEWEY, *The Quest for Certainty*

> *The lesbian also knows that nothing can replace the lack to which in fact she has resigned herself.*
>
> —TERESA DE LAURETIS, *The Practice of Love*

> *No one knowing me knows me. I am II.*
>
> —GERTRUDE STEIN, *The Geographical History of America*

UNDENIABLY, self-authorization is one of the premier themes in the great tradition of American poetry, if not in the canons of American literature itself. In the life and work of Gertrude Stein (1874–1946), arguably one of the most important American Modernists last century, the struggle for self-authorization is perhaps presented to us most clearly in that well-known period from her early life marked, on the one side, by the completion of her first book, *Three Lives* (1906), and after several turbulent years, on the other, by the publication of *Tender Buttons* (1914). The texts I shall be concerned with in this opening chapter all come near or at the end of this seven-year purgatory, as it were. As such, they can be said to represent the achievement of self-authorization that, in Gertrude Stein's own particular case, is impossible to conceive in any other terms but those having to do with writing as a dissident act of distancing described in the Introduction.[1]

---

1. David R. Jarraway, "Ammons Beside Himself: Poetics of the 'Bleak Periphery,'" *Arizona*

It can hardly seem accidental, for instance, that at the time these texts were composed, Gertrude Stein finds it possible to break free—distance herself, as it were—at last from the pernicious and overbearing influence of her elder brother Leo, who makes a permanent departure from her life in 1912. As one of her biographers observes:

> Turning to writing at this early stage appears to have been her most natural means of breaking away from Leo's paternalistic domination. Their relationship . . . was based on common pursuits and, to a degree, on shared ideas. But the intellectual initiative continued to be Leo's, and his aggressive self-assertions often silenced her and left her resentful. Somewhere along the line Gertrude apparently realized that only when she became an artist in her own right and on her own terms might she escape her brother's overzealous control.

Fueling Stein's struggle for self-authorization "on her own terms," additionally, was her burgeoning love for Alice B. Toklas, who came into her life in 1907, much to Leo's chagrin, just about the time this period of restiveness began.[2] But 1907 was also the year that William James, Stein's self-admitted "big influence" and "man among men" in her undergraduate years, published his lectures entitled *Pragmatism*. If the achievement of self-authority, therefore, is the especial hallmark of the dissident American poet, what makes this preoccupation "unique" in the writing of Gertrude Stein is its complex intrication within a polyvocal discourse that is at once feminist, sapphist, and Pragmatist. And unpacking the self-autonomous claims of each of these layers of discourse in her Modernist declaration of independence, as we shall see in turn, would fairly much amount to asserting the claims for all.

Quarterly 49 (Winter 1993), 99–116; Stephen Scobie, "The Allure of Multiplicity: Metaphor and Metonymy in Cubism and Gertrude Stein," in *Gertrude Stein and the Making of Literature,* ed. Shirley Neuman and Ira B. Nadel (Boston, 1988), 102.

2. John Malcolm Brinnin, *The Third Rose: Gertrude Stein and Her World* (Reading, Mass., 1987), 54. "Alice met Gertrude on September 8, 1907," as Harriet Chessman sums up their courtship, and "[t]heir relationship may have been consummated in the spring of 1908," with "Stein's marriage proposal to Toklas [coming] the following summer, as they vacationed in Fiesole, Italy." Harriet Chessman, *The Public Is Invited to Dance: Representation, the Body, and Dialogue in Gertrude Stein* (Stanford, 1989), 228 n. 9. For brother Leo's resentment over the introduction of this new source of emotional attachment into Gertrude's life at 27 rue de Fleurus, see Diana Souhami, *Gertrude and Alice* (London, 1991), 101–102. For Stein and Pragmatism, see James R. Mellow, *Charmed Circle: Gertrude Stein and Company* (New York, 1974), 55, Brinnin, *The Third Rose,* 28, and more generally John Patrick Diggins, *The Promise of Pragmatism: Modernism and the Crisis of Knowledge and Authority* (Chicago, 1994), 115.

In this initial section of the chapter, I want to deal with the Pragmatist context of Stein's discourse first, particularly as it manifests itself in various texts selected from *Tender Buttons*, and work up gradually to the more radical claim, in the chapter's final section, for her unique self-authorization as a writer of both feminist and lesbian texts that we encounter, for instance, in *Geography and Plays*, which were composed immediately following. In working with a Jamesian Stein to start with, I perhaps may be perceived as following a popular critical response to her work advocating that "she identified herself with male roles in both her professional and personal life" much before she eventually began "to write in her own female person." After all, as Catharine Stimpson reminds us, "no one spoke of her lesbianism until after her death in 1946."[3]

My view, however, as I shall explain more fully in a moment, is that it was a number of the ideas associated with the philosophy of Pragmatism, particularly as Stein was exposed to them under the tutelage of William James while yet a student at Radcliffe College in the late 1890s (known then as the "Harvard Annex"),[4] which provided her with sufficient warrant, from quite early on, to

---

3. Shirley Neuman, "'Would a Viper Have Stung Her If She Had Only One Name?' *Dr. Faustus Lights the Lights*," in *Gertrude Stein and the Making of Literature*, ed. Shirley Neuman and Ira Nadel (Boston, 1988), 193 n. 23; Robert K. Martin, "*The Mother of Us All* and American History," in *Gertrude Stein and the Making of Literature*, eds. Shirley Neuman and Ira Nadel (Boston, 1988), 217, 219; Marianne DeKoven, *A Different Language: Gertrude Stein's Experimental Writing* (Madison, 1983), 137); Catharine R. Stimpson, "The Somograms of Gertrude Stein," in *The Lesbian and Gay Studies Reader*, ed. Henry Abelove, Michèle Aina Barale, and David M. Halperin (New York, 1993), 643. Ironically, it was Alice B. Toklas herself who endeavored most to background the issue of Stein's lesbianism, if not efface it entirely, particularly among her biographers. To Julian Sawyer, for instance, an American academic who wanted to deal frankly with this issue in Stein's work, Toklas was provoked to respond: "You will understand I hope my objection to your repeated references to the subject of sexuality as an approach to the understanding of Gertrude's work. She would have emphatically denied it—she considered it the least characteristic of all expressions of character—her actual references to sexuality are so rare." Toklas, quoted in Souhami, *Gertrude and Alice*, 258.

4. Brinnin also notes the possible influence of other Pragmatists while Stein was at Harvard: "a course under George Santayana in philosophy and a course in metaphysics under Josiah Royce." Brinnin, *The Third Rose*, 26. The influence of William James on Stein mainly in terms of his deregulation of traditional epistemology is dealt with most thoroughly by Randa Dubnick, *The Structure of Obscurity: Gertrude Stein, Language, and Cubism* (Urbana, 1984), 90–92 (for the convergences), by Chessman, *The Public Is Invited to Dance*, 157–60 (for the departures), and by Jayne L. Walker, *The Making of a Modernist: Gertrude Stein, from "Three Lives" to "Tender Buttons"* (Amherst, 1984), 159 n. 6, 104–105 (for Stein's "conscious rebellion against some of [James'] precepts"). The issue is further dealt with by Charles Caramello, "Gertrude Stein as Exemplary Theorist," in *Gertrude Stein and the Making of Literature*, ed. Shirley Neuman and Ira B. Nadel (Boston, 1988), 5; by Henry M. Sayre, "The Artist's Model: American Art and the Question of Looking like Gertrude Stein," in *Gertrude Stein*

begin thinking (and writing) about her own same-sex orientation in unapologeti-
cally self-authenticating and self-confirming ways. Such is the radical nature of
this whole self-authorizing process, indeed, that the often oblique and tenden-
tious manner in which it is pursued can seem as if "the unspoken censorship"
necessitated by contemporaneous "social and moral taboo" to a large extent might
account for Stein's purported "linguistic disguise." But once again, it is Stein who
becomes the artist *on her own terms*. So that if we choose to postpone dealing
with her anormative treatment of sexuality, or bow to the censors and handle it
in code, or even ignore it entirely, the fault lies with our terms of reference, not
hers. "To change the world," as one of the more recent commentators on the
whole project of Pragmatism writes, "is to take possession of the language that
describes it," a point not lost on another dissident subject closer to our own time,
Roland Barthes, who also argues that "it is in the very structure of language that
power is embodied."[5] If a world excluding same-sex attachments among women
seemed to Gertrude Stein to be the one *most* worth changing, her exposure to
some of the ideas of William James would appear to have been a propitious discursive beginning.

James R. Mellow has recorded the enormous debt Stein owed to this early
leader of American Pragmatism, in a statement she made just before her death:
"'Everything must come into your scheme,' [James] said of the creative life, 'otherwise you cannot achieve real simplicity.' A great deal of this I owe to a great
teacher, William James. He said, 'Never reject anything. Nothing has been
proved. If you reject anything, that is the beginning of the end as an intellectual.'
. . . He was a man who always said, 'complicate your life as much as you please,
it has got to simplify.'" The "real simplicity" that Stein alludes to in this valedic-
tory is the knowledge about life that James had always contended one "gained
from direct experience" rather than the knowledge that one merely learned "*about*

---

and the Making of Literature, ed. Shirley Neuman and Ira B. Nadel (Boston, 1988), 24; by Ulla E.
Dydo, "Gertrude Stein: Composition as Meditation," in *Gertrude Stein and the Making of Literature*,
ed. Shirley Neuman and Ira B. Nadel (Boston, 1988), 45; by Susan E. Hawkins, "Sneak Previews:
Gertrude Stein's Syntax in *Tender Buttons*," in *Gertrude Stein and the Making of Literature*, ed. Shirley
Neuman and Ira B. Nadel (Boston, 1988), 119; and by Martin, "*The Mother of Us All* and American
History," 210. More socially and culturally resonant treatments of James in relation to Stein and other
American Modernists broadly speaking can be found in Richard Poirier, *Poetry and Pragmatism*
(Cambridge, Mass., 1992), and Frank Lentricchia, *Modernist Quartet* (New York, 1994).

5. Scobie, "The Allure of Multiplicity," 116; Cyrena N. Pondrom, introduction to *G&P*, xlix;
Diggins, *The Promise of Pragmatism*, 49; Roland Barthes, quoted in Robert K. Martin, "Roland
Barthes: Toward an 'Écriture Gaie,'" in *Camp Grounds: Style and Homosexuality*, ed. David Bergman
(Amherst, 1993), 290.

a subject" (*P*, 147). Merely learning about a subject is the complacent disposition of "rationalism," as James describes it in his lecture on "Pragmatism's Conception of Truth" (*P*, 147). Passively accepting knowledge rather than actively seeking it out from direct experience presupposes that, for the rationalist, "Reality stands complete and readymade from all eternity," and that truth "adds nothing to the content of [the Pragmatist's] experience," since, for the rationalist, reality "is supervenient, inert, static, a reflexion merely" (*P*, 147).[6]

For the Pragmatist more fully in touch with life, however, truth is not "a stagnant property" inherent in an idea but rather something that "*happens* to an idea": "It *becomes* true, is *made* true by events. Its verity *is* in fact an event, a process: the process namely of its verifying itself, its veri*fication*. Its validity is the process of its valid-*ation*" (*P*, 133, emphases retained). This validating the process of "fictionalizing" ideas in response to life's events, therefore, leads the Pragmatist away "from fixed principles, closed systems, and pretended absolutes and origins," and causes her, instead, to turn "towards facts, towards action and towards power." With this distanciated remove, James is prompted to formulate perhaps the most revolutionary statement in his Pragmatist ethos:

> Like the half-truths, the absolute truth will have to be *made*, made as a relation incidental to the growth of a mass of verification-experience, to which the half-true ideas are all along contributing their quota. . . . [Accordingly,] [s]o far as reality means experienceable reality, both it and the truths men gain about it are everlastingly in process of mutation—mutation towards a definite goal, it may be—but still mutation.[7]

6. Mellow, *Charmed Circle*, 49–50, 47. Accordingly, "Poetry must not be thought as a mere storehouse of wisdom, a treasure-trove," asserts Richard Poirier. "It is, rather, an exemplary act or instrumentality for the continuous creation of truth, an act that must be personal and private and never ending. 'To begin to begin again,' is Stein's way of putting it." Richard Poirier, "Why Do Pragmatists Want to Be Like Poets?" in *The Revival of Pragmatism: New Essays on Social Thought, Law, and Culture*, ed. Morris Dickstein (Durham, 1998), 353–54.

7. William James, "Pragmatism and Radical Empiricism," quoted in Diggins, *The Promise of Pragmatism*, 133. To the constructed and processual character of truth offered here, James would have us imagine the rationalist taking the most strenuous exception: "'Truth is not made,' he will say; 'it absolutely obtains being a unique relation that does not wait upon any process, but shoots straight over the head of experience, and hits its reality every time. . . . The bare quality of standing in that transcendent relation is what makes any thought true that possesses it, whether or not there be verification'" (*P*, 143). For a much fuller development of the view "that knowledge is produced rather than discovered" through the several generations of important American pragmatist thinkers, see Diggins, *The Promise of Pragmatism*, 39, 111, 127, 132, 136, 224, 233, 412, 416, 424, and 426.

What a woman at the turn of the century struggling with the need for self-legiti-
mation and self-authority would likely have heard most clearly in this last citation
was the mention of the mutational aspect of reality, and by implication, the ques-
tionable need to conform to any fixed principles of experience—principles invariably established by men—in view of the fact that these were subject to the process
of perdurable alteration. "The notion of a reality calling on us to 'agree' with it,
and that for no reasons, but simply because its claim is 'unconditional' or 'transcendent' is one that I can make neither head nor tail of," William James would
conclude (*P*, 152). Stein, no doubt, was perplexed to the same degree, and quite
possibly well before settling permanently on her vocation as a writer a decade
later.

"To be able to live without truth and certainty," John Diggins writes in *The
Promise of Pragmatism*, "to have the courage to face life as Melville faced the void,
is the challenge of modernism." A further aspect of that challenge, of course, is
to learn to live without authority—authority in the sense of a controlling force or
power imposed upon us from outside when "authoritative principles" like absolute knowledge or transcendent truth are thought to "regulate human affairs,"
in place of our openness and responsiveness to "the inexorable contingencies of
experience."[8] The Modernism of Gertrude Stein resides in both of these challenges. And it is difficult to imagine how they might have come to settle so ines-
capably over the length and breadth of her very large corpus had she not first
caught their fire from that teacher who "was always 'throwing off sparks'":

> Characteristically, James remained convinced that modern man could live without
> older ideas of truth and authority if he had the will to believe in himself. Such a

---

8. Diggins, *The Promise of Pragmatism*, 396, 248. "Ultimately what pragmatism offers us," this
last passage from Diggins goes on to conclude, "as Santayana noted, is the benign message that it is
better to pursue truth than to possess it, and better to regard as knowledge only those ideas that
enable us to change things according to our desires, rather than to regard knowledge as a criterion of
judgment that stands over and against our drives and desires" (248). Kant's own examples (in Foucault's extrapolation) of such a criterion of judgment, if we "accept someone else's authority to lead
us in areas where the use of [our own] reason is called for," occur "when a book takes the place of our
understanding, when a spiritual director takes the place of our conscience, when a doctor decides for
us what our diet is to be," and so forth. Foucault, "What Is Enlightenment?" 34. Hence, according
to Richard Rorty, "Pragmatism as Romantic Polytheism," in *The Revival of Pragmatism: New Essays
on Social Thought, Law, and Culture*, ed. Morris Dickstein (Durham, 1998), John Dewey's "lifelong
distaste for the idea of authority," that is to say, "the idea that experience must be subjected at some
point or other to some form of external control: to some 'authority' alleged to exist outside the process
of experience" (31, 33).

resolution liberated the human condition by making the subject aware that he or she could be the author of his or her own actions. Small wonder that the philosophy of pragmatism could be hailed by James as "an alteration in the seat of authority that reminds one almost of the Protestant Reformation."

The externally imposed supervenient authority that becomes transformed into an internally induced self-authority foregrounds the punning sense in which this latter *author*-ity proposes to foment James' reformative "alteration": namely, the "Revolution of the Word," in Eugène Jolas's famous Modernist proclamation from 1929, or what William James also had in mind a generation earlier when he referred to all truth as "discursified" (*P*, 140). Did the self-authority of American Pragmatism turn Gertrude Stein into an "author"? John Dewey, who was himself especially partial to that "alteration in the seat of authority," could have thought so. In his own case, Dewey viewed his development, perhaps like James and Stein both, "controlled largely by a struggle between . . . the schematic and formally logical, and those incidents of personal experience that compelled [him] to take account of actual material"—a struggle which registered itself, interestingly enough, "in style of writing and manner of presentation." But it was "the concrete diversity of experienced things" which ultimately settled the conflict for this second-generation Pragmatist, and from that time forward, compelled Dewey to confess, in an even more interesting parallel to Stein, that "thinking and writing have been hard work." In the Modernism of Gertrude Stein, therefore, which promises the alteration from absolute to relative truth, from fixed to mutational experience, and from permanent to processual reality, it is perhaps the authority that is made "functional rather than foundational" which counts for most.⁹ For with a functional authority, it is at last possible to begin to think how the world, for a change, might be made answerable to the individual self.

Although Stein would deny it—and understandably so, given her concern for self-authority—it is quite plausible to contend that "[t]he influence of William James can be read in every example of her work up to *Tender Buttons*."¹⁰ As a

9. Mellow, *Charmed Circle*, 47; Diggins, *The Promise of Pragmatism*, 157 (see also 372, 456); Eugène Jolas, quoted in Cary Nelson, *Repression and Recovery: Modern American Poetry and the Politics of Cultural Memory, 1910–1945* (Madison, 1989), 173–75; John Dewey, "From Absolutism to Experimentalism," in *The Philosophy of John Dewey*, vol. 1, *The Structure of Experience*, ed. John J. McDermott (New York, 1973), 5; Diggins, *The Promise of Pragmatism*, 374.

10. Brinnin, *The Third Rose*, 165. In her own defense, Stein's biographer records her riposte to this contention from 1914: "It does not follow that the strongest impression is produced by the strongest mind. It just happened by accident or circumstance that I came under the influence of William James, but I have not yet found the expression of that influence or impression." B. F. Skinner, the famous behavioral psychologist, in an inflammatory article in *The Atlantic Monthly* from 1934 ("Has

prologue to taking up the issue of authorization with respect to the matter of sexual identity later, for the remainder of this section, I would like to examine the possible impact that a predisposition toward certain Pragmatist modes of thinking might have had on the early Stein, in a sampling of texts from *Tender Buttons*. A great deal has been written about this extraordinarily baffling collection, and I don't for a moment propose to enlist any kind of ultimate interpretation or final word. Besides, in view of what we've already mentioned with respect to the relativity of truth, and the affirmation of one's own unique responsiveness to the world, a "final word" on any text by Stein would seem to be considerably beside the point. In reading her work, as Frank O'Hara, himself a voracious reader of Stein, might say, "You just go on your nerve." You try to imagine what it would be like to undergo a reading experience that you have never had before, or to deal with meaning (if that word even applies) so novel and so unexpected that you hardly know where to put it—"being in being where there was no seeing," as Stein herself might say.[11] Ideally, then, the following sampling of texts, first from "Objects," then from "Food," and finally from "Rooms," ought to prove that "Every one then is an individual being. Every one then is like many other always living, there are many ways of thinking of every one . . . a whole history of each of them" (*SSW*, 262). In reading Stein, in other words, we all find our own quite personal ways of author-izing ourselves.

It has become a commonplace in commentary about Gertrude Stein to remark upon her tireless efforts to get us to see things about the world that we had not quite been aware of before. The intense focus on "Objects" and "Food" in *Tender Buttons* might be offered as an example. But we misconstrue her project entirely if we expect to see *exactly* what she sees. Here, James is useful in helping us to understand that Stein's meticulous and minute observations of her surroundings are never meant to be mimetic representations of precise experience. For the Pragmatist, we recall, reality can never be a "reflexion" merely. Its truth is never

---

Gertrude Stein a Secret?"), likewise contended that Stein's "eccentric writing style, in *Tender Buttons* and other works, was simply a continuation of the practice she had begun with William James," but in a sharply worded letter to the magazine's editor, again she denied it. Mellow, *Charmed Circle*, 165, 484; see also Neil Schmitz, "The Difference of Her Likeness: Gertrude Stein's *Stanzas in Meditation*," in *Gertrude Stein and the Making of Literature*, ed. Shirley Neuman and Ira B. Nadel (Boston, 1988), 127, 137. As Brinnin sums up the case, "Gertrude still preferred to think of James as an influence on her personality, rather than as a source of her writing career. However, since she was shy about admitting to the slightest literary influence from any quarter, she seems to have suffered, in this instance, from a temporary case of myopia." Brinnin, *The Third Rose*, 165.

11. Frank O'Hara, *Standing Still and Walking*, ed. Donald Allen (San Francisco, 1983), 110. Stein, quoted in Brinnin, *The Third Rose*, 202.

"given," but always "made," so that if reality is "experienceable" as James asserts, Stein's reportorial mandate is "not to reflect the world but to invent it," and like the Cubist painters offering her much inspiration from this period—Picasso, Cézanne, Braque—to "[bring] to light hidden *versions* of reality."[12] In this (re)production of "versions" of reality, three important inferences would appear to follow.

First, since no ultimate, total, or final form or vision of reality exists, each attempt on the part of the artist to capture that reality must in a sense be constituted a failure, or at least, only a partial or provisional success, thus requiring the whole effort to be repeated all over again, and theoretically, for an infinite number of times thereafter, since truth is "everlastingly in the process of mutation," as noted earlier. Second, without any definitive access to ideal truth or ultimate reality—the "pretended absolutes and origins" in James' terms—the entire emphasis of artistic endeavor falls upon the openness of ongoing process rather than the closure of finalized product. Hence, Marianne DeKoven, in her important study, foregrounds the "mode of writing" in Stein that is "anarchic, undifferentiated, indeterminate, multiple, open-ended," and "opposed to objectivity, order, lucidity, linearity, mastery, and coherence." In more precise terms, "It *is* the indeterminate, anti-patriarchal (anti-logocentric, anti-phallogocentric, presymbolic, pluridimensional) writing which deconstruction, alias Jacques Derrida, proposes as an antidote to Western culture, and which Julia Kristeva proposes as an antidote to patriarchy."[13]

A third and final inference that follows from the processing of endless versions of experience would be to remark the sheer extravagance, the inordinate excess, the very hyperbolic nature of the artist's undertaking—what Stein brings clearly to the fore in heeding James' caution, mentioned previously, never to reject, but instead, to allow "[e]verything [to] come into your scheme." The emphasis here on the radically *inclusionary* aspect of the artist's project carries us, paradoxically,

12. For sample commentary, see Walker, *The Making of a Modernist*, 15, 17, Hawkins, "Sneak Previews," 122, and Marjorie Perloff, "(Im)personating Gertrude Stein," in *Gertrude Stein and the Making of Literature*, ed. Shirley Neuman and Ira Nadel (Boston, 1988), 76; Brinnin, *The Third Rose*, 128, emphasis added. In commenting on Stein's "Cubist" connection, Diana Souhami writes that what Stein and Picasso thought "they were producing was beyond realism . . . They were dismantling the components of reality and reconstructing them in their own highly individual ways . . . working at a time when 'belief in reality of science commenced to diminish.'" Souhami, *Gertrude and Alice*, 101.

13. Diggins, *The Promise of Pragmatism*, 48, 128, 133, and Dubnick, *The Structure of Obscurity*, 20, 29–30; DeKoven, *A Different Language*, xvii, and further on xviii, 5, 7, 15, 16, 20, 22–23, 24, and passim. Cf. Walker, *The Making of a Modernist*, 111–12.

to the very heart of its utter impossibility. For in the end, it is an absence towards which Stein's project is ultimately aimed—"nothing," according to James (*P*, 169, 170)—and as such, would appear to defeat even the most imaginatively inspired effort to call forth "what is just entering into experience, and yet to be named," as James describes this impossible reality, "some imagined aboriginal presence in experience, *before any belief about the presence had arisen.*" As James goes on to remark, "It is what is absolutely dumb and evanescent, the merely ideal limit of our minds. We may glimpse it, but we never grasp it; what we grasp is always some substitute for it which previous human thinking has peptonized and cooked."[14] Yet in *Tender Buttons*, Stein prefers not to be daunted by this "dumb and evanescent" present absence. Indeed, the genius of her text would appear to lie not in excluding it, but rather in turning its "ideal limit" into an extravagantly proliferating absent presence—"the absence of more," as she refers to it in the concluding "Rooms" section of *Tender Buttons* (*SSW*, 501), and thereby subverting "the tendency to deplore" a notion of reality that, until she comes to write these very words, "has not been authorized" (*SSW*, 501).

A short text entitled "Suppose an Eyes," from the "Objects" portion of *Tender Buttons*, brings nicely together all of these inferences with respect to Stein's pragmatic handling of reality:

Suppose it is within a gate which open is open at the hour of closing summer that is to say it is so.
All the seats are needing blackening. A white dress is in sign. A soldier a real soldier has a worn lace a worn lace of different sizes that is to say if he can read, if he can read he is a size to show shutting up twenty-four.
Go red go red, laugh white.
Suppose a collapse in rubbed purr, in rubbed purr get.
Little sales ladies little sales ladies little saddles of mutton.
Little sales of leather and such beautiful beautiful, beautiful beautiful.

(*SSW*, 475)

The exercise Stein sets for herself in this text, as with several others from this section, is to sustain a profusely fecundating discourse in response to a number of "objects" observed from the surrounding world—a white dress, some worn lace, sales ladies—when so many of the aspects of the medium through which the whole experience is rendered contrive against that experience's discursive con-

---

14. William James, quoted in Kathleen Wheeler, *Romanticism, Pragmatism, and Deconstruction* (Oxford, 1993), 86, emphasis added.

tinuance: the statements, for instance, all jammed in between the prefatory title at the beginning and the punctuation at the end; the sentences themselves, each starting with a capital and ending with a period; and, even the individual letters arranged within each line of the page to signify only certain words (and meanings), and not others—"a white dress is in sign," for example. With so much closure, Stein seems to be saying, how is it possible to keep the reality of true-life experience open, or, to go with the terms of her opening line, to keep something which is supposed to be "open" *still* open—"to say it is so"—even though it finds itself "within a gate," and "at the hour of closing." Even our reading of Stein too precisely on this conundrum presented by the "real" may be betraying us if we become overly complacent about ascribing to it a final meaning. The fatality of "a real soldier," after all, lies in the fact that "he can read," and if he *can* read, then he, like us, "show[s] shutting up" daily ("twenty-four"): a "red" stoppage in response to "go," or "a collapse" in response to highly charged discourse like "rubbed purr" (fur?). Better to be like the "little sales ladies," whose example bears repeating. For when they meaning-lessly meld with the "little saddles of mutton" and "[l]ittle sales of leather" through nothing more than the mere force of the poet's vocalic elisions, a certain openness to discursive continuance and renewal is implied: "beautiful beautiful, beautiful, beautiful"!

Richard Rorty, following an important train of thought in John Dewey, shrewdly observes that the Pragmatist's approach to statements like Stein's detailing the nature of observed objects is less likely to be "'Do they get it right?'" than "'What would it be like to believe that? What would happen if I did? What would I be committing myself to?'" For their discourse, concludes Rorty, "is the vocabulary of practice rather than of theory, of action rather than contemplation, in which one can say something useful about truth."[15] I find this comment provides a rather useful insight into Stein's title, "Suppose an Eyes." Run together, the words do sound very much like an injunction to "hypothesize," to suppose or imagine what it would be like actually *to see* the world proactively, from the point of view of the fluid sales ladies, say, rather than merely contemplate it reactively, through the eyes of the static soldier. What would we be committing ourselves to if we did likewise, and what might follow as a result?

In the next section, entitled "Food," Stein juxtaposes two meditations on the single topic "Milk" to enlarge upon these questions, once again, through an important contrast in perceptions. In the first apostrophe, there is much potential

15. Richard Rorty, *Consequences of Pragmatism (Essays: 1972–1980)* (Minneapolis, 1982), 163, 162.

for getting beyond the passive contemplation of sense experience imaged in terms of the ordinary blandness of "[a] white egg" and the tight containment of "a colored pan and a cabbage," all showing "settlement" (*SSW*, 487). A "real pint" "in the middle" of the text is both "open and closed," and elsewhere, "a single cold" suddenly begins to make "an excuse" for adding a second: "Two are more necessary" (*SSW*, 487). Both point to a quite palpable sense of active alteration in response to the world when "cooking, cooking" becomes the central "recognition," opening up "between sudden and nearly sudden very little and large holes" in Stein's text (*SSW*, 487). But when the "seen eye holders" steer this "best of change" in the direction of "meaning," it's as if the text has suffered a mortal wound: "the dark red, all this and bitten, really bitten" (*SSW*, 487). And it's "the best men, the very best men" who, predictably, carry it off at the close. Nonetheless, the element of "guessing" in the text's last line—possibly a reflection on the "holes" uncovered earlier—works against a completely pat ending, and thus becomes the prompt for a further meditation on "Milk," but a repetition with considerable difference, thus:

MILK
        Climb up in sight climb in the whole utter needles and a guess a whole
    guess is hanging. Hanging hanging.

Rounding back with "a guess" on the previous text's point of active egress extirpated by passive contemplation, this second text leaves us to wonder what might have emerged in that first draft of milk if settled meaning had at last given place to sudden recognition. Now, at least, we're past all halfway measures, for "a *whole* guess is hanging" (*SSW*, 487).

"Salad Dressing and an Artichoke," near the end of this second section, provides an interesting gloss on that "whole" left hanging from the previous two texts: "A whole is inside a part, a part does go away, a hole is red leaf. No choice was where there was and a second and a second" (*SSW*, 496). Stein's entire modus operandi may be seen summed up in these two single statements. For the "whole" here stands in for the Pragmatist's reality, the whole that previously became reduced metonymically to merely a "part" of its potentially incalculable meaning, leaving here "a hole" with its "red leaf" (*SSW*, 496) so reminiscent of the bloody wound when the first "Milk" in fact "does go away." With this reduction of presence to absence, Stein is left with "[n]o choice" but to move on to a second "Milk," to restore absence to presence. That act of discursive repetition, however, promises to reenact itself yet *again*—"there was a second and a second" (*SSW*,

496)—since, as Stein observes elsewhere, "the balance of a space [is] not filled but [only] created by something moving."[16] Stein's whole movement in *Tender Buttons*, then, from part to part and from section to section, in pursuit of that w/hole "space between" (*SSW*, 480) is perhaps the best evidence of how the "something" creates and, at the same time, is *itself* repeatedly created. But in order for us to keep her author-ity (and ours) fully functional, in order, in other words, to say something "useful about truth" in Rorty's term, we can only, as Stein herself states, "Read her with her for less" (*SSW*, 497). Less is, in fact, more in Gertrude Stein: "the absence of more" (*SSW*, 501).

Stein's critical essay "Composition as Explanation" (1926) is considerably outside our time-frame of 1907–14. But as a further theoretical expansion of the artistic procedures that remained with her for a lifetime, it forms a convenient bridge to the final "Rooms" section of *Tender Buttons* with which to conclude this chapter's first part. The summative link between the essay as a whole and the previous "Objects" and "Rooms" is provided by Stein's own explanation of "composition" as, quite simply, "A continuous present and using everything and beginning again": "There was a groping for using everything and there was a groping for a continuous present and there was an inevitable beginning of beginning again and again and again" (*SSW*, 518). These endlessly repeated trials of composition stretch back to the Jamesian "singularly nothing," in the first line of the text, which apparently sets them all going—"nothing," that is to say (synonymous with the lesser space of "reality" formerly), "that makes a difference a difference in beginning and in the middle and in ending except that each generation has something different at which they are all looking" (*SSW*, 513; also 519, 520). The trials of composition also extend forward, bringing Stein "to the period of the beginning of 1914" near the end of the essay, where the fateful cataclysm of war urges her to reconsider the whole notion of "romanticism" (*SSW*, 520). Because war is an aggressively violent activity, whose ultimate effect is always to induce extreme conformity within societies and institutions in order for it to be waged effectively—"the fatal unity of war," in Wallace Stevens' phrase (*SCP*, 236)—Stein searches for a viable term through which to resist "[e]verything being alike," and within which to shelter the precious historical differences of generations that

16. Gertrude Stein, "Poetry and Grammar," in *Lectures in America* (Boston, 1985), 225. Although working with a completely different text from *Tender Buttons*, Chessman, similarly, is compelled to conclude that "Otherness ('difference') is now celebrated; the hole or lacuna, which in a Freudian 'system' 'points' to such difference can now be sensed to be, not a locus of absence at all, but a rich and indefinable presence." Chessman, *The Public Is Invited to Dance*, 93. Cf. Scobie, "The Allure of Multiplicity," 116, and Dubnick, *The Structure of Obscurity*, 22.

composition itself, with its dedication to a repetitive "continuous" present, is not quite able culturally to safeguard. Thus, with the introduction of this concept into her discourse, Stein sharpens her thinking about the semantic operations of "composition" enormously. By the end of the essay, it becomes a "con-fusion" or dialectic of what she terms "distribution and equilibration" (*SSW*, 522), whose relation to each other is structured very much like that joining the two "Milk" texts earlier: on the one hand, an equilibration of sameness, meaning, and presence; and, through the "extrication" or revolution of romanticism, on the other hand, the distribution of difference, non-meaning, and absence—yet all poised to return the entire discursive economy back to equilibration once again. The repetition or revolution of Stein's discursive economy here suggests something very much like the operational field of Foucault's "enunciative function," which he describes "as a unity of distribution that opens a field of possible options, and enables various mutually exclusive architectures to appear side by side or in turn." In the broaching of possible but as yet unstated options, then, through her conception of Romanticism Stein gestures once again in the direction of reality's absent excess. What is more, her Romanticism continues to sustain the integrity of the Pragmatist project more generally, whose own "romanticism," according to John Diggins, evinces a like "willingness to plunge into a contingent world of possibility." In its deployment of distributive force, therefore, Stein's romantic composition seeks, in John Dewey's words, "to help get rid of the useless lumber that blocks our highways of thought . . . and open the paths that lead to the future."[17]

17. Michel Foucault, *The Archeology of Knowledge*, trans. A. M. Sheridan Smith (London, 1972), 106, 66, and further on 98–99; Diggins, *The Promise of Pragmatism*, 49; John Dewey, "From Absolutism to Experimentalism," 13. Richard Brodhead is not minded of such pragmatist thinking, but his own conception of romance in *The School of Hawthorne* (New York, 1986) is remarkably similar: "a literary form that aims not to be like reality—by which we mean in part, not to organize meaning as it is coded in the systems of understanding we call the real. Instead romance aims to produce its own, frankly literary world: not the one we know already but a new one, the yield of the work's own representational act. . . . Returning us to a primal state of undifferentiated possibility, this genre allows us to participate in the making of moral signification—in the heady and risky act of giving such possibility determinate shape . . . —that primal *definition* or reduction of possibility by which meaning is brought to an actual form" (193). Diggins, in the reference cited, follows closely the suggestion of Louis Hartz in *The Necessity of Choice* (1990): "When revolutionary norms move into the realm of reality they become romantic. The implementation of ideals requires a departure from rationalism. By his own route the revolutionary adopts precisely that romantic mood of indeterminacy and complexity that gets defended in reactionary thought. In the world of action the Revolution and the Reaction meet." Diggins, quoted in *The Promise of Pragmatism*, 49. Or, in the world of "romance," the "very essence" of which, according to Oscar Wilde's famous comment in *The Importance of Being*

With the exhortation, at the opening of the "Rooms" section of *Tender But-tons*, to "[a]ct so that there is no use in a centre" (*SSW*, 499), Stein thus defers to the dialectical momentum of her composition just outlined, valorizing the distribution of differences over the centralization of meanings. "If the centre has the place" in her discourse, then the question becomes: "is it possible to suggest more to replace that thing"? (*SSW*, 499). If it is a question of "A whole centre" and a "hanging" (*SSW*, 498), we recall from a similar hanging earlier that "This question and this perfect denial does make the time change all the time." Then, Stein affirms, "there is distribution" (*SSW*, 499). What is so vexatious, however, about making a proper entry into this decentered economy of difference is its failure to provide us with any of the conventional signposts of discursive activity: "A silence is not indicated by any motion, less is indicated by a motion, more is not indicated it is enthralled. So sullen and so low, so much resignation, so much refusal and so much place for a lower and an upper, so much and yet more silence, why is it not sleeping a feat why is it not and when is there some discharge when. There never is" (*SSW*, 501). In a word, Stein's composition "suggests nothing" (*SSW*, 501).[18]

Gradually, however, as we begin to realize, following Stein's own lead, that it is we ourselves whom her writing purposes most to empower, and start to focus attention less on our own doubts about her writing and more on our own energy and resourcefulness in engaging it, the game begins to change: "The name is changed because in the little space there is a tree . . . [and] in every space there is a hint of more, all this causes decision" (*SSW*, 504–505). Stein refers to this change as one involving "current" (*SSW*, 505), and I take her to mean by this that now our own energies begin to find their outlet in the production and circulation of text. And whereas before, there seemed to be "no virtue" in "disturbing a centre," while her rooms had seemed so "vacant" (*SSW*, 506), now "there is plenty of room" to "question more and more," and sufficient comfort to feel "a room is big

Earnest, "is uncertainty"—a "saving uncertainty," according to Richard Poirier, quoted in Giles Gunn, "Religion and the Recent Revival of Pragmatism," in *The Revival of Pragmatism: New Essays on Social Thought, Law, and Culture*, ed. Morris Dickstein (Durham, 1998), 413.

18. Or her composition suggests "distance," if we pick up on the proliferation of silences in the passage just quoted. Ray Carney establishes this linkage in an excellent comment in *American Vision: The Films of Frank Capra* (Hanover, 1996): "In a novel or story by Proust, Conrad, Woolf, or Joyce, or in a film by Dreyer, Bergman, Antonioni, Fellini, or Fassbinder, intensities of feeling and imagination are, in effect, openings out of the world of ordinary social and verbal life. They are escape hatches out of the traps and confinements of routine social structures and institutional systems of discourse . . . [and] characters granted such momentary richness of consciousness stop participating practically in society and the world entirely and stare *into the distance in silent rapture*" (336–37, emphasis added).

enough," when the "centre [is] no distractor" (*SSW*, 505, 506). With this "change in organization," therefore, it seems pointless to complain of the endlessness of this final section's "Rooms." Their more than ample space is there at the end of *Tender Buttons* to show "that there is not so much extension as there would be if there were more choice in everything" (*SSW*, 507). And without the "show of choice," so Stein concludes, there can be no "translat[ion]" of authority (*SSW*, 508). If this final installment of her writing, then, succeeds in making "a wide place stranger," it's only because "a wideness" itself "makes an active center" (*SSW*, 508).

Poetry, according to Charles Bernstein, has its "outer limit" and its "inner limit."[19] Up to this point, we've mostly been concerned with the outer limit of poetry in the writing of Gertrude Stein, that is to say, with its relation to the existential content—objects, food, rooms—of the outside material world. But when James talks about reality in terms of "the merely ideal limit of our minds," dealt with earlier, there's also the sense in which reality constitutes an "inner limit"—the limit of personal, subjective psychic experience, within the rooms of the human mind. With the shift from the outer and objective to the inner and subjective, we shall continue to remain focused on the issue of Stein's self-authority in this final part of the chapter. But somehow, immersed in the entirely *human* element of subjective knowledge, we sense that this issue will be harder for us to *control*—a word which will begin to absorb more and more of our attention as we proceed. Stein, I'm fairly convinced, felt the same way. Throughout "Composition as Explanation," for example, she is happy to celebrate the "continuous present" of the new kind of romance-writing she is all the while promoting. But only until the year 1914 and war are mentioned. After that, the text seems to darken considerably—clearly, this innovative time-sense she intuits is fraught with enormous difficulty—and remains that way until it quickly draws to a close: "This is the thing that is at present the most troubling and if there is the time that is at present the most troublesome the time-sense that is at present the most troubling is the thing that makes the present the most troubling. There is at present . . . expression and time, and in this way at present composition is time that is the reason that at present the time-sense is troubling. . . . Now that is all" (*SSW*, 522–23). Why, we might wonder, does Stein appear so perplexed by the sense of continuous time as it relates to expression here? And more importantly, what bearing might this

19. Charles Bernstein, *A Poetics* (Cambridge, Mass., 1992), 66.

concern have upon her newly confirmed sense of author-ity—confirmed, at least, up until the war years?

We can begin to gain a purchase on Stein's anxiety over her writing from about this time by understanding, first of all, the reason for her attaching such importance to its intense temporality. For it is her writing's continuous time-sense, driving as it does the dialectic of distributive difference and equilibrated sameness in face of some ungraspable and yet to be named reality—it is this time-sense that holds her composition open to contingency, multiplicity, and variety, and assures her continuous sense of self-authority in the process. What is more, if we now begin to view the ungraspable as that ideal inner limit set by the interiority of psychic experience, Stein's continuous time-sense makes promise of a subjectivity whose claim can never be "self-sufficient, transparently self-conscious, and self-identical," but a subjectivity itself open potentially to infinite construction, given its constitution as the "endless repetition" of an (im)possible "absent ideal."[20] The new spin that temporality puts on self-authority thus points it in the direction of authentication within the contexts of gender and sexuality. But here the risks begin to multiply for a writer like Stein.

As she explains in "Composition as Explanation," writers "creating the modern composition authentically are naturally only of importance when they are dead because by that time the modern composition having become past is classified and the description of it is classical" (*SSW*, 514). The regrettable implication

20. Judith Butler, "Lana's 'Imitation': Melodramatic Repetition and the Gender Performative," *Genders* 9 (fall, 1990): 1–18. Butler's formulations for subjectivity are most apt here, forming a vital intersection with James' pragmatism, whose own "ideal limit," at the impossible interface between repeated representation and evanescent reality—"mother nature," he calls it (*P*, 62)—exactly parallels "the primary prohibition against an original experience of maternal presence" in "Lacanian discourse," thereby providing "an occasion to generate a limitless series of phantasms which effectively multiply the aims and directionalaities of desire . . . [yielding] a multiplication and diversification of imaginary strategies" (13), or as Stein remarks, "a center confused with lists [and] series" (*SSW*, 519). In grasping "always some substitute" for reality, but never the thing itself (William James, quoted in Wheeler, *Romanticism, Pragmatism, and Deconstruction*, 86), James would further agree with Lacan's suggestion "that the 'real' is obliquely contained in the repetitive act . . . which establishes substitutability as the indeterminate site of the real" (Butler, "Lana's 'Imitation,'" 14). Hence, Stein's "*Act* so that there is no use in a centre," in *Tender Buttons* (*SSW*, 498), since, in her famous tag from *Lectures in America*, "there is no there, there" (218). Teresa de Lauretis, working with the psychoanalysis of Jean Laplanche and the Pragmatism of Charles Sanders Peirce in *The Practice of Love: Lesbian Sexuality and Perverse Desire* (Bloomington, 1994), contrives to construct a parallel argument to the foregoing, viz., "Both the sexual object constructed in fantasy and the immediate object constructed in semiosis are contiguous but displaced in relation to the real; and hence the homology of fantasy (in sexuality) and semiosis with regard to the subject's relation to the object of representation" (305).

of Stein's observation is that the true Modernist can write nothing of importance in life, her reputation as a writer of "romantic" (as opposed to "classical") composition residing entirely in her dissident status as an "outlaw" throughout all of that time (*SSW*, 514). "Acceptance," if it comes at all, is earned when "the thing created becomes a classic"—a thing whose "characteristic quality . . . is that it is beautiful" (*SSW*, 515). If there is to be any surviving death in *this* life for the writer, we sense the tremendous pressure being brought to bear on the modern artist to surrender her authority to the discourse of Classicism. Thus, at the outer limit of her project, the removal of the continuous time-sense from the representation of reality is likely to presence it in some form of "realism," and even Gertrude Stein herself was famously known to go that route with the publication of *The Autobiography of Alice B. Toklas* (1933), a book that brought her instant fame and a great deal of money besides.[21]

At the inner limit of reality, however, the removal of the rhetoric of temporality in yielding to the clamor for "acceptance" could mean only one thing: the surrender of alternative forms of gendered subjectivity to the pathology of abjection, in exchange for the authority of a heteronormative lie. Both outer and inner limits of discourse, if handled just this way, come together in George Steiner's remark that "heterosexuality is the very essence of . . . classic realism," which prompts him further to note that "homosexuality could be construed as a creative rejection of the philosophic and conventional realism, of the *mundanity* and extroversion of classic and nineteenth century feeling." In such terms, Stein's "absence of more" opens up a queer "distance" between a classically closed and a romantically open notion of selfhood that Guy Hocquenghem links to "homosexuality" that, in his Steinian formulation, "questions again and again the certainties of existence." Sue-Ellen Case makes the similar observation that "Oscar Wilde brought [his] artifice, wit, irony, and the distancing of straight reality and its conventions to the stage," following the suggestion of Michael Bronski, closer to our own day, that "Wit and irony provide the only reasonable modus operandi in the American Literalist Terror of Straight Reality."[22] Now Stein is able to

21. Walker, *The Making of a Modernist*, 16–17; Souhami, *Gertrude and Alice*, 190–96.

22. George Steiner, quoted in Jonathan Dollimore, *Sexual Dissidence: Augustine to Wilde, Freud to Foucault* (New York, 1991), 307; Guy Hocquenghem, *Homosexual Desire*, trans. Caniella Dangor (Durham, 1993), 53; Sue-Ellen Case, "Toward a Butch-Femme Aesthetic," in *The Lesbian and Gay Studies Reader*, ed. Henry Abelove, Michèle Aina Barale, and David M. Halperin (New York, 1993), 298. The "black" subject, no doubt, is dissident in quite similar terms as the "queer," since the "distancing" signed by both, as Hortense Spillers recently argues, "might be regarded as the mark of self-displacement in the social given." Hortense Spillers, "'All the Things You Could Be by Now, If Sig-

maintain some sense of control over (or distance from) the terror of realism threatening her authority as a lesbian writer by indulging the continuous time-sense of her modern composition: in the passage previously cited from "Composition as Explanation," for instance, "trouble" is repeated *five* times in as many lines. But as a control maintained in face of, if not precisely founded upon, a perpetual lack of acceptance for lesbian authorship now, and in the future, what could it matter?

What must have made the struggle for self-authority through temporality even more troublesome for Stein was the toll it exacted in terms of the loss of sibling support and fraternal love. From a very early age, she and her brother Leo formed a deeply affectional alliance in response to a distant and invalid mother and an overbearing and tyrannical father, the latter in particular sparking a resentment so intense in both that it was eventually "to include *all* fathers." As time wore on, however, it was Leo, ironically, who more and more would assume the role of patriarchal authority, mounting his claim for control and mastery of his sister, not unexpectedly, on the basis of a demand for greater realism in her work:

> A writer, he felt, should aim only at fitting meaning to purpose with the exquisite precision of a jeweler. . . . As early as 1907, Leo had made a series of drawings of an abstract nature, but he was dissatisfied with the results and may very likely have extended his impatience with abstractionist art to include Gertrude's experiments . . . [for] it became apparent that she had found in [abstractionist] writing the one means by which she could gain ascendance over Leo and that she would no longer allow her progress to be curbed.[23]

The introduction of Alice B. Toklas into Gertrude's life shared with her brother in Paris in the years leading up to the war succeeded only in heightening even further the crisis taking shape around the struggle for self-authority. For what

mund Freud's Wife Was Your Mother': Psychoanalysis and Race," *Boundary 2* 23 (summer 1996): 112. And as in Stein's queer distancing, Spillers too views verbal discourse—"speaking"—as "both process and paradigm to the extent that signifying enables the presence of an absence and registers the absence of a presence, but it is also a superior mark of the transformative, insofar as it makes something by cutting through the 'pure and simple' of the 'undifferentiated' gaps and spacings of signifiers" (118). According to Spillers, "This movement across an interior space demarcates the discipline of self-reflection, or the content of a self-interrogation that 'race' always covers over as an already-answered. But for oneself, another question is posed: Where might I become, insofar as . . . ? To the extent that 'I' 'signs' itself 'elsewhere,' represents itself beyond the given, the onus of becoming . . . rebounds on the one putting the question" (119).

23. Brinnin, *The Third Rose*, 16–17, 10, 80. Cf. Souhami, *Gertrude and Alice*, 113.

Gertrude and Alice both began producing together now "was beyond realism, or 'things remembered,' or 'reconstruction from memory.' They were dismantling the components of reality and reconstructing them in their own highly individual ways [and Gertrude] felt that this subjective expression put them into the vanguard of the twentieth century." Having all the while contended that "[Gertrude's] basically stupid and I'm basically intelligent," Leo eventually dissolved the relationship with his sister for good in 1913. Despite a couple of half-hearted attempts by Leo to reconcile the differences with his sister, for the remainder of her lifetime, for her part, "Gertrude apparently welcomed the estrangement and made no serious effort to repair the break."[24]

Gertrude may have welcomed the break with Leo. Nonetheless, I think it's fairly safe to assume that their highly pitched battle over the right to assert what was really true in life—a battle essentially for authoritative control over how their world ought ideally to be represented—left Gertrude deeply troubled. In "A Portrait of F. B." (1913), composed the year Leo left 27 rue de Fleurus for good, we find a great deal of Gertrude's frustration spilling over into the text in the form of bitter sarcasm:

> Praise the lion and the rat, see the morsels fairly, show the swimming of the rat show the rabbit winning. Bestow the light and chase it there, see the hall is dimmer, see the lightening everywhere see the lightening dimmer. . . . Make no dinner in the morning, make it in the evening, see the same and see it there, see it in the morning . . . say no more and undertake what is so ridiculous that there is no time to say that and any how what is the abuse of an intention, why should there be etiquette, why is there every lightening, why if the season is the same is there summer, when is there more night than in winter.
>
> (G&P, 176)

If Leo might be thought to be the lion in this passage (and perhaps also the rat, and the rabbit who always wins the race), Gertrude imagines herself in the somewhat petulant position of insisting on merely doing the opposite to him. If dietary protocol demands that dinner be made in the evening rather than the morning, then she, "undertak[ing] what is so ridiculous," prefers to "see it in the morning": "why should there be etiquette"? If Leo prefers "lightening everywhere," then she will see dark everywhere—"more night than in winter." In a battle for authority,

24. Souhami, *Gertrude and Alice*, 101; Leo Stein, quoted in Brinnin, *The Third Rose*, 311; Chessman, *The Public Is Invited to Dance*, 228 n. 11; Souhami, *Gertrude and Alice*, 140, 153; Mellow, *Charmed Circle*, 296.

one either controls, or is oneself controlled. And to a large extent, this fairly much represents Leo and Gertrude's epistemological standoff. In Leo's championing the position of realism, he represents the "traditional quest for foundations and first principles . . . searching to get at the truth of things by thinking thoughts that are true to the way things are and consistent with other thoughts." Gertrude, to the contrary, assumes "the nature of things to be a succession of events in which nothing is fixed and everything is in change and transition":

> No longer could the reality of things be a matter of photographic representation, copied in the mind like a "kodak fixation," as Dewey put it. . . . With pragmatism, . . . ideas are tested in experience in view of their observable outcomes, as opposed to being measured against some standard that is atemporal and external to experience. [Accordingly,] the rational meaning of ideas would lay in the future since only the future, and not the past, could be subject to *alteration and control.*[25]

As this passage indicates, then, whether one found oneself nourished by ideas in the past, or ideas in the future, the positions could hardly be distinguishable one from the other if it was a fixation on authoritative control that ultimately served as their overriding purpose and governing rationale. "A turn of the table does not mean that cups are there," as Stein's "Portrait" goes on to reveal, "it means that there is no loneliness" (i.e., unique distinction or separation). In sum: "It does not mean any little thing" (*G&P,* 177).

Stein's favorite reading (in addition to detective stories and *Clarissa Harlowe*) was William Shakespeare. With the eve of war serving as backdrop, one can't help thinking that she must very much have been minded of another brother, eager to colonize his sister's independence of mind and singularity of spirit, in the author from whose work she would read a play "every few days." "The canker gall[ing] the infants of the spring," as Ophelia's importuning elder brother Laertes remarks, "too oft before their buttons be disclos'd" (*Hamlet,* I.iii), in one sense, depicts a predatory situation that seems to fit both sisters precisely. And the line quite possibly suggested to Gertrude the title for her *Tender Buttons,* completed the previous year.[26] But in another sense, Stein could hardly have thought Ophelia's plight at all matched her own, if she felt the key to her pursuit for unique self-authorization might lie in fashioning herself into a mirror-image of her brother's own controlling identity. Yet this appears to be the very troubling

25. Diggins, *The Promise of Pragmatism,* 39, emphasis added. See further on 19, 24, 38, 154, and 471.

26. Brinnin, *The Third Rose,* 61, 374; Pondrom, *G&P,* 424.

impasse—"the abuse of an intention" in the previous citation, perhaps—that the
continuous present of her composition had brought her by 1913: "A clatter registered has a calming center. That is the outlasting of a sight of all. If it is possible
that there is the result then certainly no one would think so. Every one does.
There is no sense in such a history. There is no sense at all. Not a bit of broom
has the window open, not a bit" (*G&P*, 177). Ensconcing herself at the "calming
center" of her Paris apartment for all the important painters and poets and writers
of the day to see, in prospect of such closure—not even "the window open"—
Stein seems to sense that her whole project as an American Modernist lesbian
poet has been betrayed if, as in the earlier passage, she can "say no more": "There
is no sense in such a history. There is no sense at all."

Judith Butler has recently argued the case for *uncontrollability* in feminist and
gay politics, and one is prone to speculate whether or not a similar notion might
have suggested itself to Stein as just the insight needed to work through the troublesomeness that her quest for a distinct sense of authorship had incurred when
revolved from an overly controlling and exclusionary sense of identity. Writes
Butler:

> The singular and authoritative homophobic figuration . . . cannot be opposed by
> remaining within the terms of that binary fight, but by displacing the binary itself
> through producing again and again precisely the discursive *uncontrollability* of the
> terms that are suppressed by regulatory violence. . . . The task is not to resolve or
> restrain the tension, the crisis, the phantasmatic excess induced . . . but to affirm
> identity categories as a site of inevitable rifting, in which the phantasmatic fails to
> preempt the linguistic prerogative of the real. It is this incommensurability of the
> phantasmatic and the real that requires . . . to be safeguarded . . . to make that
> rift, that insistent rifting, into the persistently ungrounded ground from which . . .
> discourse emerges.[27]

27. Judith Butler, "The Force of Fantasy: Feminism, Mapplethorpe, and Discursive Excess," *Differences* 2 (spring 1990): 120–21. Cf. Judith Butler, *Gender Trouble: Feminism and the Subversion of
Identity* (New York, 1990), 66–72. Domestic trouble should also be included here, as Robert K. Martin notes: "Stein wants to create a continuous present not only of language but also of self, an eternally
renewing and transforming identity that cannot be confined to the permanent past of marriage . . .
[since] [t]he desire of marriage to freeze the other in a past time brings it inevitably into conflict with
the need of the individual to change" Robert K. Martin, "*The Mother of Us All* and American History," 216. As a further elaboration on "identity categories" that Butler perceives as "a site of rifting,"
or in terms of this study, "distancing," John Champagne observes: "What Foucault terms 'the reality
of discourse' is a necessarily inadequate attempt to name the rift between unthinkable heterogeneity
and the sign, a rift that humanism attempts to fill with recourse to concepts such as experience." John
Champagne, *The Ethics of Marginality: A New Approach to Gay Studies* (Minneapolis, 1995), 198 n. 15.

res- -ture t?
in dn ?. L

If Stein proposed to move her composition forward, she perhaps realized she was not likely to succeed by turning the tables on Leo, and prolonging the "binary fight" by arrogating his authority to her self. Instead, her sense of unique self-authorization would be achieved by displacing that authority onto a continuous distancing of selfhood "as a site of rifting" precisely through an *enlargement* of composition's repeated troublesomeness rather than its curtailment. By locating her authority in non-authority, so to speak, she gestures toward that "ungrounded ground" that places identity beyond the control of *all* categories and classes, and joins the outer to the inner limit of her poetry in revealing "that there is a resistance to identity at the very heart of psychic life."[28]

In so doing, Stein thus ushers her dissident authorship, finally, into a future of potential acceptance based on *nothing more*—"say no more," "the absence of more"—than the fluid distribution of an excess of subjective space, what she perhaps calls, in this final passage of "Portrait," "the practice of Nileing":

> Bake a table, the rest is empty, see the plate first, the first is distributed, see the arrangement the arrangement is in the curling Christmas.
> Bet more than sugar, copy no more principally, restrict more decoration, repeat the needle. There is made.
> So to see and so to go and so to turn the list around, so to go and so there is the practice of Nileing. Plainer sheets have simple stripes. (*G&P*, 177)

The an(nihil)ation here of controlling authoritative categories—"copy no more"—suggests a possible "arrangement" that gives a Christmas-like new birth to the subject in a repeated turning, curling, or nileing around an empty "rest"—an incommensurable reality that Teresa de Lauretis designates as the "lack" to which Stein becomes resigned, and elsewhere refers to as "the symbolic space of excess and contradiction . . . or imaginary space in which [the difference between characters and roles] configures a lesbian subject-position."[29]

28. Jaqueline Rose, *Sexuality in the Field of Vision* (New York, 1986), 91.
29. De Lauretis, *The Practice of Love*, 227, 110, and further on 224–25. Ed Cohen explains, similarly, in "Foucauldian Necrologies: 'Gay,' 'Politics'? Politically Gay?" *Textual Practice* 2 (spring 1988), how "Foucault repeatedly assesses the significance of gay experience as a space of possibility, of creativity, and not just as a 'sexual' identity but as a 'way of life,'" and finds further corroboration in de Lauretis' notion (in *Alice Doesn't: Feminism, Semiotics, Cinema* [Bloomington, 1984]) of subjectivity as "an ongoing construction, not a fixed point of departure or arrival" (91, 100 n. 15). In the reference cited here, de Lauretis' formulation is based on a film-text, but a poem can be like a film, as the passage from Stein shows, "by disallowing a univocal spectatorial identification with any one character or role or object-choice, and foregrounding instead the relations of desire to fantasy and

In the end, Stein's "turn[ing] the list around"—presumably, the list of subject positions—argues for "the speculative character of identity," so that "[w]hat survives the ravages of time," in her discourse, "is not an identity but a question of identity." The question of identity, in this optional rather than problematic sense, would lead her much later to the paradoxical formulation in the *Geographical History of America* (1936), "No one knowing me knows me. I am I." But undoubtedly, it's the "nileing" of subjectivity in this redoubled i-dentity—"the terrible *fluidity* of self-revelation," according to Henry James (preface to *The Ambassadors*)—in a text like "A Portrait of F.B.," that can eventually transport her there.[30] For "There is the rate," as its final stanza declares, "that makes no more" (*G&P*, 177).

The notion of a fluid subjectivity through which to maintain her composition's radical sense of both temporality and authority is perhaps a final debt Stein owed to William James. For it was his concept of a "stream of consciousness," one of the critical hallmarks of Modernism, that construed consciousness not as an essentialized state of being, but whose "liquid metaphor impl[ied] a Whitmanesque continuous becoming."[31] "Sacred Emily" (1913), a poem composed the same year as the previous "Portrait," and with which we might conclude, veritably overflows with the continuous alteration of states of feeling and thought unbounded through time:

> Rose is a rose is a rose is a rose
> Loveliness extreme.
> Extra gaiters,
> Loveliness extreme.

---

its mobility within the fantasy scenario" (*Practice of Love*, 122)—safeguarding, in other words, the "incommensurability of the phantasmatic and real," as Butler earlier observes, and refers to elsewhere (following Lacan, again) as "a *fêlure* of or in the subject, the division that multiplies into the dissimulating trajectory that 'is' the subject." Butler, "Lana's 'Imitation,'" 14.

30. Karin Cope, "Painting after Gertrude Stein," *Diacritics* 24 (spring-summer 1993): 201, 197; Gertrude Stein, *Geographical History of America, or the Relation of Human Nature to Human Mind* (New York, 1973), 77; Henry James, quoted in Ira B. Nadel, "Gertrude Stein and Henry James," in *Gertrude Stein and the Making of Literature*, ed. Shirley Neuman and Ira B. Nadel (Boston, 1988), 88. Echoing de Lauretis' invocation of symbolic "lack" just mentioned, John Champagne, *Ethics of Marginality*, observes that "such positionings will always necessarily be contingent, provisional, subject to slippage—that is, subject to deconstruction . . . so that it becomes impossible to speak of something like 'the homosexual' except as a determined and *vacant place* in a discourse, a place that, by definition, cannot be filled once and for all" (65, emphasis added).

31. Diggins, *The Promise of Pragmatism*, 127.

Sweetest ice-cream.
Pages ages page ages page ages.

. . . .

Able able able
A go to green and a letter spoke a go to green or praise or
Worships worships worships.
Door.
Do or.

(*G&P*, 187)

I would like to think that the "door" opened up in this last citation tropes a kind of portal through which Stein's pragmatism flows seamlessly into her feminism and sapphism, hence melding the two parts of my own argument together.

Thus, when we stand back from this passage, we perhaps see how Stein's sapphism *repeats* (does over = do'er = door) her pragmatism, in the way that "sexuality remains fluid and everchanging," like James' stream of consciousness, "evolving through adult life in response to internal and external vicissitudes: flexible, anarchic, ambiguous, layered with multiple meanings, *offering doors* that open to unexpected experience . . . [in] the search for pleasure and expansiveness that motivates visions of political change and human connection." Accordingly, James' opposition to rationalism for its exclusionary logic's resistance to such expansiveness is Gertrude Stein's as well:

> Reason purses.
> Reason purses to relay to relay carpets
>
> . . . .
>
> Cunning saxon symbol
> Symbol of beauty.
> Thimble of everything.
> Cunning clover thimble.
> Cunning of everything.
> Cunning of thimble.
> Cunning cunning.
>
> (*G&P*, 186)

Her unique self-authorization, therefore, locates itself in a position quite outside mainstream culture's narrow logocentric "thimbology," a discursive site from which she can then resist patriarchy's "official symbol systems" by deploying them "to both reveal and mock dominant culture": "rose is a rose is a rose."[32]

---

32. Carole S. Vance, "Pleasure and Danger: Toward a Politics of Sexuality," in *Pleasure and Dan-*

But that discursive distancing, as we know, was also the site of Emily Dickinson's unique authority, displaced through "play, parody, duplicity, evasion, illogic, silence, role-playing, and renunciation."[33] Gertrude Stein can honor Dickinson's dissident subjectivity in the title of her text, therefore, because a symbolic absence or distance underwrites her sacred identity as a writer—"Gold space gold space of toes. / Twos, twos. / Pinned to the letter" (G&P, 183)—rather than essentializing orders of meaning and truth "Begging to state begging to state begging to state alright / Begging to state begging to state begging to state alright" (G&P, 182).

"Sacred Emily" thus becomes a tribute to a writer whose work, like Stein's favorite Shakespeare, is sutured over an engima—"So great so great Emily. Sew grate sew grate Emily" (G&P, 182)—a tribute to an author-ity that, like Hamlet's skewed custom, is perhaps "More honour'd in the breach than the observance" (Hamlet, I.iv).[34] And the miracle is that the custom has survived, in the repetition of the writer, Gertrude Stein, herself:

> Put something down.
> Put something down some day.
> Put something down some day in.

ger: Exploring Female Sexuality, ed. Carole S. Vance (London, 1989), 22, emphasis added, 15. Cf. DeKoven, A Different Language, xvii. "[T]he opposition between rational analysis and emotional immediacy was one of Stein's central preoccupations during the early years of her career," Jayne Walker writes in The Making of a Modernist, and explains it further in the context of sibling rivalry already referred to: "Identifying her brother Leo's failures with his excess of rational control and redefining her own intellectual stance in opposition to his, she began to regard all analytic thought as a barrier to the unmediated experience that nurtures creativity" (37, 104, and further in 161 n. 17). Walker's argument elsewhere that Stein "declar[es] her rejection of James's philosophical pragmatism" (104) may thus be more rightly perceived as a rejection of brother Leo's "version" of the philosophy, which Mellow implies Leo completely misunderstood in any case (Charmed Circle, 54), although Walker is careful to note that Stein "never abandoned her early commitment to James's teachings" (104–105).

33. Paula Bennett, "The Pea That Duty Locks: Lesbian and Feminist-Heterosexual Readings of Emily Dickinson's Poetry," in Lesbian Texts and Contexts: Radical Revisions, ed. Karla Jay and Joanne Glasgow (New York, 1990), 107.

34. "'Suture,'" as Joan Copjec writes (following Jacques-Alain Miller), "'names the relation of the subject to the chain of its discourse.' It is an account of the subject's, of meaning's coming into being . . . [that] says that there are no fully constructed subjects or objects outside discourse which must then be integrated into a social structure. Nor is there any unified subject or object outside discourse that governs it. The subject is, instead, simultaneously constituted and dislocated by speech" Joan Copjec, "Sex and the Euthanasia of Reason," in Supposing the Subject, ed. Joan Copjec (New York, 1994), 27, 38.

> Put something down some day in my.
> In my hand.
> In my hand right.
> In my hand writing.
> Put something down some day in my hand writing.
>
> *(G&P,* 185)

The excess of repetitions from this passage midway through the text are brought
to a halt with, appropriately, a quadruple iteration of the phrase "Never the less"
(*G&P,* 185). As a further inaugural, accordingly, to the "absence of more" that
promises to follow, Stein ultimately channels her lines' unstoppable flow, near
the end of the poem, through her own enigmatic identity as "hubbie," the lesbian
lover of "pussy," that is, Alice B. Toklas: "Excessively illigitimate. / Pussy pussy
what what" (*G&P,* 187). The inscrutable double "what" capping this excess is
intended to show only "Mercy for a dog," which Stein positions dumbly immediately following (*G&P,* 187). "I am I," she was once reported to have declared,
"because my little dog knows me," then added, "That does not prove anything
about you it only proves something about the dog."[35] For the readers of this doubly emphatic dumb cadence, therefore, the two *what*s present a final portal
through which Stein's struggle for unique self-authorization can perhaps pass out
of her life, and begin to take hold of our own, through the prodigal variety and
alterity of a love that, going the distance, has yet futurally to legitimate:

> A go to green and a letter spoke a go to green or praise or
> Worships worships worships
> Door.
> Do or.
>
> *(G&P,* 187)

---

35. Souhami, *Gertrude and Alice,* 111; Mellow, *Charmed Circle,* 327.

Chapter 2

William Carlos Williams' "Secret Gardens":
Cultural Criticism in the Distance

The first task of thought is to criticize the all-embracing commensurability.
—THEODOR ADORNO, MINIMA MORALIA.

The poem . . . is the construction in understandable limits of [one's] life.
—WILLIAM CARLOS WILLIAMS, AUTOBIOGRAPHY

*The expert in thought is one who has skill in making experiments to intro-
duce an old meaning into different situations and who has a sensitive ear
for detecting resultant harmonies and discords.*
—JOHN DEWEY, EXPERIENCE AND NATURE.

ONE of the least-remarked-upon aspects of *The Autobiography of William Carlos Williams* that the poet published in 1948 is that having to do with the presentation of subjectivity in any number of its forms, figures, and fashions— and these mostly dissident or forbidden. The presentation of the forbidden forms of subjectivity is where Williams' fascination with words leads him in several places in his *Autobiography*—words "full of a perfection of the longest leap, the most unmitigated daring, the longest chances" (*A*, 288)—and he hardly seems less fascinated with all of the depictions that result. Collectively, they take on a kind of secret life, he states at one point: "a secret life I wanted to tell openly—if only I could—how it lives, secretly about us as much now as ever" (*A*, 288). And the cure for this secret longing-to-tell not unexpectedly lies, once again, in the daring of words. For it is by their "medicine" that the poet gains entrance to "these secret gardens of the self," and by their "permission" that "another world" is revealed to "the poor, defeated body," with all its "gulfs and grottos" (*A*, 288). What is particularly fascinating about Williams' secret gardens, moreover, are the variability and range of identities they open up within the quite specific context of individual subjectivity in the decade or so, on the *Autobiography*'s account, *prior to* the 1920s, the period when it is generally conceded that Williams' vocation as a practicing poet was officially established. Because this chapter (like the last) will be primarily concerned with the poet's writing in this initial stage of his career, I would like to dwell a bit further on Williams' earliest and most primordial representations of selfhood. For it is within them, as I shall argue, that Williams' cultural criticism first begins to take shape, and within them, too, that the possibilities and limits of such criticism would more or less become set for the long vocation of writing that was later to burgeon.

It is perhaps fair to say that the representation of dissident forms of subjectivity is one of the most compelling experiments in Williams' *Autobiography*, at least in the earlier chapters. One thinks, for instance, of the hapless day-laborer, "a big lump of a man in dirty overalls," whom the poet-doctor encounters one day during the course of his internship at the old French Hospital in New York City (circa 1906–1908), in Chapter 15. "When we saw him," Williams recounts, "he was messed up generally, bleeding from the mouth and nose and . . . unconscious," and so "[I] told the girls to undress him." Nothing at the hospital, however, has quite prepared doctor and nurses for what happens next:

> I went back to sit in the chair at the chart desk but almost at once heard the girls cry out and come piling from behind the screen. . . . I went and was not a little astonished at what they had discovered. The man was a big guy, a plump specimen in bloody clothes, but when they had begun to remove the outer clothing, they found he had on a woman's silk chemise with little ribbons at his nipples; that his chest and finally his legs were shaved; that he wore women's panties and long silk stockings. The girls wouldn't have anything more to do with him.
>
> (*A*, 82)

What is perhaps no less astonishing are the injured workman's wife who, when notified of her husband's somewhat bizarre attire, "said merely that he liked that sort of thing," and the laborer's intimate, white-haired friend, "one of the most prominent [names] in the state," who comes daily to inquire after the condition of the unconscious man until he eventually dies, and his body is "returned to the wife for a decent funeral" (*A*, 82–83).

Or take this next unusual episode, related in the chapter entitled "Hell's Kitchen," which follows the above:

> The police had brought in a young girl who had been plenty roughed up. We didn't usually care for that sort of case, but under the circumstances the nurses had to

straighten her out at least a little. They discovered that it was not a girl at all, but a boy. He had apparently been soliciting trade in doorways and the street entries to the various houses on the block, the usual two-bit stand-up, when one of his customers got wise to him. For the boy or young man had an inflated rubber replica of the female genitalia pulled up and strapped between his legs to make him marketable. It must have gone fine for a while until this guy found himself cheated, got his hands on the thing and then hauled off and clipped the vendor on the jaw.

(*A*, 99)

The prosthesis in this vignette, by contrast to the previous, no doubt raises the art of cross-dressing to a more practiced height. Still, the art is one the experience of which Williams himself was given to indulge in from time to time in his own youth. From his college years, for instance, there is the boast that his "Tit Willow" from *The Mikado* for the Mask and Wig Club at Penn presented "a round, smooth face, as shown by the half-tone in the Philadelphia *Bulletin*," and the boast is further puffed by the somewhat vain speculation that had his legs been equal to it, "I should have got the part of a handsome girl in the varsity production which followed" (*A*, 52). But the art of cross-dressing is one in which Williams had acquired a bit of experience before going to college. Three years previously, at the age of sixteen, in the ninth chapter, entitled "Paris" (circa 1899), he recollects making a visit to his Tante Alice on her birthday, dressed entirely in his mother's clothes:

cross-dressing

I hadn't got ten feet from our street doorway—Alice lived in the next block—when my hat began to give me trouble. I leaned my head to this side then to that, but people began to look at me and I became jittery. But I kept on, got to the proper entry, climbed the three flights of stairs and had the satisfaction of having Alice take me in her arms crying, "Ma chère Hélène!"

(*A*, 57)

What conclusions, then, might we be invited to draw from all of these unusual anecdotes?[1]

1. Among these early episodes, we should perhaps not neglect to include Williams' curious amusement over Ezra Pound's role as one of the women of the chorus in the production by the senior class at Penn of Euripides' *Iphigenia in Aulis,* in the original Greek, at the Philadelphia Academy of Music. "The fellow who played the Messenger was superb that night," recounts Williams, "and got an ovation for the impassioned delivery of his lines. But Ez was as much the focus of attention, *at least for me.* He was dressed in a Grecian robe, as I remember it, a togalike ensemble topped by a great blond wig at which he tore as he waved his arms about and heaved his massive breasts in ecstasies of

Bernard Duffey, in a recent reading of the Williams canon following the theory of Kenneth Burke, puts forward the suggestion, although he does not elaborate upon it to any great extent, that "a central and little-considered motive in Williams's writing was to gain a sense of regenerated and remade self." Williams was, Duffey explains, "an 'expressive' as well as a 'mimetic' poet, and what he chose to express at length and in detail was his experience of and with a self clear and free of demands not of its own accepting."[2] A self "clear and free of demands," demands imposed upon it by some external source of control or authority, forges a direct link to the argument that Theodor Adorno elaborates in his landmark essay "Cultural Criticism and Society," an essay, as I shall later reveal, that can usefully serve to explain several of the leading tenets of Williams' own cultural criticism, both in the early prose and poetry. But before advancing to this next stage of my own argument, we might just pause for a moment to notice what demands may already have been thrown up in the way of the free expression of dissident forms of subjectivity in the episodes from Williams' *Autobiography* previously recounted.

Recall, for instance, the reaction of the nurses to the unconscious workman accoutred in female attire earlier—nurses who, once privy to the man's highly secretive alternative to orthodox sexual expression, in Williams' words, "wouldn't

---

extreme emotion" (*A*, 57, emphasis added). Photographs of Pound in period-costume in this production are reproduced in Daniel Hoffman, ed., *Ezra Pound and William Carlos Williams: The University of Pennsylvania Conference Papers* (Philadelphia, 1983), 44–45. Theatricality, of course, encourages the kind of experimenting with self-identity that Williams clearly had an interest in from his earliest years. Ross Posnock's expansion of this point in *The Trial of Curiosity: Henry James, William James, and the Challenge of Modernity* (New York, 1991) is "theatricalized, stylized self-representation that escapes the 'monotonous,'" and "a heterogeneous, theatrical self [that] bristles with the mobility and impurity of internal difference, of something not wholly itself" (58, 59; see also 12, 22, 55, 57, 166, 170, 173, 185, and 186). Michael Paul Rogin develops a similar set of issues in *Subversive Genealogy: The Politics and Art of Herman Melville* (Berkeley, 1985), 235–36. Almost two decades later in the *Autobiography*, and certainly well beyond the transgender role-playing of his youth, when Williams is given to relate his rejection of the homosexual advances of Marsden Hartley, it should again be curious for us to note a sense of ambiguity attached to the more normative identity Williams intends categorically to construct for himself in this encounter (Chapter 29): "He [Marsden Hartley] told me I *would* have made one of the most charming whores of the city" (*A*, 173; the emphasis here, interestingly, is Williams' own).

2. Bernard Duffey, *A Poetry of Presence: The Writing of William Carlos Williams* (Madison, 1986), 44. Much later in his study, Duffey is given to observe that it was because "Williams found multiplicity to be the necessary condition, against the unitary thrust of philosophy and science" that in all likelihood served as the impetus for "making subjective assertion possible" (184). This astute, but again unelaborated, comment I hope also to extend in much of the argument that follows.

have anything more to do with him" (*A*, 82). In what seems an almost perfect gloss on this passage in his *Minima Moralia*, Theodor Adorno would tend to understand the rigidified view of orthodox sexuality presented by the nurses here in terms of a "common consent to the positive" that, acting almost like "a gravitational force," "pulls all downwards." As Adorno elaborates further, this positive capitulation to social conformity with respect to identity "shows itself superior to the opposing impulse by declining to engage it." Thus,

> [i]ntellectual debility, affirmed as a universal principle, appears as vital force . . . [a] hidebound insistence on arbitrary opinion in the absence of any proof, in short the practice of reifying every feature of an aborted, unformed self, withdrawing it from the process of experience and asserting it as the ultimate That's-the-way-I-am, [that] suffices to overrun impregnable positions. . . . [Consequently,] the cynical trumpeting of their own defect betrays an awareness that . . . the objective spirit liquidates the subjective.
>
> (*MM*, 184)

The anecdotes retold from Williams' *Autobiography* earlier would appear to make it plain, then, that as with Adorno, the self for the poet is formed to no intractable or stabilizing "universal principle" but that immersed in "the process of experience" (a telling phrase, as we shall later see). It is given to take up what by all rights ought to be "impregnable positions," dissident subject positions that might give the lie to the hidebound tendency among some to reify, to objectify, and ultimately, to liquefy human identity. "In many people," as Adorno states elsewhere, it is perhaps "an impertinence to say 'I,'" since "the wave of the future" would seem to augur continuously for "the critical construction of being"—a future Williams himself would foresee (*A*, 26)—thus making allowance for "all possibility of subjective deviation" (*MM*, 50, 218, 189).

Williams, of course, would not have read Adorno. But in the initial period of his writing career with which we are concerned, he *was* reading an American philosopher whom Adorno highly approved; namely, John Dewey.[3] Adorno's

---

3. Theodor Adorno, *Negative Dialectics*, trans. E. B. Ashton (New York, 1973), 14; Posnock, *Trial of Curiosity*, Chapter 5. In his more recent "The Politics of Nonidentity: A Genealogy," *Boundary 2* 19 (winter, 1992), which turns out to be largely a redaction of the "Coda" to his magisterial performance in *The Trial of Curiosity*, Posnock confirms the link between Adorno and Dewey by emphatically stating: "Dewey refuses to follow William James in his plunge into the flux and is actually closer to Adorno, who begins *Negative Dialectics* with a critique of Bergson (a critique equally applicable to William James) and a salute to Dewey. By taking seriously Adorno's rarely noticed late praise of Dewey (which he repeats in *Aesthetic Theory*), I hope to encourage a rapprochement between

bow in the direction of the process of experience in the above commentary sets us before Dewey's own masterwork, *Experience and Nature* (1925), as a significant source for contextualizing much of the cultural criticism contained in Williams' early work composed through the 1920s.

Crucial to that criticism, if Williams' concern for the representation of a multifaceted human identity is any indication, would be the relentless suspicioning of any categorical claims to an absolutizing and totalizing Truth—Adorno's "universal principle" as an intellectual debility, once again. So that Williams would find very much to recommend Dewey's own suspicioning of thought which merely "manipulates received objects and essences," as in the case of philosophers who solely insist upon "the certainty of the immediately and focally present or 'given,'" and substitute "a general character for an immediate this" (*EN*, 182, 283; see also 131, 135, 180, 305, 345, and 350). "For the immediately given is always the dubious," Dewey continues this last citation, "[and] it is always a matter for subsequent events to determine, or assign character to. . . . [Hypothetically] [i]t were, conceivably, 'better' that nature should be finished through and through, a closed mechanical or closed teleological structure, such as philosophic schools have fancied. But in that case the flickering candle of consciousness would go out" (*EN*, 283–84). "Having relieved philosophy of its grander pretensions," then, as Robert B. Westbrook argues in his monumental *John Dewey and American Democracy* (1991), "Dewey continued his effort to redefine its mission as cultural criticism."[4] And central to that mission would therefore be, as in Williams' own cultural agenda, the foregrounding of human identity as a constructed or

---

two traditions of social theory usually deemed irreconcilable" (38). For further expansions on the relation between Dewey and Williams, see Mike Weaver, *William Carlos Williams: The American Background* (Cambridge, Eng., 1977), 32–35; Paul Mariani, *William Carlos Williams: A New World Naked* (New York, 1981), 336; Peter Schmidt, *William Carlos Williams, the Arts, and Literary Tradition* (Baton Rouge, 1988), 27–28; Brian Bremen, *William Carlos Williams and the Diagnostics of Culture* (New York, 1993), 151–52; and Lisa Steinman, "Once More with Feeling: Teaching *Spring and All*," *William Carlos Williams Review*, 10 (spring, 1984), who generally concludes that "Williams seems . . . to have found much of lasting value in Dewey" (11 n. 6), a view that the present chapter will attempt at greater length to corroborate below.

4. Robert B. Westbrook, *John Dewey and American Democracy* (Ithaca, 1991), 369. Clarifying the imbrication between philosophy and culture more fully, Westbrook adds later: "Dewey realized that, in stripping philosophy of any claim to access to a truth beyond that assayed by science . . . he was leaving philosophers with a far more modest cultural role than that to which they had traditionally aspired. It was, nonetheless, a role requiring great courage, for, in the service of their culture, philosophers might well call into question its apparent goods [*sic*] and thereby risk, at least figuratively, the fate of Socrates" (373; see further 371 and 540).

invented or fabricated notion, a human self not born but made, hence one that was infinitely discoverable rather than one that was essentially, intrinsically, or generically recoverable, as those early vignettes from Williams' *Autobiography* only too well substantiate.

Dewey sums up the case admirably in an important place in *Experience and Nature*, as follows:

> The individual, the self, centered in a settled world which owns and sponsors it, and which in turn it owns and enjoys, is finished, closed. Surrender of what is possessed, disowning of what supports one in secure ease, is involved in all inquiry and discovery; the latter implicate an individual *still to make*, with all the risks implied therein. For to arrive at new truth and vision is to alter. The old self is put off and the new self is only forming, and the form it finally takes will depend upon the unforeseeable result of an adventure. . . . Only by identification with *remaking the objects* that now obtain are we saved from complacent objectivism. Those who do not fare forth and take the risks attendant upon the formation of new objects and growth of a new self, are subjected perforce to inevitable change of the settled and close [*sic*] world they have made their own. (*EN*, 201, emphases added; see also 141, and further, 191 and 351 for the opposing view)

Saving ourselves from "complacent objectivism" in this revolutionary approach to conceptualizing identity, of course, resonates strikingly with Adorno's discrediting of that "objective spirit," so anxious to contain procreant subjectivity at the unformed level of homogeneous liquefaction, in the passage remarked upon earlier. But how, we might well wonder, would this adjuration against objectivism square with the cultural proclivities of a poet who, from his earliest work and onwards, would exhort us, as in the well-known *Paterson* from 1927, to say: "no ideas but *in things*" (*WCP*, 263–64)? We entirely misunderstand the program of Williams' cultural criticism in such early writing, however, if we fail to understand precisely how Williams would have us position ourselves in relation to "things," which as it turns out, is not in any way an invocation to objectivism in the conventional (i.e., commodifying, reifying) sense of the term.[5] Adorno's essay "Cultural Criticism and Society" (1967) can best explain why, as can Williams' own *Embodiment of Knowledge* (1928), which, as an important cultural document in its own right, anticipates that of Adorno in several important ways. The join between them, once again, lies in Dewey, as we shall see. In order, therefore, to

5. See Joseph N. Riddel, *The Inverted Bell: Modernism and the Counterpoetics of William Carlos Williams* (Baton Rouge, 1991), 129, 131.

apprehend properly Williams' privileging of "things" in some of the early poetry that we shall come onto shortly, we would do well to rehearse, for a final time, the theoretical triangulation among these three thinkers from the point of view of the slightly altered cultural perspective concerning their ideas in (or about) things.

However we choose to theorize it, cultural criticism is a Modernist phenomenon, and in newly addressing the relation between the mind and its world, is in the very first instance interested to know what difference it makes to have a human society immanently at the center of that world rather than some theological or spiritual or transcendent entity, as in former times. To paraphrase Michel Foucault, though in a slightly altered context, cultural criticism is a discourse with "attitude," an attitude, albeit deliberate and difficult, yet one that nonetheless "consists in recapturing something that is not beyond the present instant, nor behind it, but *within* it." For Theodor Adorno, in the essay "Cultural Criticism and Society," what is centrally lodged *within* the social present is "the anonymous sway of the *status quo*," so that it now becomes the perpetual task of the typically modern mind instrumentally to wrap itself around this new anthropological order, on the model of economic exchange, either by constantly producing "what is always the same," or by constantly identifying with the "powers" that be with the view to altering or transforming the status quo.[6]

With respect to the second response to human experience in particular, cultural criticism will then seek to view a method by which the mind might resist the endemic reification and ultimate "mutilation of man," construed as the fatal inheritance of Modernist Enlightenment rationality. This method of resistance it finds solely in the mind's willingness to put itself (back) into its dialectical relationship "with the material conditions of life." By "dialectical" here, Adorno, in

6. Michel Foucault, "What Is Enlightenment?" 39; Theodor Adorno, "Cultural Criticism and Society," in *Prisms*, trans. Samuel Weber and Shierry Weber (Cambridge, Mass., 1986), 21, 23, 25. For an alternative reading to something like the same two models of cultural response presented here, see Susan Buck-Morss, *The Origin of Negative Dialectics: Theodor W. Adorno, Walter Benjamin, and the Frankfurt Institute* (New York, 1977), 186, 189. John Dewey perhaps has both incipiently in mind when he refers to an "oscillation between surrender to the external [Positivism] and assertion of the inner [Idealism]" (*EN*, 200). Either way, both approaches to experience sustain the notion of a dualism between subject and object which Dewey's "ultimate 'dialectic,'" like that of Adorno and Williams' that I am about to outline, will attempt to explode by ridding itself of "Romanticism" (*EN*, 189), no doubt a species of fetishized utopian Idealism that Adorno would attribute once again to intellectual debility in his "Subject and Object," in *The Essential Frankfurt School Reader*, ed. Andrew Arato and Eike Gebhardt (New York, 1982), 499, and further in his "Portrait of Walter Benjamin," in *Prisms* (Cambridge, Mass., 1986), 239. See also Martin Jay, *Adorno* (Cambridge, Mass., 1984), 63.

true deconstructive fashion, intends the kind of relation between self and world that consciously would bring to the fore, for better or worse, the very "untruth" that any truthful statement itself is usually made to the detriment or at the expense of. In other words, the mind establishes a *negotiable* relation to experience (hence, the phrase "*process* of experience" noted earlier), and the well-intentioned cultural critic always insists on knowing the material (i.e., the economic, historical, social, political, etc.) conditions by which things come to be known, and perhaps beyond that, to be believed. There are no givens, no faits accomplis in Adorno's dialectical model; today's gain, depending on contingency and circumstance, could very well become tomorrow's loss. Accordingly, "Dialectics means intransigence towards *all* reification." Indeed, "the semblance of unity and wholeness grows with the *advance* of reification." The "immanent procedure" of the cultural pundit's dialectical, material criticism Adorno, therefore, sums up as follows:

> It takes seriously the principle that it is not ideology in itself which is untrue but rather its pretension to correspond to reality. Immanent criticism of intellectual and artistic phenomena seeks to grasp, through the analysis of their form and meaning, the contradiction between their objective idea and that pretension. It names what the consistency or inconsistency of the work itself expresses of the structure of the existent. Such criticism does not stop at a general recognition of the servitude of the objective mind, but seeks rather to transform this knowledge into a heightened perception of the thing itself.[7]

This extraordinary passage, unusually lucid for Adorno, perhaps takes us to the heart of Frankfurt School cultural criticism, which, as the final statement shows, like Williams, is firmly focused on the perception of things. In what remains of this chapter, therefore, I would like to elaborate upon three important ways the passage intersects with some of the early prose and poetry of William Carlos Williams, in the shadow of John Dewey. In doing so, I propose to outline a kind of "prolegomenon" to the cultural criticism of Williams that would serve to un-

---

7. Theodor Adorno, *Prisms* (Cambridge, Mass., 1986), 24, 28, 31 (emphasis added), and 32. See also Jay, *Adorno*, 21–22. An astonishing passage from Dewey's *Experience and Nature* would appear to paraphrase this last statement of Adorno almost precisely: "There is a difference in kind between the thought which manipulates received objects and essences to derive new ones from their relations and implications, and the thought which generates a new method of observing and classifying them. It is like the difference between readjusting the parts of a wagon to make it more efficient, and the invention of the steam locomotive. One is formal and additive; the other is qualitative and transformative" (*EN,* 182).

dergird much of Williams' later writing, while also establishing its more general relevance to the distanciation of Modernist poetic discourse more particularly described in the preceding and following chapters.

First, it would appear only inevitable that if one is to propound a dialectical rather than a given or recoverable relation to experience in the method of the cultural critic previously described, that Adorno should first want to clear important epistemological ground by attacking the truth-of-correspondence theory of reality, to which Ideology apparently lays claim. As Adorno was shrewdly given to remark elsewhere, and which Williams the autobiographer would surely have applauded, "the more artists have journeyed into the interior, the more they have learned to forgo the infantile fun of imitating external reality" (*MM,* 214). We can only be scandalized by Williams' "secret gardens" recounted in the *Autobiography,* as Williams himself clearly was not, if we are predisposed to view subjectivity as formed to some fixed and fungible ideological status quo exhibited by so many of the culture industry's prime-time media idols that we are perpetually exhorted to emulate.[8] But because idolatry, and ideology to which it is related, are fabrications or inventions merely, like anything else in experience, they ultimately have nothing to correspond *to.* Nor do we. "Shakespeare's, 'To hold the mirror up to nature,'" as the *Autobiography* tells us, is "as vicious a piece of bad advice as the budding artist ever gazed upon. It is tricky, thoughtless, wrong. It is NOT to hold the mirror up to nature that the artist performs his work. It is to make, out of the imagination, something not at all a copy of nature, but something quite different, *a new thing,* unlike any thing else in nature, *a thing advanced and apart from it*" (*A,* 241, emphases added). In this passage, then, "to copy" is really what Adorno means by imitating. Imitation, for Williams, however, is quite different—in fact, is just the opposite. "To copy," as he explains, "is merely to reflect something already there, inertly. . . . But by imitation[,] we enlarge nature itself, we become nature or we discover in ourselves nature's active part. This is enticing to our minds, it enlarges the concept of art, dignifies it to a place not yet fully realized" (*A,* 241).[9] Along precisely these same Coleridgean lines, discovering in ourselves "nature's active part" becomes, for John Dewey, the "discovery of inner experience . . . at the individual's command":

> It implies a new worth and sense of dignity in human individuality, a sense that
> an individual is not a mere property of nature, set in place according to a scheme

8. Max Horkheimer and Theodor W. Adorno, *Dialectic of Enlightenment,* trans. John Cumming (New York, n.d.), 144–45.

9. See also William Carlos Williams, *The Selected Letters of William Carlos Williams,* ed. John C. Thirlwall (New York, 1984), 297.

independent of him, as an article is put in its place in a cabinet, but that he adds something, that he makes a contribution. It is the counterpart of what distinguishes modern science, experimental, hypothetical; a logic of discovery having therefore opportunity for individual temperament, ingenuity, invention.

(*EN*, 143; cf. 332 and 350)

Dewey concludes the above train of thought by noting that this new "world of inner experience"—"another world," in the citations from Williams' "secret gardens" back in my introduction—is entirely dependent upon "an extension of language" (*EN*, 143). But this notion of a linguistic or rhetorical construction of experience (see further *EN*, 181, 186, 188–89, 346, and 350) was one of the genuinely revolutionary pronouncements in several of the prose interpolations within the collection of poems entitled *Spring and All*, published by Williams in Paris in 1923. There, we are instructed that the value of the imagination "consists in its ability to make words," and that its unique power, in consequence, consists in "giv[ing] created forms reality, [or] actual existence" (*WCP*, 207). As in the later *Autobiography*, therefore, we are cautioned about Shakespeare's "stabilizing the copyist tendency," and in its place, given a right appreciation of Shakespeare's imagination in actually raising him "NOT TO COPY [his fellows in scientific training], not to holding the mirror up to them[,] but to equal, to surpass them as a creator of knowledge, as a vigorous, living force above their heads" (*WCP*, 208–209; further on 194 and 235). It seems necessary, then, within these theoretical clarifications, for Williams to distinguish between "realism" ("likeness to 'nature'") and "reality itself" ("enlargement—revivication of values," in the additive sense of "contribution" touched on previously in the passage from Dewey [*WCP*, 204]). Ideology, accordingly, can be true in the sense earlier discussed by Adorno if its correspondence is of a "likeness" to nature, that is, "realistic." But "realism" is not its only option. Denying ideology *other* options is what then becomes untrue. In the end, it is left up to the imagination to decide what all the possible options are, a complete repertoire of which Williams calls "the world of the imagination," and it is *only* this mental or linguistic, as against an existential or actual, world that men (*sic*) can know, and *only* this world that men can properly understand as "reality" (*WCP*, 215).

But what can they know of this "reality"? Feelings, mostly: "the dynamization of emotion," "force [. . .] recognized in a pure state," "the wave [of] rhythm" (*WCP*, 215, 219, 221)—most of what is subsumed under Raymond Williams' well-known definition of experience as the "structures of feeling." Not very much, really. But that is precisely the point. In the "secret gardens" of *Spring and All* we

are made to experience what William Carlos Williams calls the "jump" between fact and reality, a jump which ultimately has us "sliding into nothing" (*WCP*, 221). And yet, it is exactly that jump into nothing "on which reality rides": "It is the imagination—It is a cleavage through everything by a force that does not exist in the mass and therefore can never be discovered by its anatomization" (*WCP*, 225). Still, having said *this* much about imaginative reality has at least uncovered *something*—a kind of "distance" in which all cultural criticism might be thought to take form or shape, but whose status must ultimately remain "empty" in the parallel Lacanian formulation of Slavoj Žižek since (as in Williams) "the compulsion to *encircle* again and again the site of the lost thing, to *mark* it in its very impossibility . . . will [always] enable us to discern signs of the New."[10]

In face of the apparent contradiction that "something" will come of "nothing," we come on to a second important aspect of Williams' early work, once again shadowed by the writing of John Dewey. In the most general sense, *The Embodiment of Knowledge* would appear to be a "philosophical" text, as the title gives out. But time and again we're repeatedly frustrated to comprehend exactly what "knowledge" Williams would disclose to us as embodied, which perhaps may explain why the work was rejected for publication in the *Dial* by Kenneth Burke in early 1933, and would remain unpublished in Williams' lifetime.[11] Yet the same contradiction confronts us in the work of Adorno, which Adorno himself tried to head off in an essay, "The Actuality of Philosophy," also written early in his career (1931), that, interestingly, wasn't published in *his* lifetime either. There, Adorno was quite emphatic in stating that the idea of philosophy was not the transmission or embodiment of truth at all, but instead, its "interpretation": "In

10. Raymond Williams, *Marxism and Literature* (Oxford, 1977), 132; Slavoj Žižek, *For They Know Not What They Do: Enjoyment as a Political Factor* (New York, 1991), 152, 272–73, emphases retained. The figure of the leap into nothing previously that begins in Williams' "The Wanderer" (1917), and that will be featured prominently later in his *Paterson*, is one that Adorno is especially partial to as well, for instance in Poe and Baudelaire, where "the concept of newness emerges": "the plunge into the abyss, no matter whether hell or heaven, '*au fond de l'inconnu pour trouver du nouveau*' [in the depths of the unknown to find the new] . . . is an unknown threat that the subject embraces and which, in a dizzy reversal, promises joy." Adorno, *Prisms*, 235. Cf. "the abyss of relativity" in *MM*, 128.

11. The rejection by as problematic a "philosopher" as the neo-Pragmatist Kenneth Burke is a tissue of ironies, as Mariani briefly records: "Burke had spotted John Dewey's influence in the *Embodiment* as a weakness, but Williams rejoined strongly that if all he'd done was merely follow Dewey in the manuscript he would 'vomit and quit—any time.' Still, Burke wrote to say he couldn't use *The Embodiment*." Mariani, *William Carlos Williams*, 336. Undoubtedly, "John Dewey's influence" may be the only thing ringing true here, where it is openly acknowledged, for instance, in *EK*, 7 and 113.

this remains the great, perhaps the everlasting paradox: philosophy persistently and with the claim of truth, must proceed interpretively without ever possessing a sure key to interpretation; nothing more is given to it than fleeting, disappearing traces within the riddle figures of that which exists and their astonishing entwinings. . . . Thus it reaches so few 'results.'"[12] The fleeting, disappearing traces of knowledge here, with the emphasis tipped instead in favor of their un-riddling, are our best warrant, I would argue, for suggesting that what both Adorno and Williams are in fact writing in these texts is criticism—cultural criti-cism—where the problematic of imaginative reality, in the highly qualified sense previously unpacked in Williams' prose, once again takes center stage in Adorno's important use above of the word "nothing." And if that "nothing," on which the cultural critic's imagination rides, presents us with a veritable world of forms by which to make its reality known, as Williams had argued, then we need to start thinking about that "nothing" not as the blank refusal of knowledge, but instead, in the truly contra-dictory sense of knowledge's own complete and utter permis-sion: no-one-thing, some-thing, every-thing.

Williams teases out—should we say embodies?—the quite fruitful contradic-tion of his nothing/something collocation in *The Embodiment of Knowledge* as follows:

> I assert that the whole is greater than all its parts and that since no one knows anything about it[,] all proofs are invalid—as prohibitions—except relatively to its own set of conditions and *ad interim* while one must proceed, as always, with the business of existence by measures always greatly in question . . . [for] nothing exists in the parts of his exercises which can be anything but insignificant and unworthy of him. . . . But nothing can be forced. We must stick to the proven rules, as far as they are proven . . . but beyond them exists something else.
>
> (*EK*, 61)

12. Theodor W. Adorno, "The Actuality of Philosophy," *Telos* 31 (1977): 126. Philosophy, the passage concludes, "must always begin anew and therefore cannot do without the least thread which earlier times have spun, and through which the lineature is perhaps completed which could transform the ciphers into a text" (126). The entire citation needs to be set alongside an almost identical one from Dewey: "the claim of philosophy to rival or displace science as a purveyor of truth seems to be mostly a compensatory gesture for failure to perform its proper task of *liberating and clarifying mean-ings*, including those scientifically authenticated. For, assuredly, a student prizes historic systems rather for the meanings and shades of meanings they have brought to light than for the store of ultimate truths they have ascertained" (*EN*, 332–33, emphasis added). Similar animadversions against the traditional conceptions of philosophy and science can be sampled in Williams (*EK*, 68–69, 87, 112, 123, and passim).

The alternation, in this passage, between the Nothing of wholes, invalid proofs, and questions, as against the Something of parts, proven rules, and significances, underscores the dialectical method of the cultural critic, described earlier by Adorno, as she or he addresses at once the truth and non-truth expressive of "the structure of the existent," what J. Hillis Miller calls "a kind of negative visibility."[13]

Further, because that existent is a process—experience as the "actualization" of constructed meaning, in Dewey's terms, rather than meaning itself (*EN*, 189, 291)—Williams can be even more precise about the contradiction of his dialectical procedure, viewing it as a making and an escaping and then a making all over again, *ad infinitum*, quite like a perpetual-motion "machine," that picks up on the several notations of imaginative force and power already alluded to. What propels this machine is frankly a "mystery." Perhaps this is so because "[t]he embodiment of knowledge can have no meaning but the escape from its [meaning's] domination as a fetish of knowledge itself" (*EK*, 62, 63), what Cornel West has infamously and more generally tagged "evasive" in an important study, *The American Evasion of Philosophy*.[14]

To sum up this second contradictory aspect of the poet's cultural criticism, a consideration of some of Williams' early poetry may be helpful. "To Have Done Nothing," item VI from the 1923 *Spring and All* (*WCP*, 191–92), while it legitimately "may be taken as a demonstration of Stein's Cubist theories in action,"[15] for our purposes, is likely best understood as a (re)mapping of the contradictions

13. J. Hillis Miller, "Williams," in *The Linguistic Moment: From Wordsworth to Stevens* (Princeton, 1985), 386, and further on 364, 387, and 388. Brian Bremen, in his recent cultural diagnosis of the Williams canon in *William Carlos Williams and the Diagnostics of Culture*, expands exhaustively upon several variations of Williams' dialectical method only roughly sketched here: between poetry and prose (10, 163), language and history (12), recognition and independence (58), self and other (70, 104, 147, 161, 164, 168, 198), history and modernity (122), past and present (125), and other dialectical combinations (further on 25, 28, 41, 42, 67, 73, 91, 98, 126, 134, 139, 161, 197, and 199). Though the term "dialectical" is not expressly invoked, Duffey's version of the method is defined as an "interplay between background and foreground," thus establishing "a middle ground as imagination's realm," and his elaboration is elegant and precise: "Background is what is assumed as given. Foreground is what may be made of it by refocus, translation. The two enact their dance with greater or lesser elegance and completion." Duffey, *A Poetry of Presence*, 223. Riddel places a similar dialectical construction on "dance" here in *The Inverted Bell*, 222, 253, 294, and 298. Hillis Miller's version is that of "a technique [for] the juxtaposition of the disparate." Hillis Miller, "Williams," 377.

14. William Carlos Williams, *The Selected Essays of William Carlos Williams* (New York, 1969), 256; Cornel West, *The American Evasion of Philosophy* (Madison, 1989), esp. 230–39.

15. See Schmidt, *William Carlos Williams, the Arts, and Literary Tradition*, 76 n. 19.

no [illegible] everything

and paradoxes of the cultural critic's dialectical approach to experience. The "nothing that I have done . . . made up of / nothing," in the opening stanzas of the poem, suggestively transforms itself into an "everything" that is "capable / of an / infinity of / combinations" that have quite specific material relations to moral, physical, and religious codes. Hence, "everything / and nothing / are synonymous" (*WCP*, 192). The infinity, here, which shatters any correspondent authorization of the political and social coding, foregrounds instead the critic's own "power" either to maintain the current historical embeddedness of discursive forms and institutional practices, or to transform the cultural space by constructing alternatives for any (or all) of them in their place. Doing "nothing," then, can go in two completely opposite directions at once in the poem, which thus accounts for both its "con[-]fusion," as well as its "perfect[ion]" in the very last line.

In any case, its very empowerment of the critic by way of that no-one-thing—"energy *in vacuo*," as Williams succinctly puts it—that commands such centrality in the poet's text, and perhaps for the first time makes it possible for us "to believe in writing," as Michel de Certeau so memorably puts it, "precisely because legitimized by 'nothing,' it legitimizes the other and ceaselessly begins." The poet's (along with the critic's) perpetual provocation by this other, this *vacuo*, no doubt explains so many of the variations of it we're likely to encounter through much of Williams' other early poetry: "the guts of shadows" in "Sub Terra" (*WCP*, 64), "the high sea" in "In Harbor" (*WCP*, 69), "the fixing of an eye / concretely upon emptiness" in "Virtue" (*WCP*, 89), "life's endless profusion" and "exquisite diversity" in "When Fresh, It Was Sweet" (*WCP*, 248), to cite only a few instances. And no doubt, too, all are magnetically pointing to the lode of "radiant gist" awaiting us in Williams' last work, which Joseph Riddel was one of the first poststructural readers of the poet to relate to the "lack" in language itself "that calls for the new signs, the additive or supplementary signs [that] makes necessary the infinite substitutions without which, one might say, a new language, or new beginning, a 'new measure,' would be impossible."[16]

16. Michel de Certeau, quoted in Iain Chambers, *Border Dialogues: Journeys in Postmodernity* (New York, 1990), 103; Riddel, *The Inverted Bell*, 236–37. For a further expansion of Williams' "energy *in vacuo*" previously, see Žižek's notion of a "distance separating the locus of Power as such from those exerting Power at a given moment." Žižek, *For They Know Not What They Do*, 267. In a context closer to my own, see Bremen, *William Carlos Williams and the Diagnostics of Culture*, 197: "The empowerment of the individual is the radiant gist of Williams's culture, and as such, *Paterson* maps out the strategies to break down those forces that block the flow of communication, credit, poetry, and knowledge," and so forth, and Bremen's Chapter 5 (160–99) on "The Radiant Gist" more generally.

My point would be that all of these references to the *distancing* effects of verbal discourse that establish an undeniable linkage to Gertrude Stein's poetic project outlined in the last chapter also make it fairly clear that Williams had a very strong cultural agenda from his earliest years, based on an extraordinarily complex and uncompromisingly theoretical vision that "nothing" quite takes us to the core of.[17] Nonetheless, as Williams records in *The Descent of Winter* from 1928, "poetry should strive for nothing else, this vividness alone, *per se*, for itself," for the "realization of this has its own internal fire that is 'like' nothing," and it is "[t]hat thing, the vividness which is poetry by itself, [and that] makes the poem" (*WCP*, 302).

The invocation to "things" in this last excerpt carries us to a third and final aspect of Williams' early work having to do with cultural criticism's transformation of objective knowledge into, in Adorno's words once again, "a heightened perception of the thing itself."[18] To get there, however, I need to creep up on Williams' "energy in *vacuo*," once again, but from a slightly altered perspective. The best gloss on this important line Williams himself provides in *The Embodiment* when he realizes that the new theory of knowledge that he is attempting to construct—"tenets of a new mythology" as he calls it—would be just "as useless as the old" if ever, even for a second, the meaning of the words themselves and the assertion of control that meaning would imply should once come to displace "the making of them words" (*sic*), a making as a kind of "broad sweep through which to assert their power":

> [Them words] would or might be composed as real objects to mould the psyche of peoples over again, thus reasserting their own powerful   and by blasting away the stultifying association with the old mythology which has denied them their dynamic potentialities by fixing them in meanings which prostitute the intelligence.
>
> (*EK*, 19)

17. "[T]he closer we / look at a word, the greater the distance / from which it stares back," writes the contemporary Language poet Charles Bernstein, quoted in Bob Perelman, "Write the Power," *American Literary History* 6 (spring 1994): 322. Although Bernstein here apparently cites an aphorism by Karl Kraus, elsewhere in a recent "Autobiographical Interview" conducted for *Boundary 2* 23 (summer 1996), he also acknowledges his enormous debt to the writing of Gertrude Stein from quite early on in his career (34–35)—writing, the "bizarreness [of whose] silent call"—dissident distanciation, in terms of the present study—"holds out the promise of endlessness signification," in Perelman's apt description from "Write the Power" (322).

18. Adorno, "Cultural Criticism and Society," 32.

That rather gaping hole following the word "powerful" in the above passage, in quite graphemic terms, is perhaps Williams' best assurance that the force of his own expression—the "cleavage through everything . . . that does not exist in the mass," we recall (*WCP*, 225)—can *never* allow words ultimately to rigidify into "real objects," and so cancel their best and most dynamic possibilities, in proxy to a disciplinary and controlling knowledge.

Hillis Miller's categorical suggestion, therefore, that "[a] primordial union of subject and object is the basic presupposition of Williams' poetry" accords only too well with "[t]he violence of equality-mongering" underwriting "the insatiable identity principle" problematized by Adorno, and would for that reason tend to be vehemently resisted by cultural criticism.[19] Thus, John Dewey talks about the expressive potentiality for knowledge in terms of "dispositions and attitudes" that operate to much the same effect as Williams' powerful words:

> [W]hile capable of being distinguished and made concrete intellectual objects, [they] are never separate existences. They are always *of, from, toward,* situations and things. They may be studied with a minimum of attention to the things at and away from which they are directed. The things with which they are concerned may for purposes of inquiry be represented *by a blank,* a symbol to be specifically filled in as occasion demands. But except as ways of seeking, turning from, appropriating, treating things, they have no existence nor significance.
>
> (*EN,* 195, emphasis added)

As a poetic transcription of the above two citations with their blank holes and yawning spaces, Williams offers us "The rose is obsolete" in *Spring and All,* an extraordinarily dynamic poem in the process of casting aside an old mythology, in the highly conventional image of the rose, and of putting on a new. Mythology's confrontation with the source of its own power occurs near the beginning:

> The edge
> cuts without cutting
> meets—nothing—renews
> itself in metal or porcelain—
>
> whither?
>
> (*WCP,* 195)

19. Hillis Miller, "Williams," 360; Adorno, *Negative Dialectics,* 143, 142.

And its continuous transformation in thrall to the power of "nothing" enlarges and extends the meaning of the rose exponentially—"becomes a geometry"—for the entire length of the poem:

> The rose carried weight of love
> but love is at an end—of roses
>
> It is at the edge of the
> petal that love waits
>
> Crisp, worked to defeat
> laboredness—fragile
> plucked, moist, half-raised
> cold, precise, touching
> What
>
> The place between the petal's
> edge and the
>   (*WCP*, 195)

In the above sequence, each of the four units of thought draws a blank at its end, seemingly mute in the face of what has carried it thus far, yet at the same time charged with an energy to continue onwards in quest of some "infinitely fine, infinitely / rigid" thing, a process that Williams images as the penetration of "the Milky Way," in the penultimate stanza, and of "space" in the concluding word (*WCP*, 196). Through the highly charged course of "The rose is obsolete," what both these final spatial metaphors—exceedingly apt variations on the ones drawn previously from *The Embodiment* and Dewey—play up is the frank impossibility of words to keep apace of things, of things to deliquesce into words, and the excess of stratospheric energy sustaining both impossibilities that Williams refuses to foreclose upon with any terminal punctuation. The same high-energy impasse greets us in other early poems as well, for instance, in "Spring Strains" from *Al Que Quiere!* (1917):

>   But—
> (Hold hard, rigid jointed trees!)
> the blinding and red-edged sun-blur—
> creeping energy, concentrated
> counterforce—welds sky, buds, trees,
> rivets them in one puckering hold!

> Sticks through! Pulls the whole
> counter-pulling mass upward, to the right,
> locks even the opaque, not yet defined
> ground in a terrific drag that is
> loosening the very tap-roots!
> (WCP, 97–98)

or, these opening stanzas from an untitled entry for 9/30 in the much later Descent of Winter (1928), once again:

> There are no perfect waves—
> Your writings are a sea
> full of misspellings and
> faulty sentences. Level. Troubled.
>
> A center distant from the land
> touched by the wings
> of nearly silent birds
> that never seem to rest—
> (WCP, 292)

Hence, to return approximately to where this chapter began, if we can imagine in these poems human subjectivity standing in place of the rose, a spring day, or the very words on the poet's page, we understand fully Williams' rage in the previous extract from *The Embodiment* at the presumption of his own words being composed "as real objects to mould the psyche of peoples over again." And not just a rage at denying words "their dynamic potentialities" by having them fixed in psychic meaning now, but rage at the denial of dynamic potentialities within an alterable and transformative subjectivity as well. The indecipherable space that Williams in much of his early writing opens up between words and things, a space that the poet won't even try to name, thus speaks directly to the incommensurate quality of dissident identity as we watch it unfold in *The Autobiography*, and more generally, to human thought itself, whose first task is to criticize an all-embracing commensurability (*MM*, 55).

Williams' description of his writing, in that last excerpt, as a sea whose center is "distant from the land," to conclude, presents us in sum with our best take on "no ideas but in things." In Theodor Adorno's important prose fragment, "Keeping one's distance," which crucially links up with Williams on this issue, we noted in the Introduction that essential to all thought "is an element of exaggeration, of overshooting the object, of self-detachment from the weight of the factual" (*MM*, 126; see also Adorno, "Portrait of Walter Benjamin," 240). Such exaggeration frequently becomes a droll source of comedy in Williams' penchant for particular description in the early poetry: "the old man who goes about / gathering dog lime . . . is more majestic than / that of the Episcopal minister" (*WCP*, 71), or "With what deep thirst / we quicken our desires / to that rank odor of a passing springtime!" (*WCP*, 92), or "You exquisite chunk of mud / Kathleen . . . teach them a dignity / that is . . . the dignity / of mud!" (*WCP*, 106–107), and so forth. Adorno's point, and surely Williams' in much of this mildly hyperbolic observation, is to underscore the incommensurability of all thought, and once again, to raise the whole issue of reality as a problematic. "For thought," as Adorno elaborates his important distance, "must aim beyond its target just because it never quite reaches it, and positivism is uncritical in its confidence of doing so, imagining its tergiversations to be due to mere conscientiousness. A transcending thought takes its own inadequacy more thoroughly into account than does one guided by the control mechanism of science" (*MM*, 127–28).

By "transcending" here, and not "transcendent," note that Adorno has in mind, as in Williams' obsolete rose, the perpetual figuring and disfiguring of nature that is the frustration of all ideas in face of their restive and boundless expressive power. To this extent, accordingly, Adorno's discursive "distance" would corroborate Williams' "space" of "nothing" and Dewey's "symbol" of "blank" discussed earlier—a collocation of tropes that Pragmatist cultural critic Ray Carney refers to as an "expressive gap" whose "insistent occurrence . . . [becomes] one of the most distinctive and familiar aspects of American art":

> That is why it appears in one form or another in so much American expression, in the work of Homer and Hopper, for example, in terms of almost exactly the same visual metaphor as it does in [Frank Capra's films]: an enormous physical space or distance that is looked across, gestured across, or visionarily traversed in an effort to reach across it to bridge it . . . beyond all social forms, manners and expressions.

Yet it's on the very point of reaching across this distance that such thinking, and cultural criticism in general, imperils itself by seeming to champion an undecidability and indeterminacy—"calculated indeterminacy" is Marjorie Perloff's exacting formulation (129)—and in so doing, threatening to empty it of all historical resonance, as some would accuse most poststructuralist thought, and of all political engagement.[20]

Williams' "no ideas but in things" could be construed as one answer to the charge that his "secret gardens" are apolitical, and woefully do have quite definite limits. But this chapter would not exist had Williams had absolutely no interest in ideas, and so I want to conclude it by pointing to a quite different idea of limits and thus "distance" Williams' cultural criticism from the pejorative sense of limits just alluded to. Stuart Hall, in an important essay entitled "Cultural Studies and Its Theoretical Legacies" (1992), addresses a very palpable "tension" that we experience in all cultural criticism, and that we perhaps run into here, in the case of William Carlos Williams. Hall endeavors to explain this tension by suggesting that when one works on culture, "you have to recognize that you will always be working in an area of displacement," that there will always be "something decentered about the medium of culture, about language, textuality, and signification, which always escapes and evades the attempt to link it, directly and immediately, with other structures" (284). He cites Edward Said on what some of these other structures might be: classes, academies, corporations, nations, races, genders, and the like. But Hall is also shrewdly mindful of discursive structures like "the intertextuality of texts," "sources of power," "site[s] of representation and resistance," and so forth—structures that the cultural critic ought to find *equally* compelling. In sum, then, the crux of the matter comes down to this: "that culture will always work through its textualities—[yet] at the same time[,] that textuality is never enough." Nonetheless, Hall concludes, cultural critics must learn to live with this tension between theoretical displacement and practical intervention, because without holding together "theoretical and political questions in an ever irresolvable but permanent tension," cultural studies will have insisted upon "some final theoretical closure," and will thereby "have renounced its 'worldly' vocation."[21]

Hall's astute and persuasive outlining of this supervenient tension in cultural

20. Carney, *American Vision*, 338; Marjorie Perloff, *The Poetics of Indeterminacy: Rimbaud to Cage* (Evanston, Ill., 1983), 129. For the important distinction earlier between "transcending" and "transcendent," see Posnock, *Trial of Curiosity*, 73. On the ahistorical brief against poststructuralist thought, Donald Pease offers perhaps one of the most trenchant articulations of this position: "By reducing the complex activity of Western culture to a 'tracing' operation that erases cultural memory, poststructuralism relieves those attached to the Old World of any pain accompanying their memories of a lost past. For when reduced to these traces the lost past can be forgotten without too much regret" Donald Pease, *Visionary Compacts: American Renaissance Writings in Cultural Context* (Madison, 1987), 163; but 168 and 231 suggest some backpedaling.

21. Stuart Hall, "Cultural Studies and Its Theoretical Legacies," in *Cultural Studies*, ed. Lawrence Grossberg, Cary Nelson, and Paula Treichler (New York, 1992), 284.

criticism is coordinate with the distance we find opening up in Williams, bounded as it is by the limit of ideas, on the one hand, and by the limit of things on the other. And his argument is coordinate, too, with Adorno's further qualification that such distance should never be thought as "a safety-zone," but instead, "as a field of tension," for "[Distance] is manifested not in relaxing the claim of ideas to truth, but in delicacy and fragility of thinking . . . [that reveals] the impossibility of a coincidence between the idea and what fulfills it" (*MM*, 127). The "safety-zone" version of Williams' cultural space would be the argument for its turning back political and social and historical investment into something linguistically indeterminate and materially inconsequential, Perloff's dubious insistence, for example, that "Williams' 'wheel / barrow' exists nowhere but in the words on the page." The "tension-field" version, the one we have been tentatively mapping in relation to his "secret gardens," to the contrary, would argue that the kind of self-detachment to be found within Williams' limits leaves cultural space sufficiently open "so that instead of merely reproducing being [the self] can, at once rigorous and free, [actually] determine it" (*MM*, 126–27). As Laurie Langbauer recently writes (citing Barbara Johnson), "There is politics precisely *because* there is undecidability," and Langbauer goes on convincingly to show how poststructuralism's recognition of subjectivity's always already thorough mediation of things (the ultimately unrepresentable category of "the everyday" in Henri Lefebvre, for instance) politicizes reality as a field of tension by imparting to it positions and markers "rather than a stable referent."[22]

The several dissident variations of the self reviewed earlier from Williams' *Autobiography* politicize subjectivity in precisely this way: "as a shifting marker," in his cultural criticism, "it tends to point in many, even opposite directions," and "[w]hat it marks is precisely the impossibility of its definition."[23] The word "secret," therefore, would seem appropriate to the poet's gardens in this sense. But again, "secret" ought not to consign his art to the quietism of opaque self-reflec-

22. Perloff, *Poetics of Indeterminacy*, 129 n. 20; Laurie Langbauer, "Cultural Studies and the Politics of the Everyday," *Diacritics* 20 (winter 1992): 48–49, emphasis added. As a variation of my title foregrounding the "distance" between ideas and things as a "limited" field of tension in Williams' criticism, Langbauer observes that Lefebvre "insists that 'the limitations of philosophy—truth without reality—always and ever counterbalance the limitations of everyday life—reality without truth'" (50). In the "Distance" fragment, Adorno goes even farther, to suggest that the "experience of its limit" is what allows philosophy to exist "within whatever conceptual area has been marked off for it," since "to think [a limit] is, according to Hegel's superb insight, the same thing as to cross it" (*MM*, 128). I develop a quite similar line of argument in Chapter 6 of my *Wallace Stevens and the Question of Belief:* "Velocities of Change: Nothing Exceeds like Excess," 224–51.
23. Langbauer, "Cultural Studies and the Politics of the Everyday," 50.

tion. Shakespeare is the "prime example" of "the 'mystery' of writing" not because he vaporizes so easily within the "false scantling of the classroom," but because "nearly anonymous, [he] is the 'mystery' of writing, and *must be* ingeniously explained": "the unsolved vessel of the clarification *I seek*" (*EK*, 99–100, emphases added).

Williams' "Elsie," again from *Spring and All*, is perhaps a more well known example of the garden-variety "shifting subject" in the early work—"under some hedge of choke-cherry / or vibernum— / which they cannot express—" (*WCP*, 217)—whose "broken brain . . . great / ungainly hips and flopping breasts" resist completely what Adorno calls "the pressure of identity" ("The Essay as Form" 165), and in her secretive mystery, thus makes the "pure products of America / go crazy" (*WCP*, 217). As one further addition to the expanding cultural vision of a young poet that makes its own powerful contribution to the populous Modernist American landscape by expanding its distance, Elsie, like all Williams' other dissident subjects, registers the "*[f]reedom* of thought denot[ing] the freedom of *thinking*" subtending the "tentative hypotheses, trials or experimentings that are unguaranteed" in that vision, and which, according to John Dewey, "puts some portion of an apparently stable world in peril" (*EN*, 182).[24] Within these tentative hypotheses, I would contend, are to be found all the Modernist possibilities of Williams' cultural criticism, as well as the source of its unique power. Together, they constitute a "chemical experiment or discovery fraught with ter-

24. T. W. Adorno, "The Essay as Form," trans. Bob Hullot-Kentor, *Telos* 32 (1984): 165. In such terms also, Adorno imparts to "great philosophy" a like cultural vision. He writes: "If, with the disintegration of all security within great philosophy, experiment makes its entry; if it thereby ties onto the limited, contoured and unsymbolic interpretations of aesthetic essays, then that does not appear to be condemnable. . . . For the mind (*Geist*) is indeed not capable of producing or grasping the totality of the real, but it may be possible to penetrate the detail, to explode in miniature the mass of merely existing reality." Adorno, "The Actuality of Philosophy," 133. Adorno's predilection for essay-writing noted here, explains in addition, perhaps, the fragmentary tentativeness of so much of Williams' early prose that we've only barely sampled: "He writes essayistically who writes while experimenting, who turns his object this way and that, who questions it, feels it, tests it, thoroughly reflects on it, attacks it from different angles, and in his mind's eye collects what he sees, and puts into words what the object allows to be seen under the conditions established in the course of writing." Adorno, "The Essay as Form," 164. I develop some of these ideas at greater length in my "The Novelty of Revolution/The Revolution of Novelty: Williams' First Fiction." *William Carlos Williams Review* 18 (spring 1992): 21–33. "Experiment, of course," Ross Posnock remarks, "is Dewey's pragmatist watchword." "The Politics of Nonidentity" 55. For further expansion of this inveterate preoccupation, see *EN*, 29, 59, 60–61, 66, 98, 129, 132, 138, 143, 156, 160, 161, 179, 182, 201, 265, 328, 338, 346, 350, and 353.

rific consequence for the world," the poet himself would say, because they, "at best, quite truly mean nothing," in Williams' own special distanciating use of that term (*EK*, 119). "It is only in isolate flecks that / something / is given off," so his "Elsie" concludes, "No one / to witness / and adjust, no one to drive the car" (*WCP*, 219).

Chapter 3

"Montage of an Otherness Deferred":
Dreaming Subjectivity in Langston Hughes

> *Our identities are often provoked by what we oppose.*
> —Jeffrey Escoffier, "The Limits of Multiculturalism"

> *In the Vietnamese language . . . [w]hen you talk to someone you establish a relationship. Such a self concept is a way of experiencing the other, of ritualistically sharing the other's essence and cherishing it. In our culture, seeing and feeling the dimension of harm done by separating self from other requires somewhat more work. Very little in our language or culture encourages looking at others as parts of ourselves.*
> —Patricia J. Williams, *The Alchemy of Race and Rights*

> *A subject who points to him or herself as subject-in-process, a work that displays its own formal properties or its own constitution as work, is bound to upset one's sense of identity—the familiar distinction between the Same and the Other since the latter is no longer kept in a recognizable relation of dependence, derivation, or appropriation.*
> —Trinh T. Minh-Ha, "Documentary Is/Not a Name"

THE otherness "deferred" in my title plays off, or perhaps I should say (indulging an old black cultural game remarked by Henry Louis Gates), *signifies upon* a later book of poetry by Langston Hughes entitled *Montage of a Dream Deferred* (1948). In that six-part suite of poems trained on Harlem life, Hughes offers enough of a variety of dream-postponements to suggest that the deferral of dreaming itself is perhaps willful, if not a little perverse. Yet otherness oftentimes strikes us as willful and perverse in just this way. The perverse otherness of black literature, for instance, oftentimes for theorists provides the most compelling reason for maintaining its clear separation from rival traditions and competing canons. "I would suggest that judgments on Afro-American 'modernity,'" Houston Baker has observed, "that begin with notions of British, Anglo-American, and Irish 'modernism' as 'successful' objects, projects, and processes to be emulated by Afro-Americans are misguided . . . [since] Africans and Afro-Americans . . . have little in common with Joycean or Eliotic projects." Paul Lauter echoes Baker's plea for a distinguishing separation by noting that "fundamental organizing principles [of standard American anthologies]," until only quite recently, "[have] seldom been altered to accommodate the fact that the significant literary work of African Americans cannot be understood as an expression of 'European culture' in an 'American environment.'"[1]

But even the contextualization of an "American environment" would appear to be an insufficient basis upon which to dissolve the otherness of Hughes' African American project. Overmastering literary traditions, after all, exist in America as well as in Europe. And even Alfred A. Knopf, for years Hughes' major publisher in the States, could barely restrain its disdain in the face of Hughes' refusal to conform to the hierarchical aesthetic dictates of more mainstream (i.e., WASP, masculinist, middle-class) canonical figures. "When Wallace Stevens visited the office," a Knopf official once later recalled to Hughes' biographer, long after the poet's death, "people were in awe of him. We treated him like a lord. Hardly anybody cared about Hughes. As far as I am concerned, he wrote baby poetry, poor stuff. If we had to go out to lunch with him, say to a French restaurant in mid-town, it was kind of embarrassing. He was a nice enough guy, but you couldn't get around the race thing."[2]

1. Henry Louis Gates, Jr., "Talkin' That Talk," in *"Race," Writing, and Difference,* ed. Henry Louis Gates, Jr. (Chicago, 1986), 407; Houston Baker, *Modernism and the Harlem Renaissance* (Chicago, 1987), xv–xvi; Paul Lauter, "Race and Gender in the Shaping of the American Literary Canon: A Case from the Twenties," in *Feminist Criticism and Social Change,* ed. Judith Newton and Deborah Rosenfelt (New York, 1985), 3.

2. Arnold Rampersad, *The Life of Langston Hughes, vol. 2: 1941–1967: I Dream a World* (New York, 1988), 120. Karen Jackson Ford, "Do Right to Write Right: Langston Hughes's Aesthetics of Simplicity," *Twentieth Century Literature* 38 (fall 1992), summarizes the generally mainstream critical reception of Hughes' work affirmed here, even to his last book (in 1967): "the poems are superficial, infantile, silly, small, unpoetic, common, jejune, iterative, and, of course, simple. Even his admirers reluctantly conclude that Hughes's poetics failed" (437). For more positive criticism, especially on matters relating to the complexity of Hughes' technique and musical style, see Theodore R. Hudson, "Technical Aspects of the Poetry of Langston Hughes," *Black World* (1973): 24–45; Onwucheka Jeme, *Langston Hughes: An Introduction to the Poetry* (New York, 1976); and Baxter Miller, *The Art and Imagination of Langston Hughes* (Lexington, 1989).

In taking up the issue of deferral in the otherness of Langston Hughes' poetry more generally, and the otherness underwriting his treatment of dissident subjectivity more specifically, I myself make no claim in this chapter for having got around "the race thing." Part of my argument, in fact, will be to suggest, particularly when I come onto the roundness or circularity in Hughes' handling of subjectivity, that race was perhaps an issue that the poet, unlike his contemporaries such as Alain Locke and Countee Cullen, would not care at all to lead us beyond. I *can*, however, right from the start, get beyond a certain animus held against his work, in the animadversions of "baby poetry" and "poor stuff" brought on by its specious comparison to either mainstream European or American culture. To do so, I think myself much better advised in following Henry Louis Gates' lead, and in the very first instance, "turn[] to the black vernacular tradition . . . [in order] to isolate the signifying black difference through which to theorize about the so-called Discourse of the Other."[3]

It would hardly seem possible to isolate the "signifying difference" in the discourse of Langston Hughes by seeking to establish a correspondent relationship between it and that of other communities or cultures. In an important journal-entry from 1929, Hughes articulates his "ultimate hope," beginning with his earliest work; namely, "To create a Negro culture in America—a real, solid, sane, racial something growing out of the folk life, *not copied from another,* even though surrounding[,] race." The statement echoes Hughes' more strenuous like-sentiments in his earlier essay "The Negro Artist and the Racial Mountain" from 1926, in which he declares that "the mountain standing in the way of any true Negro art in America" represents the "urge within the race toward whiteness, the desire to pour racial individuality into the mold of American standardization, and to be as little Negro and as much American as possible."[4]

Hughes' almost pathological resistance, in these comments, to the standardization, homogenization, or reduplication of personal experience presents us with a first level of insight into an otherness that we perceive to be in a constant state

---

3. Henry Louis Gates, Jr., *Loose Canons: Notes on the Culture Wars* (New York, 1992), 69.

4. Arnold Rampersad, *The Life of Langston Hughes*, vol. 1: *1902–1941, I, Too, Sing America* (New York, 1986), 173 (emphasis added), 130. Hughes concludes the essay by resoundingly underscoring the point: "We younger Negro artists who create now intend to express our individual dark-skinned selves without fear or shame. If white people are pleased we are glad. If they are not, it doesn't matter. We know we are beautiful. And ugly too. . . . If colored people are pleased we are glad. If they are not, their displeasure doesn't matter either. We build our temples for tomorrow, strong as we know how, and we stand on top of the mountain, free within ourselves." Quoted in Rampersad, *The Life of Langston Hughes*, 1:131.

of deferral throughout much of his work. Take, for instance, these opening lines
from Hughes' early "Afro-American Fragment":

> So long,
> So far away
> Is Africa.
> Not even memories alive
> Save those that history books create,
> Save those that songs
> Beat back into the blood—
> Beat out of blood with words sad-sung
> In strange un-Negro tongue—
> So long,
> So far away
> Is Africa.
>
> (*HCP*, 129)

Here, songs, like history books, endeavour "with words" to replicate black experience in the evanescent image of Africa: "So long, / So far away." Yet to the extent
that words seem capable of internalizing a determinate degree of reality which is
"Africa"—experience beaten "back into the blood"—a proportionate amount of
experience would appear, simultaneously, to be foreshortened or foreclosed—
beaten "out of blood"—by those very same words. We might almost be tempted
to educe a certain strain of Pragmatist thought in the opening and closing of
personal experience in Hughes' text, a kind of "self-sustaining in the midst of
self-removal" that William James contends "characterizes all reality and fact, [as]
something absolutely foreign to the nature of language."[5]

In the Pragmatist take on reality, "Something forever exceeds, escapes from
statement, withdraws from definition," James contends, and that something—
arguably Hughes' "racial something" mentioned previously—can only "be
glimpsed and felt, not told." Reflecting on this "so little known" passage from
James, Giles Gunn instructively observes: "The life of experience is therefore one
of constant movement beyond the linguistic formulations to which it gives rise,
and it makes no difference to the reality of our experience that we have no names
for its connective and transformative tissue. Its processes of relation and transition are still as real and as consequential as the places where they carry us." In his

---

5. William James, quoted in Giles Gunn, *Thinking Across the American Grain: Ideology, Intellect, and the New Pragmatism* (Chicago, 1992), 113.

recent *Color and Culture*, Ross Posnock remarks more particularly on the transitional aspect of Pragmatism as foregrounded in the African American context under the long shadow cast by philosopher W. E. B. Du Bois, a former student of James: "[Ralph] Ellison declares that [Alain] Locke sensed above all that Modern American culture was 'the experience of human beings living in a world of transition.'" Hence for Ellison, "turbulent transition" summarizes "the pragmatist legacy" by "reinstating, in Dewey's phrase, 'what is left over . . . excluded by definition from full reality,' what goes astray by eluding or disrupting the reign of system." Concludes Posnock: "Pragmatist pluralism is, to borrow [Zora Neale] Hurston's words, 'disturbing to the pigeon-hole way of life,' for it disinters what various forms of absolutism—identity claims grounded in biology, ethnicity, foundational philosophy, nationalism, or white supremacy—seek to keep buried: tangled and muddied overlap, 'motley mixtures.'"[6] Not unexpectedly, therefore, a similar withdrawal (or deferral) of motley or muddied experience, signed once again by Africa, flickers darkly at the end of Hughes' "Afro-American Fragment":

> I do not understand
> This song of atavistic land,
> Of bitter yearnings lost
> Without a place—
> So long,
> So far away,
> Is Africa's
> Dark face.
>
> (*HCP*, 129)

The image of Africa's "Dark face" in the poem's closing lines serves to reinforce the otherness of experience—the black difference—in the tradition of "true Negro art" that Hughes labored for over four decades to establish in America.

---

6. William James, quoted in Gunn, *Thinking Across the Grain*, 113, 112, 113–14; Ross Posnock, *Color and Culture: Black Writers and the Making of the Modern Intellectual* (Cambridge, Mass., 1998), 189. Houston Baker's terms for the Pragmatist's "life of experience" are "form" and "mask," and his elucidation of them uncannily matches not only the meaning, but also the very phrasing, in the passage cited from James: "It is difficult to convey notions of *form* and *mask* in the exact ways that I would like, for the mask as form does not exist as a static object. Rather it takes effect as a center for ritual and can only be defined—like form—from the perspective of action, *motion seen* [James' "glimpsed"] rather than 'thing' observed [James' "told"]." Baker, *Modernism and the Harlem Renaissance*, 17, emphases retained. For experience as an ultimately "unknowable reality" elsewhere in James, see *P*, 70–71.

Furthermore, in Hughes, the collocation of darkness, Africa, and facial (non)-identity, in one form or another, directs our response to a surfeit of experience that severely problematizes our tendency to rationalize, systematize, or categorize reality, and thereby, call an end to it. In "Negro," for instance, the surplus or deferral lies in "depths": "I am a Negro: / Black as the night is black, / Black like the depths of my Africa" (*HCP*, 24). In "As I Grew Older," the darkness is shattered and the night is smashed, but the surfeit is nonetheless sustained in what results: "To break this shadow / Into a thousand lights of sun, / Into a thousand whirling dreams / Of sun!" (*HCP*, 94). "The Negro Mother" brings the experience of the previous two poems together: "Look at my face—dark as the night— / Yet shining like the sun with love's true light." Yet it is the very unfathomableness of the Negro mother's experience that prevents us from according her any *specific* identification: "I am the child they stole from the sand / Three hundred years ago in Africa's land. . . . Three hundred years in the deepest South: / But God put a song and a prayer in my mouth" (*HCP*, 155). Ultimately, Hughes' surplus otherness directs our responses to a certain *lack* at the heart of black experience, a lack within the very word "b*lack*" that Hughes himself suggests in the appropriately titled "Consider Me"—"What I lack, / Black, / Caught in a crack / That splits the world in two"—and whose final lines neatly sum up the overriding effect of an otherness perpetually deferred: "Consider me, / Descended also / From the / Mystery" (*HCP*, 386). Noting the phrase "the mystery of American identity" repeated several times in Ralph Ellison's own work, Posnock is reminded "that American identity is not a preordained given to discover and to know but instead eludes adequate definition and offers the experience of bewilderment," for, according to Ellison, "it is in the very *spirit* of art to be defiant of categories."[7]

Langston Hughes shipped out to Africa for almost a full year, in 1923, much before taking up writing as a full-time vocation once back in America. According to his biographer, mystery would appear to have been the key to that extraordinarily formative experience, right from the poet's first embarkation: "Africa! The continent was a mystery known to few black Americans. . . . Hughes stood there awhile in the darkness, salt spray blowing in his face . . . as the *West Hesseltine* surged into the dark. Toward Africa!" This description is perhaps most useful in helping us to understand how Africa could enter Hughes' poetry as *a figure*, particularly in its association with darkness and dreaming, for the willed mystery, the uncertainty, or the indeterminacy—what I have been calling the deferred otherness—of black experience. And in Hughes' early work, we are particularly

7. Posnock, *Color and Culture*, 202–203.

struck by the large number of texts that play about this figure. For the little "snail," in the Blakean lyric of that title, "Weather and rose / Is all you see, / Drinking / The dewdrop's / Mystery" (*HCP*, 233). "Fantasy in Purple" exhorts us to "blow one blaring trumpet note of sun," and "go with me / to the darkness / where I go" (*HCP*, 56). While in "Havana Dreams," the image of the face surfaces, once again, to underscore the enigmatic character of all human endeavor:

> Perhaps the dream is only her face
> Perhaps it's a fan of silver lace—
> Or maybe the dream's a Vedado rose—
> (*Quien sabe?* Who really knows?)
> (*HCP*, 173)

As with the lack, earlier, that splits the world in two, so Hughes' mysteries land us, in "Border Line," on a "difference" between "living and dying" and between "here and there"—borderline mysteries that ultimately, in the poem, constitute a "distance" that "Is nowhere" (*HCP*, 325). The nowhere, however, of Hughes' "distance"—a distance so resonant with its several other Modernist deployments in this study—is hardly meant to be dismissive of life's mystery. As Robert Young remarks in a related context, distance, through its mediation by language, "posits a relation of sociality, whereby the self instead of assimilating the other[,] opens itself to it through a relation with it," and thus sustains "the radical separation" as well as "the strangeness" of the other as a kind of revelation.[8]

In *The Signifying Monkey,* Henry Louis Gates puts forward the important suggestion that "The 'finding of the voice' of the speaking subject in a language in which *blackness is the cardinal sign of absence* is the subject of so much of Afro-American discourse." Gates's association of black experience with "absence,"[9] for

8. Rampersad, *The Life of Langston Hughes*, 1:71–72; Robert Young, *White Mythologies: Writing History and the West* (New York, 1990), 13.

9. Henry Louis Gates, Jr., *The Signifying Monkey: A Theory of African-American Literary Criticism* (New York, 1988), 40n. Later in Gates' theoretical treatment, this association is supported with the further observation that "[t]he blackness of black literature is not an absolute or a metaphysical condition, as Ellison maintains, nor is it some transcending essence that exists outside of its manifestations in texts. Rather, the 'blackness' of black American literature can be discerned only through close readings," that is, through the "specific uses of literary language that are shared, repeated, critiqued, and revised." Gates, *The Signifying Monkey*, 121. Cf. also Gates' comment, in his "Editor's Introduction: Writing 'Race' and the Difference It Makes" in *"Race," Writing, and Difference*, 5, that "[r]ace has become a trope of ultimate, irreducible difference between cultures, linguistic groups, or adherents of specific belief systems." In such terms, race gestures towards a condition of "nonidentity," according

which the writer of color, as speaking subject, is then adjured to lend his or her voice—this association, I would argue, is one that began to congeal quite early in the poetry of Langston Hughes, in the ideas such as mystery, lack, difference, and absence, all clustered, as we have seen, about the more general notion of a deferred otherness or distance. Moreover, if Africa served to trope the idea of asserting that otherness or going that distance in texts more broad-ranging in their representation of black experience, it was the Harlem ghetto in New York that the poet's discourse figuratively settled upon, as the quintessential image of difference in Hughes' more concentrated and focused view of American urban life. Darkness, undoubtedly, formed the link between Africa and Harlem, for it was "[t]he sheer dark size of Harlem," Hughes records, "that intrigued [him]." Yet it was Harlem itself that constituted "the lifelong source of his finest inspiration," his biographer recounts, "a living, breathing, vibrant black community in all its colors and classes, virtues and vices, dreams and fears":

> [Hughes] was not romantic about Harlem, which had changed dramatically since his arrival there twenty years earlier [in 1921]. Still relatively safe, it was not as safe as it had once been; several people he knew had been mugged at least once. . . . But Harlem was home . . . [and] he blended effortlessly with the dark flow of life on which he and his art had always depended.[10]

Harlem's "dark flow of life," in this account, once again foregrounds the signifying difference so central to the representation of reality as Hughes conceives it. "Likewise," an important text in the *Montage* sequence noted earlier, is perhaps pivotal in the representation of Harlem's darkness:

> The Jews:
>   Groceries
>   Suits
>   Fruits
>   Watches
>   Diamond rings
>   THE DAILY NEWS

---

to Posnock, "what in *Dark Princess* [W. E. B. Du Bois] calls 'divine anarchy,'" and Zora Neale Hurston "cosmic" when she observes: "the stuff of my being is matter, ever changing, ever moving, but never lost; so what need of denominations and creeds [when] . . . I am one with the infinite and need no other assurance." Posnock, *Color and Culture*, 85. Similarly, "[James] Baldwin's namelessness announces his Americanness." Posnock, *Color and Culture*, 231.

10. Rampersad, *The Life of Langston Hughes*, 1:56, and 2:60.

> Jews sell me things.
> Yom Kippur, no!
> Shops all over Harlem
> close up tight that night.
>
> Some folks blame high prices on the Jews.
> (Some folks blame too much on the Jews.)
> But in Harlem they don't answer back,
> Just maybe shrug their shoulders,
> "What's the use?"
> . . . .
> Sometimes I think
> Jews must have heard
> the music of a
> dream deferred.
>
> (*HCP*, 424–25)

Predictably in this text, the "deferred dream" that is Harlem in the final line reiterates what makes Africa so darkly mysterious, analyzed previously: its imperviousness to rational or logical penetration ("in Harlem they don't answer back"), and therefore, its resistance to a fully linguistic elucidation ("close[d] up tight"). What is more, the focus on "Jews," already well-established symbols of disruption and difference in Modernist representation,[11] defers the appearance of Harlem's black denizens perhaps to other texts in Hughes' sequence, in characterizations anticipated to be "likewise," and thus here, reiterates Harlem's darkness as the cardinal sign of its black people's absence. A poem so tight-lipped about the *real* character of Harlem life can only mock its own words in meaningless signs and exasperated shrugs: "What's the use?"

But it would be a mistake to construe Harlem in all of these interpretive refusals as an empty signifier in Hughes' later discourse, a linguistic counter or cultural marker dried up "like a raisin in the sun" (*HCP*, 426). Harlem suffers not from an attenuation of meaning, if its roaring Jewish storefronts above are any indication, but rather from meaning's excess in the Jamesean conception of experience: "overflow[ing] its own definition . . . [and] open[ing] out and run[ning] into the more."[12] In "Projection" (*HCP*, 403–404), for instance, the *discordia concors* that places Sammy Davis cheek by jowl with Marian Anderson, Paul Robeson with

11. See Iain Chambers, *Border Dialogues*, 138 n. 11.

12. William James, quoted in Posnock, *Color and Culture*, 10–11.

"Moms" Mabley, that pits the Savoy and "jitterbugging" against Seventh Avenue
and the "Renaissance," or that would have the Abyssinia Baptist Church lie down
beside St. James Presbyterian—such a rollicking, roistering, raucous mélange of
disparate tastes and variegated temperaments can only excite a healthy palate for
experience, hardly beggar it. Yet even the excitement of the palate would only
leave it wanting more. For surely the "projection" in the poem's title has more to
do with the desire for experience, not the satisfaction or satiation made possible
by any particular presentation of that experience. Hence, in the poem entitled
"Deferred," the fact that one may never go to France does not prevent the Har-
lemite from studying French at night school; nor does the lack of "a decent radio"
extinguish the need "to take up Bach" (HCP, 413–14).

What keeps the dream distanced or "deferred" in this poem, and several others
where the phrase becomes insistently repeated ("Dream Boogie" [HCP, 388],
"Tell Me" [HCP, 396], "Boogie 1 a.m." [HCP, 411], "Dime" [HCP, 420], etc.)
is no one thing. Built into that "certain / amount of nothing / in a dream deferred"
("Same in Blues" [HCP, 427]) is the desire that, punningly, would turn no[one]-
thing into everything, if Harlem might only be large enough, or have the stamina
to withstand "all its colors and classes, virtues and vices, dreams and fears," in
Rampersad's phrase, strongly enough. If blackness is the cardinal sign of distance,
then Harlem in all of its deferred dreams—its "nothing"—is that blackness' most
particular signifier, just as Africa is perhaps its most universal. In all of the instances just rehearsed, Harlem therefore becomes the perfect evocation for blackness, since, as Kimberly Benston persuasively argues, "Blackness, far from being
inextricable from the paradoxes of its articulation, finally transcends representation," and all "Afro-American cultural expression" that would tie it down to some
essentialist Ding-an-sich. Hughes indulges a continuous montage of dream-
deferrals in his representation of Harlem because the otherness of black experience, according to Benston, "does not inhere in any ultimate referent but is renewed in the rhythmic process of multiplication and substitution generated from
performance to performance," and accordingly, becomes "a dynamic producer of
richly differing signifying perspectives . . . 'seething with possibilities.'"[13]

The one identity or representation that Hughes does risk attaching consis-
tently to Harlem is that of the female. Generally in his poetry, women suffer
intolerable hardships at the hands of black men: for example, in "Misery" ("A

13. Kimberly W. Benston, "I Yam What I Am: The Topos of (Un)naming in Afro-American
Literature," in Black Literature and Literary Theory, ed. Henry Louis Gates, Jr. (New York, 1990),
172, 173.

good woman's cryin' / For a no-good man" [*HCP*, 77]), in "Lament over Love" ("Gonna think about my man— / And let my fool-self fall" [*HCP*, 70]), in "Ballad of the Girl Whose Name Is Mud" ("The guy she gave her all to / Dropped her with a thud" [*HCP*, 256]), and so forth. But in its specific association with Harlem, as the distanciated image of darkness and mystery, female identity in Hughes presents us with something quite other:

> Take Harlem's heartbeat,
> Make a drumbeat,
> Put it on a record, let it whirl,
> And while we listen to it play,
> Dance with you till day—
> Dance with you, my sweet brown Harlem girl.
>
> (*HCP*, 393)

In this brief excerpt from "Juke Box Love Song," Hughes' discourse is fully trained on the character and quality of experience that sets Harlem life apart as a unique culture, that is to say, on the seething possibilities, picked up in the insistent rhythms and repetitions of its music. And it is these possibilities that allow his discourse to transcend the specific representation of men and women in the closure of a constraining and containing sameness, and instead, to open out onto a new and more dynamic level of difference, hence equality and freedom.[14] On this level, too, as I mentioned earlier, we begin to give some serious thought to alternative forms of American Modernism, critically dismantling the notion that modernity comes handed down to us, monolithically, in only one traditional shape, or in only one canonical condition.

Hughes' "sweet brown Harlem girl" is thus given to us in deference to an *alternative* modern consciousness, and in this light, her representation should not surprise us. As Iain Chambers sums up the case: "In philosophical, literary, historical and critical considerations of modernity the figure of woman has invariably been presented as the symbol of all that is mysterious, unknown and uncontrollable. . . . Such a figure stands for that excess in feeling and being that breaks the bounds of reason and threatens its exercise of power. It is therefore a figure of

---

14. As John Lowney recently remarks, "bebop's hybrid style reflected the social heterogeneity of Harlem while registering the jarring but liberating impact of a new urban environment. Improvisation became a means for negotiating but also inventing new racial—an interracial—identities." John Lowney, "Langston Hughes and the 'Nonsense' of Bop," *American Literature* 72 (spring 2000): 365.

the displaced, the hidden, the unrecognized" (107).[15] Mystery, absence, nothingness, and excess in Chambers' astute commentary allow it to become a rather
appropriate gloss on Hughes' handling of the female-figure in relation to Harlem's deferred otherness. One might be tempted to go even further, and perhaps
imagine that the characterization of Alberta K. Johnson, the female-persona in
another memorable Harlem sequence, *Madam to You,* was what Hughes really
had in mind when Chambers speaks of a female-figure constituting a threat to
powerful reason through an excess of feeling. To a meticulously logical census-
taker, for instance, who demands to know the meaning for "K" in Alberta's middle name, the woman lashes out: "My mother christened me / ALBERTA K. /
You leave my name / Just that way!" ("Madam and the Census Man" [*HCP*,
355]). Although Alberta will say only "K— / And nothing more," nonetheless,
she strikes us as someone a bit too sure of herself, a bit too confirmed in her own
sense of identity. In this standoff, it is not likely that her "nothing" is that abyss
that will suck in her overly sensible census man, or any other calculating, manipu-
lating patriarch. Perhaps here, we are reminded once again of the Jews in another
Harlem poem who "don't answer back" (*HCP*, 424), but instead, allow their mysterious distance to be construed as an invitation for the reader to construct their
identity in any number of dissident ways.

With the mention of distanciated identities, I want to shift attention now to that
very important area in Langston Hughes' poetry where the deferral of otherness
becomes not just the rhetorical principle of a more discriminating Modernism,
but in more personal terms, a veritable article of faith in the context of social and
cultural politics. Specifically, I mean to address that area in Hughes' discourse in
which our attention shifts from experience *outside,* in the external world, to experience *inside,* within the human individual, that is to say, to the more particular
realities of racial thought and gendered consciousness. In a word, and for the
remainder of this chapter, I want now to examine the import of otherness deferred in Hughes' treatment of subjectivity, and the significant bearing we might
perceive this to have in relation to a certain cultivation of distance in the Modernist American poetic text.

From the start, I think it is important to make a critical distinction between

15. Iain Chambers, *Border Dialogues,* 107. For an alternative, feminist expansion of the view of
"'woman' as the unknown, the unsayable, the indecipherable, as that excess which signifies the 'other'
for the philosophers of crisis and difference (from Nietzsche to Derrida)," Chambers additionally
directs our attention to the work of Alice Jardine in *Gynesis* (1985). Chambers, *Border Dialogues,* 138
n. 11. Cf. the parallel use of this material in my own *Wallace Stevens and the Question of Belief.*

two kinds of subjectivity that we have already touched upon in Hughes' poetry, in laboring to make the separation, say, between Alberta K. Johnson and Hughes' "brown Harlem girl": on the one hand, a specific and individualized character that can be designated, and named, and on the other, a more generalized figure or type that can only be alluded to or gestured toward, but never directly identified. The distinction between a "referred" subjectivity, in the former case, and a "deferred" subjectivity, in the latter—"dissident," in a word—is perhaps what is needed at this point. And with respect to the latter, Houston Baker's notion of a "mask" may help to take us even closer to deferred or dissident subjectivity as a kind of "symbolizing fluidity," that is to say, "a momentary and changing same array of images, figures, assumptions, and presuppositions that a group of people . . . holds to be a valued repository of spirit."[16]

More important still, I think it is useful to try to understand that while both kinds of subjectivity in my examples from Hughes are joined together in their designation as female, although it would be impossible for a man to occupy the space of the referred instance of Alberta Johnson, it would be entirely probable— indeed, beneficial—for a man to conceive the deferred instance of Hughes' brown Harlem girl as one likely to inform his own subjectivity in an untold number of hypothetically imaginable ways. As a figure for fluidity and alterity, she foregrounds the conditionality of subjectivity for men (and women), and in the very character of her non-referential, non-representational no-thing-ness, opens up an infinite space of possibility for being different, and for existing otherwise. In this connection, one may be reminded of the primal experience that Henry Louis Gates recounts from his early youth, when his mother rose one day in church to give substance and direction to words he had mindlessly forgotten during a public

16. Baker, *Modernism and the Harlem Renaissance*, 17. My reading of Baker's "mask" as a kind of deferred subjectivity undoubtedly lends itself well to a species of radical democratic discourse that would better allow for, in Howard Winant's words, "the permanence of racial difference in US society." Howard Winant, "Postmodern Racial Politics in the United States: Difference and Inequality," *Socialist Review* 20 (January 1990). As Winant further explains, "When claims of universality are relaxed, the effect is to recognize the *fluidity* of racial themes in US politics and culture and to accept both the continuity and the variability of race in sociopolitical arrangements and cultural life." A notion of deferred or dissident subjectivity thus comes into its own "when it is possible to recognize both the necessary permanence and ongoing *instability* of racial meanings and identities in the contemporary United States" (133, 134, emphases added). Remarking on black identity as an "open-ended" and "fluid continuum," Posnock cites Ralph Ellison to the same effect, noting his stance "as part of a pragmatist lineage" with Ellison's words: "we are representative not only of one but of several overlapping and constantly shifting social categories" in a "whirlpool" of motion. Posnack, *Color and Culture*, 186.

recitation. "I realized," Gates reflects, that "much of my scholarly and critical work has been an attempt to learn how to speak in the strong, compelling cadences of my mother's voice," and what is more, that "learning to speak in the voice of the black female is perhaps the ultimate challenge of producing a discourse of the critical Other."[17]

By this time, it perhaps goes without saying that, over and over again, the poetry of Langston Hughes rises to the challenge of producing a discourse of the critical other—a discourse, in other terms, of a differing, distanciated, hence, deferred subjectivity. Had Langston Hughes, at some point during his long career as a writer, learned to speak in the voice of the black female? After close to thirty years of sedulous and unstinting effort, his biographer seems to think so:

> Surfacing now [i.e., in the early 1950s] perhaps, at last, was the obverse self-image, which had been latent in him from the start—his sense of himself, in his most intimate role as a poet, as mother (hardly father) to the race, rather than its princely child. Early poems such as "Mother to Son" and "The Negro Mother" had indicated the presence of this essential capacity, even if it had been only sparingly invoked. Now, as an object of his own will, he was moving irrevocably from confidence that Langston Hughes heroically, epically, could determine the future—that is, save and deliver his race—toward the tender hope that his "children," nurtured by him, would do so.[18]

Apart from the specific attribution of a certain kind of female identity to the male writer in this important characterization, I think what is especially noteworthy here is the manifestation of that feminine sensibility in Hughes' openness to change, that is clearly demonstrated by the gradual *turning* in the poetic representation of his self from epic hero to nurturing mother.

The turning here puts us in mind, once again, of the whirling of his brown

---

17. Gates, *Loose Canons*, 41–42. More recently, the lesson has been reaffirmed for Gates by the words of Hortense Spillers, in her well-known essay "Mama's Baby, Papa's Maybe," where Spillers asserts: "The African-American male has been touched, therefore, by the *mother*, handled by her in ways that he cannot escape, and in ways that the white American male is allowed to temporize by fatherly reprieve. This human and historical development—the text that has been inscribed on the benighted heart of the continent—takes us to the center of *an inexorable difference* in the depths of American women's community . . . [namely,] the Law of the Mother. . . . It is the heritage of the *mother* that the African-American male must regain as an aspect of his own personhood—the power of 'yes' to the 'female' within." Hortense Spillers, quoted in Gates, *Loose Canons*, 40, second emphasis added.

18. Rampersad, *The Life of Langston Hughes*, 2:40.

Harlem girl back in "Juke Box Love Song" (*HCP*, 393), whose circling subjectivity, in the context of deferred otherness, makes promise of a permanently variable state of alteration. The turning also recalls the Pragmatism of William James, and the experience of self-sustaining in the midst of self-removal. As Richard Poirier refurbishes this thought, Hughes' deferred subjectivity might be equated to what Poirier describes as the "Emersonian individual, of which James's individual is a version, [and which] 'turns' continually and quizzically on its own doubled and fractured self, aware that one part is apt to be saying more than some other part can accept. . . . [Hence,] the result is that we do not ever fully mean what we say or say what we mean." In which case, Langston Hughes might respond, better to say nothing.[19]

However, when we finally *do* mean what we say with reference to subjectivity, or say what we mean, when all the parts of our selfhood blend into one complete, coherent, and coordinate mass, with no more surplus, no more excess, no further twistings or doublings or turnings, then we arrive at the state that Langston Hughes calls the "Final Curve":

> When you turn the corner
> And you run into *yourself*
> Then you know that you have turned
> All the corners that are left.
>   (*HCP*, 368)

With no options left to construct subjectivity in alternative forms, or to make expedient choices among forms already extant, the deferred subject passes into the stratifications and the solidifications of its referred counterpart, and in so doing, forgoes any further possibility of social activism or political agency. In such terms, Alberta Johnson hands over her *final* word to the census man, and the dream of subjectivity is over. Hughes, therefore, would find much to recommend

---

19. Poirier, *Poetry and Pragmatism*, 68. And "nothing" is precisely what the Emersonian individual is led finally to conclude, according to Poirier, elsewhere: "The self for Emerson appears only *in* its workings, *in* its actions with words—*in* movements which turn back against any self . . . as it may have been constituted even a moment ago. That immediately prior self becomes only one more object of scrutiny [recall Hughes as "an object of his own will" in Rampersad, above]. Better, then not to *assert* a self; do not 'prate,' only 'speak' in some more pliant way, or say nothing." Poirier, *Poetry and Pragmatism*, 67, emphases retained. Similarly, "the act of turning or troping," remarks Posnock, "is itself at the heart of pragmatism's stance toward experience," and finds that "pragmatist method . . . to have been particularly congenial to the intellectually voracious W. E. B. Du Bois." Posnock, *Color and Culture*, 110, 121; further on 122, 130, 141, and 316 n. 5.

in Stephen Melville's recent comment that "No calculus guarantees the unfinishable precision of our language; its necessary obliquity approaches *no final ideal curve*. Around every circle another can be drawn, and the resulting figure is resolutely and irresolvably complex." The thought here forms a vital intersection with Hughes' own introduction to an anthology of poems on racial minorities by Walt Whitman, entitled "The Ceaseless Rings of Walt Whitman." In this essay, "Whitman's 'I' is not the 'I' of the introspective versifiers who write always and only about themselves"; rather, "the Whitman spiral is upward and outward toward a freer, better life for all, not narrowing downward toward death and destruction." Ideally, in the words of Emily Dickinson echoing Hughes in "Final Curve," "We meet no Stranger but Ourself."[20]

The most important political implication of the complex circularity of deferred subjectivity, of course, is its resistance to the kind of foundationalizing or essentializing of human character that inevitably leads to the verticals of hierarchy, from the viewpoint of class, and of segregation from the perspective of race. "Merry-Go-Round" subverts both of these fatal tendencies:

> Down South where I come from
> White and colored
> Can't sit side by side.
> Down South on the train
> There's a Jim Crow car.
> On the bus we're put in the back—
> But there ain't no back
> To a merry-go-round!
>
> (*HCP*, 240)

With no prospect in sight to the ending—"there ain't no back"—of the infinite revolving of individualities, in the playful consciousness of the child being nur-

20. Stephen Melville, "Oblique and Ordinary: Stanley Cavell's Engagements of Emerson," *American Literary History* 5 (spring 1993): 189, emphasis added; Langston Hughes, "The Ceaseless Rings of Walt Whitman," quoted in Rampersad, *The Life of Langston Hughes*, 2:112; Emily Dickinson, *The Letters of Emily Dickinson*, ed. Thomas H. Johnson (Cambridge, Mass., 1960), 3:348. Hughes' notion of a deferred subjectivity, as I am attempting to account for it in a dissident sense, would thus support Michael Omi and Howard Winant's notion of "[r]acial formation . . . understood as a *process* . . . through which new instabilities and contradictions emerge at a subsequent historical point and challenge the pre-existing system once more." Michael Omi and Howard Winant, "By the Rivers of Babylon: Race in the United States (Part 1)," *Socialist Review* 71 (September–October 1983): 50.

tured by Hughes here, the intolerable verticality of an exclusionary racism is
turned on its ear, and an emancipatory horizon of democratic superfluity is set in
its place. The poem "Crossing" labors to make a similar point. There, the child's
"lonely" experience of finding itself "up on a mountain" or "down in the valley" is
crossed with the possibility of standing "out on a prairie," with all one's friends
"right there," and savoring another kind of loneliness, a more individuating,
hence, empowering sense of separateness and integrity, of unique difference, that
surely comes with the realization that "as far as I could see / Wasn't nobody on
that prairie / Looked like me" (*HCP*, 251).

The kind of crossing in this text that values difference more for what it in-
cludes for the deferred subject than what it excludes for the referred, is precisely
what renovates difference for Edward Said, to whom its ideology so often becomes "an instrument to relegate the rights of others to an inferior or lesser
status." As in Hughes, "an awareness of the supervening actuality of 'mixing,' of
crossing over, of stepping beyond boundaries" points difference in the direction of
"more creative human activities than staying inside rigidly policed borders,"
thereby putting the lie to the notion that there can (or ought to) be "any such
thing as a pure race, a pure nation, or a pure collectivity, regardless of patriotic,
ideological, or religious argument."[21] Nor, in a related text such as "Cross," can
we entertain even the notion of a pure self, according to Hughes. "Being neither
white nor black" fills the protagonist with remorse that he should have once
cursed his "white old man" one moment, and his "black old mother" the next,
now that both parents are dead (*HCP*, 58). The rank impossibility of policing the
borders of racial purity is, thus, the hideous impasse to which "Mulatto" is ultimately led: "*Git on back there in the night, / You ain't white*" (*HCP*, 100). Ironically, the muteness of nature in this poem seems to hold out the greater hope for
tolerance than either of its hateful, racializing interlocutors:

> The Southern night is full of stars,
> Great big yellow stars.
> O, sweet as earth,
> Dusk dark bodies
> Give sweet birth
> To little yellow bastard boys.
>   (*HCP*, 100)

21. Edward Said, "An Ideology of Difference," in *"Race," Writing, and Difference*, ed. Henry
Louis Gates, Jr. (Chicago, 1986), 41, 43, 41, emphasis added.

The crucial distinction in Hughes between the referred and the deferred subject, as I have been elucidating it, perhaps hinges most on this last point—what Theodor Adorno has called "the mythical deception of the pure self," which enlarges in the former case to favor some form of "original entity [or] monad," and diminishes, proportionately, in the latter, in order to privilege "a social division of the social process" (*MM*, 153). That the social process is divided among a vast number of competing identifications—racial, ethnic, sexual, religious, and so forth—further suggests, as well, why the former would pathologize otherness in the dependent and appropriative relation it establishes to it (according to Trinh T. Minh-Ha), and why the latter would valorize otherness, in its relation of ritualistic sharing and caring (according to Patricia Williams). What cannot be gainsaid, in each case, is the fact of *relationship* itself, and the imperative of difference internalized in any act of self-constituting negation. Now a subject of reference can deny that relative difference, negate the negation, as it were, in an act of racial purity or ethnic cleansing. But as Judith Butler astutely observes, even a racist thrives on relationship: "he cannot be white without blacks and without constant disavowal of his relation to them[,] for [i]t is only through disavowal that his whiteness is constituted, and through the institutionalization of that disavowal that his whiteness is perpetually—but anxiously—reconstituted."[22] Toni Morrison makes the same point from the opposite direction, viewing, much in Hughes' terms, "the elaborate deferment" of Jim's final escape in *Huckleberry Finn*

22. Trinh T. Minh-Ha, "Documentary Is/Not a Name," *October* 52 (1990): 95; Patricia J. Williams, *The Alchemy of Race and Rights: Diary of a Law Professor* (Cambridge, Mass., 1991), 62; Butler, *Bodies That Matter*, 171. Butler amplifies her point elsewhere by noting that "[t]hat which is not included—exteriorized by boundary—as a phenomenal constituent of the sedimented effect called 'construction' will be as crucial to its definition as that which is included"; hence, "an abjected outside . . . is, after all, 'inside' the subject as its own founding repudiation" (245 n. 8, 3). Thus, as Richard Dyer argues, "It is the actual dependency of white on black in a context of continued white power and privilege that throws the legitimacy of white domination into question." Richard Dyer, "White," *Screen* 29 (winter 1988): 48. Similarly, in "Here Be Monsters" (from *The Price of the Ticket*), James Baldwin observes: "each of us, helplessly and forever, contains the other—male in female, female in male, white in black, and black in white. We are a part of each other. Many of my countrymen appear to find this fact exceedingly inconvenient and even unfair, and so, very often, do I. But none of us can do anything about it." James Baldwin, quoted in Henry Louis Gates, Jr., "The Welcome Table," in *English Inside and Out: The Places of Literary Criticism, Essays from the Fiftieth Anniversary of the English Institute*, ed. and intro. by Susan Gubar and Jonathan Kamholtz (New York, 1993), 60. "We needed to hear these words two decades ago," Gates remarks on the Baldwin citation. "We need to hear them today" (60). All of these comments might then persuade us to emend Jeffrey Escoffier's statement "Our identities are often provoked by what we oppose" ("The Limits of Multiculturalism," *Socialist Review* 21 [summer-fall 1993]: 71): our identities are *always* provoked by what we oppose.

as the necessary indication to the humanitarian that "freedom has no meaning . . . without the specter of enslavement . . . the signed, marked, informing and mutating presence of a black slave."[23]

"Theme for English B," arguably Hughes' most important poem in the *Montage* sequence, explodes the notion of a racially pure self, as much as the protagonist's white writing-instructor would insist on it, in the egregious simple-mindedness of the text's opening exhortation:

> *Go home and write*
> *a page tonight.*
> *And let that page come out of you—*
> *Then, it will be true.*
>
> (*HCP*, 409)

"I wonder if it's that simple?" the student is given to reflect. With Harlem firmly fixed as the backdrop to his exercise, the writer eventually comes to realize that neither his self, nor the words that form the social and cultural extension of that self, exist in a vacuum. Their interiority ("Me—who?") comes to mean only as a function of what is exterior ("Harlem, I hear you") just as the exteriority of Harlem forms to meaning only in relation to the tiny interior of the bed-sitter the student rents downtown at the Y. Eventually, this web of co-implicated relativity comes to overtake even the instructor uptown. And the call for intuitive self-expression, at the beginning of the poem, policing the rigidly symmetrical relation between self and other, writing and reality, black and white, comes completely unraveled by the end:

> You are white—
> yet a part of me, as I am a part of you.
> That's American.

23. Toni Morrison, *Playing in the Dark: Whiteness and the Literary Imagination* (Cambridge, Mass., 1992), 56 (52 and 64–65 are related). Morrison's valuable insight ought not, by some, to be viewed as an apology for slavery. Her argument, to the contrary, merely underscores the complex relation that threatens to become effaced in the referred subject's clamant rage for purity and order. The "crossings of identification of which it is itself composed" have still to be dealt with, as Butler notes, that is, "the kinds of contestatory connections that might democratize the field of its [identity's] own operation." Butler, *Bodies That Matter*, 115. But as Patricia Williams observes, "Very little in our language or culture encourages looking at others as parts of ourselves." Patricia Williams, *The Alchemy of Race and Rights*, 62. Elsewhere, Williams, in a rather Hughes-like idiom, makes ominously plain what the willfully disconnected subject chooses to ignore at its peril: "So-called enlightened

> Sometimes perhaps you don't want to be a part of me.
> Nor do I often want to be a part of you.
> But we are, that's true!
> As I learn from you,
> I guess you learn from me—
>
> (*HCP,* 410)

As in "Merry-Go-Round" previously, we can make no clear determination as to where the intrication of human identity either begins or ends from this point onward. Once again, discourse makes promise of an infinitely revolving subjectivity. And what seems quintessentially "American," in this instance, can only be the dream of its endless deferral.[24]

Before concluding this overview of the treatment of dissident subjectivity in Hughes, there is one final issue, both in the life and work, upon which the dream of deferral is at last able to help us secure a successful purchase. "Café: 3 a.m." brings this issue to an immediate focus:

> Detectives from the vice squad
> with weary sadistic eyes
> spotting fairies.
> > *Degenerates,*
> > some folks say.
>
> But God, Nature,
> or somebody
> made them that way.
>
> Police lady or Lesbian
> over there?
> > *Where?*
>
> (*HCP,* 406)

---

others who fail to listen to these voices of demonic selves, made invisibly uncivilized, simply make them larger, more barbarously enraged, until the nearsightedness of looking-glass existence is smashed in by the terrible dispossession of dreams too long deferred" (145).

24. My analysis of this particular text, as well as others previously referred to, thus finds itself at a considerable remove from the view that Hughes is "a poet who equates simplicity with truth," that "cultivating a thematics and aesthetics of simplicity is essential—poetically and politically," and that, therefore, "Simplicity *is* truth in Hughes's vision." Ford, "Do Right to Write Right," 440. To cite the student's quandary in "English B," once again, "I wonder if it's that simple." But perhaps my objection really lies in Ford's statement that "utter simplicity is *the only* adequate response to a dislocated life in an urban ghetto in a racist country" (454). I shall return to this issue a bit later.

In this brief text, we are once more presented with the familiar situation of a referred subjectivity almost immediately displaced by a deferred one. The male gaze of the detectives' "sadistic eyes" aims to objectify a truant sexuality, through disciplinary categories either prescribed (Nature, folks) or ordained (God, somebody), with the view to punishing the very outlaws of the heterosexual regime whose criminalized abjection is required to sustain that regime's own lawful hegemony. That the purity police require degenerates and fairies as much as these require the vice squad for the purpose of their own, mutual self-authentication is suggested in the poem's inability to prize apart lesbian and police-lady in the final lines: "over there? / *Where?*"

But Hughes' larger satirical project in the poem's ending is perhaps also to problematize the failure of *all* disciplinary or referential categories. "In writing my recent study of lesbian fiction from 1969 to 1989," Bonnie Zimmerman recently discloses, "I found myself constantly falling into the trap of generalizing a lesbian subject, even as I attempted to show the failures of such generalization. Pulled between the desire to affirm a historical lesbian collective identity and to 'destabilize' . . . that identity by introducing the discourses of differences within, I did not entirely satisfy either goal."[25] The otherness of deferred subjectivity in Langston Hughes' poetry would suggest that a primary investment in some totally stable, categorizable, representable identity was likely what may have been misplaced in Zimmerman's undertaking in the first place. Indeed, this kind of investment, it seems to me, is what accounts for so much of the misguided speculation about Langston Hughes' own sexuality throughout his lifetime. Was he, or was he not, gay?

Hughes' purported youthful "affairs" with women (Laudee Williams, Sylvia Chen, Elsie Roxborough, etc.), and his purported rebuffing the homosexual advances of Alain Locke and Countee Cullen, would all appear to support the opinion of longtime friends and associates (Bruce Nugent, Paul Bontemps, Raoul

25. Bonnie Zimmerman, "Lesbians Like This and That: Some Notes on Lesbian Criticism for the Nineties," in *New Lesbian Criticism: Literary and Cultural Readings*, ed. and intro. Sally Munt (New York, 1992), 8. Cf. Gillian Spraggs' comment, along similar lines, from the same volume in "Hell and the Mirror: A Reading of Desert of the Heart," *New Lesbian Criticism: Literary and Cultural Readings*, ed. and intro. Sally Munt, (New York, 1992), 125: "lesbianism, like heterosexuality, takes many different forms; . . . it is neither a willed perversion nor an arbitrary curse but a choice, a particular way of solving the problems presented by the condition of being a woman; and . . . it is not lesbianism in itself that ought to be placed at issue, but 'its manner of expression in actual living.'" For more on "the policing of identity" in the gendered context of Hughes' poem, see Butler, *Bodies That Matter*, 117.

Abdul, etc.) that the poet was definitely not gay.[26] On the other hand, people such as composer Jan Meyerowitz, and some especially in his domestic circle in the later years, thought quite differently: "Around the streets of Harlem in the sixties," an anonymous source divulges to his biographer, "everyone knew that Langston Hughes was gay. We just took it for granted, as a fact. He was gay, and there was no two ways about it." Still others were happy to form an opinion somewhere in between: Arthur Koestler, for instance, who found Hughes a warm and amiable companion, but who at the same time detected in him "a grave dignity, and a polite reserve" that translated into "an impenetrable, elusive remoteness which warded off all due familiarity"; or Carl Van Vechten, who, after thirty years of friendship with the poet, admitted that he "never had any indication that [Hughes] was homosexual or heterosexual," since "he seemed to thrive without having sex in [his] life" at all. Arnold Rampersad's own summation of the whole issue is thus conclusively inconclusive: "The truth about his sexuality will probably never be discovered. If Hughes indeed had homosexual lovers, what may be asserted incontrovertibly is that he did so with almost fanatical discretion. On this question, every person curious about him and also apparently in a position to know the truth was left finally in the dark. He laughed and joked and gossiped with apparent abandon, but somehow contrived to remain a mystery on this score even to his intimates." So Eric Garber is persuaded that although Hughes may have been "at least sporadically homosexual, the exact nature of his sexuality remains uncertain."[27]

If Hughes ever was "out" as a homosexual, the period of the Harlem Renais-

26. Rampersad, *The Life of Langston Hughes*, 1:96, 265, 331; 1:92, 98; 2:149, 239, 279.

27. Ibid., 2:177, 335; 1:260, 133; 2:336; Eric Garber, "A Spectacle of Color: The Lesbian and Gay Subculture of Jazz Age Harlem," in *Hidden from History: Reclaiming the Gay and Lesbian Past*, ed. Martin Duberman, Martha Vicinus, and George Chauncey, Jr. (New York, 1990), 326. Garber may be a bit more conclusive on the issue, given his description of Hughes' living arrangement in a small rooming house on 137th Street tagged as the "Niggerati Manor," and well known for its "considerable interaction between black and white homosexuals": "According to theater critic Theophilus Lewis, 'It was said that the inmates of [this] house spent wild nights in tuft hunting and the diversions of the cities of the plains and delirious days of fleeing from pink elephants'" (329). Garber takes part of the title for his essay from a chapter in the first volume of Hughes' autobiography, "Spectacles of Color" (in *The Big Sea: An Autobiography* [New York: Thunder's Mouth Press, 1986]), which opens with a description of Hughes' fascination with the notorious drag-balls of the Hamilton Club Lodge in Harlem's famed Rockland Palace Casino (273–74). An additional historical analogue to Hughes' sexual tergiversation in the early modern period might be found in the work of Gertrude Stein, once again, who, Renate Stendhal observes, "used every possibility of the English language to neither reveal nor conceal her gender . . . [but instead,] chose to leave the question open." Renate Stendhal, "Stein's Style: A Passion for Sentences," *Harvard Gay and Lesbian Review* 2 (spring 1995): 20.

sance, during which he came to prominence with the publication of his first book, *The Weary Blues* (1926), was indeed favorable. Spanning roughly the years between the end of the First World War, at the height of the "Great Migration" of southern blacks to northern industrial centers, and the onset of the "Great Depression," and the lifting of Prohibition in the early 1930s, the Harlem Renaissance was made famous through the efflorescence of literary discourse by several of its gay or gay-identified young writers, including Countee Cullen, Wallace Thurman, Bruce Nugent, and Claude McKay, under the mentorship of the period's two chief artistic patrons (also gay) Carl Van Vechten (a white novelist) and Alain Locke (a Howard University professor).[28]

But even though Hughes as a gay-identified writer may have experienced significantly more tolerance for his arguable alignment with same-sex practitioners in his early years, there nonetheless was considerable pressure upon him and those in his artistic circle, even at that time, to conform to more visibly mainstream, heteronormative expectations. "Many middle-class and churchgoing African-Americans," as George Chauncey recently observes, were inclined to associate homosexuals "with prostitutes, salacious entertainers, and 'uncultured' rural migrants as part of an undesirable and all-too-visible black 'lowlife' that brought disrepute to the neighborhood and 'the race.'" Taking his lead from the cultural historian Hazel Carby, Chauncey adds further:

> the figure of the sexually irresponsible woman became one of the defining tropes of middle-class African-American discourse, a symbol of the dangerous social disintegration that urbanization could bring . . . [since] racist ideology used those images so effectively to stigmatize all black women as morally debased. Similarly, the 'womanish-acting' man became a special threat to middle-class black men because their masculinity was under constant challenge by the dominant white ideology. As a white middle-class discourse, the attacks on homosexuals were usually but a

28. George Chauncey, *Gay New York: Gender, Urban Culture, and the Making of the Gay Male World, 1890–1940* (New York, 1994), 264, who guardedly adds "possibly Langston Hughes," to the list enumerated here. SDiane A. Bogus (citing Chris Albertson's *Bessie* [1972]) also notes "that during the 1920s and throughout the 1930s 'most urban Blacks—whether they indulged or not, accepted homosexuality as a fact of life.'" SDiane A. Bogus, "The 'Queen B' Figure in Black Literature," in *Lesbian Texts and Contexts: Radical Revisions*, ed. Karla Jay and Joanne Glasgow (New York, 1990), 280. Further historical background on these matters is also provided by Eric Garber, "A Spectacle of Color," 318–319; Alden Reimonenq, "Countee Cullen's Uranian 'Soul Windows,'" *Journal of Homosexuality* 24 (spring-summer 1993): 143–45, and David Levering Lewis, *When Harlem Was in Vogue* (New York, 1989), Chapter 3, whose account sometimes verges on the homophobic, esp. 66, 77, and 87.

part of a wider attack on men and women who threatened the social order by
standing outside the family system.

The willful "mystery" surrounding Hughes' sexuality pointed to by Rampersad
could thus correspond to a commonly accepted pattern of "closeted openness"
indulged by several Harlem Renaissance artists partially to circumvent the oppression of mainstream racial and sexual ideologies mounted from *both* sides of
the color line. Yet in terms of his privileging a deflective as opposed to a reflective
notion of subjectivity developed through much of his work, Hughes' resistance
to such ideological oppression was perhaps more programmatic than the "don't
ask, don't tell" stance of either sexual mystery or the conditional closet is able to
suggest.[29]

29. Chauncey, *Gay New York,* 253–54. See also Bogus, "The 'Queen B' Figure in Black Literature," 280–81. Hughes' bending to heteronormative expectations may even be experienced posthu-
mously, as evidenced in the recent video *Looking for Langston,* directed by Isaac Julien, currently a
popular offering at lesbian and gay film festivals across the country. Isaac Julien, *Looking for Langston,*
16mm., English (Toronto: Full Frame [distributor], 1989). I had originally been somewhat baffled
by the title of this short-subject film, given the fact that none of Hughes' poems appeared to be used
as texts in the several scripted voice-overs, until it was pointed out to me by an anonymous reader of
this chapter that the Hughes estate jealously safeguards his heterosexuality as a matter of historical
record. I was enlightened to discover that the film's opening with a poem by Hughes read silently
(the estate would not permit quotation), along with its somewhat acerbic title, were all the film-
makers could do to protest the proprietary legal claim Hughes' executors had staked out on his embattled sexuality. Given the appalling state of this controversy, there is thus considerable point in director
Julien's subsequent remark, on the issue of desire, that "filling the lack in everybody is quite hard
work really . . . [since] [t]he burden of representation weighs on each of us quite heavily." Isaac Julien
et al., "Filling the Lack in Everybody Is Quite Hard Work, Really . . . : A Roundtable Discussion with
Joy Chamberlain, Isaac Julien, Stuart Marshall, and Pratibha Parmar," in *Queer Looks: Perspectives on
Lesbian and Gay Film and Video,* ed. Martha Gever, Pratibha Parmar, and John Greyson (New York,
1993), 56. Sadly, as Lauren Berlant and Michael Warner contend, "the idea that queerness can be
anything other than a pathology or an evil, let alone a good, cannot even be entertained yet in most
public contexts." Lauren Berlant and Michael Warner, "What Does Queer Theory Teach Us about
X?" *PMLA* 110 (summer 1995): 345. Alden Reimonenq in "Countee Cullen's Uranian 'Soul Windows,'" uses the oxymoron of "a closeted openness" in particular to explain Countee Cullen's straddling the twin perils of "fear of discrimination," on the one hand, and "[t]he combination of
machismo and fundamentalism in the Black community," on the other, within an artistic career that
evolved through two separate marriages (one to the daughter of W. E. B. Du Bois), four or five
known relationships with gay Americans, and several French lovers, and that produced enough quality poetry to deem him the "poet laureate" of the Harlem Renaissance (152, 163, 155, 157, 143). Eric
Garber, in "A Spectacle of Color" (327), makes similar mention of the "sexually ambiguous" proclivities of Wallace Thurman and Claude McKay. Chauncey elsewhere interprets the secretiveness about
being gay additionally in terms of class, noting that about this time, "the cultural stance of the queer

Rampersad's further mention, then, of darkness is perhaps a more significant qualifier in his overall assessment of Hughes' sexuality, bringing us, in a manner appropriate to the poet, back to the approximate condition of that black otherness, with which we began. But surely by now, otherness itself should enrich our suspicion concerning "the truth" of Hughes' sexuality, about whose form all of the previous commentators to one degree or another appear convinced, whether that "truth" could definitively be made known or not. It is as if we have been spirited back to the position of the writing-instructor in "English B": "Go home and write a page tonight, and let that *sexuality* come out of you—then, it will be true." I, myself, wonder if it can be that simple. If we learn anything at all from the deferred otherness that provokes the dream of dissident subjectivity in Langston Hughes' work, I think we can at least feel fairly confident in rejecting the view that Hughes could have had "no interest whatsoever" in the subject of sexuality.[30] If what has been said about his poetry in this chapter is at all convincing, it is quite likely that Hughes could only have had *too much* interest in the subject. At least, too much not to want to commit himself, either in his life or his work, to one single category or label, identification or orientation, bearing or practice.

The view that Hughes was "a sexual blank," and that "his libido, under stimulation or pressure, seemed to vanish into a void"—such a view, though not quite in the self-effacing way the commentator intends, takes us closer to how I think we ought finally to be framing the issue. For Hughes' dealing with sexuality, both in his life and his work in a programmatically non-committal way, would appear to fly directly in the face of a quite clear and consistent pressure to categorize manliness so as to assert its pride of place within black culture, and to contain any visible threat to that categorical assertion of power both from within the culture (from the point of view of gender and class), and from without (from the point of view of class and race). The backdrop to this whole asseveration of manly prowess, of course, was the so-called invention of heterosexuality itself which, by the time of the Harlem Renaissance, had clearly emerged for middle-class men in general as "a new, more positive way to demonstrate their manhood . . . as a distinct domain of personhood," essentialized in terms of their "exclusive desire

embodied the general middle-class preference for privacy, self-restraint, and lack of self-disclosure," and further, that "middle-class men were more observant of the moral injunctions against nonmarital sexual behavior propagated by their class than working-class men," perhaps to the extent that "almost all self-identified middle-class gay men considered themselves marked, to some degree, as gender deviants as well as sexual deviants, even if they tried to recast that difference in terms of cultural sophistication or sensitivity." Chauncey, *Gay New York,* 106, 119, and 126.

30. Rampersad, *The Life of Langston Hughes,* 1:289.

Hughes' sexuality — resistant to essentializing categories in black art [handwritten marginalia]

for women" and their "renunciation of such intimacies with men." "They became heterosexuals, that is," as George Chauncey once again observes, "only when they defined themselves and organized their affective and physical relations to exclude any sentiments or behavior that might be marked as homosexual."[31] The hegemonic hetero-homosexual binary thus cemented firmly into place early in the twentieth century had little tolerance for the man who, like Hughes and several of his colleagues, would prefer more inclusively to express an equal preference for *both* sides of the dichotomy, or what was no doubt thought even worse, a preference for *neither*. From the normative vantage of the sexual mainstream, such a man is plainly out of (in the sense of beyond) control. And whether that out(side-d)ness manifests itself as a sexual blank or void in real life, or as a model of subjectivity resistant to essentializing categories in black art, Hughes' going the distance, as it were, of that deferred otherness renders the omnivorous search for the "truth" of his dissident sexuality hopelessly beside the point.

Those who would expect Hughes to be more visibly forthcoming with respect to his sexuality are perhaps searching for a more politically resonant poet as well. How else to combat the demonization of race in terms both of the pathologies of gender and class convergent in the "womanish-acting" man, noted previously, unless there were the visible presence of a gay poet actively engaged in saying and and doing otherwise? But precisely because it is the virtue of a deferred subjectivity ever fully to mean what we say and say what we mean, as Hughes' poetry instructs, that we are relieved of the moral injunction to make categorical commitments with respect to sexuality, or anything else about our person. As Amitai Avi-Ram convincingly argues in the parallel cases of Claude McKay and Countee Cullen, "What the words of the poem tell us about the poem is that its meaning cannot be controlled," so that given the "undecidability of [its] categories," "[t]he subject's knowledge of his own inability to know [becomes] the moment of his *liberation* from the prison of the binary structure of race" (and given the present context, I would add, sexuality as well).[32]

Curiously, therefore, Hughes' cultural positioning, once again, as a man out of control represents his poetry's moment of greatest social empowerment. For in that moment of complete otherness, and liberated fully from categorical contain-

31. Ibid., 1:298; Chauncey, *Gay New York*, 117, 120, 120–21.
32. Amitai Avi-Ram, "The Unreadable Black Body: 'Conventional' Poetic Form in the Harlem Renaissance," *Genders* 7 (1990): 39. As in the case of Hughes' own acategorical treatment of dissident subjectivity in the sexual context, therefore, "Only by looking at the pragmatic use the poem makes of its own essential unreadability," Avi-Ram concludes, "can its political force be made conscious and appreciated" (43–44).

room for maneuvering

ment, he enters fully into the dream of subjectivity at a time, not too far removed from his own, when the individual was once "aware, to one degree or another, of the variety of competing sexual ideologies available in his culture, which gave him some room for maneuvering among them." And though his own subjectivity, as with most dreams, has been shrouded for posterity in darkness, the invisibility in the past that once betokened for Hughes the fact that most people did not want to see him, can now make promise for the present, and for the future, as Catharine Stimpson remarks in the parallel case of lesbian subjectivity, "that no identity is stable enough to claim the reassurances of permanent visibility."[33]

So while Hughes the writer turns the issue of his own sexual "truth" away from the referred subjectivity within which it is hypothetically lodged and, in terms of the problematic burden of representation, leaves it revolving instead about its deferred other, in the end, we may be given to wonder: Why so much concern? Is this need *to know* the truth sparked by the enormous appetite in our culture, as Stuart Alan Clarke contends, for images of black men "misbehaving" that ultimately channel into our more general "Fear of a Black Planet"? Or is our demand triggered, as Eve Kosofsky Sedgwick contends, by that "estrus of manipulative fantasy" that makes our search for truth "a silkily camouflaged complicity in oppression," conditioned by "Fear of a Queer Planet"? If the answers to these questions lie somewhere buried in the "real life" of Langston Hughes, it would hardly be like him to hasten to show us just where. He would probably hand us a poem like "Neighbor," instead:

> In Harlem
> when his work is done
> he sets in a bar with a beer.
> He looks taller than he is
> and younger than he ain't.
> He looks darker than he is, too.
> And he's smarter than he looks,
>
> . . . .
>
> *Sometimes*
> *he don't drink.*
> True,
> he just
> lets his glass
> set there.

(*HCP*, 421)

33. Chauncey, *Gay New York*, 126; Catharine Stimpson, "Afterword: Lesbian Studies in the

Exactly who is the man that can be darker and smarter than he actually looks, or taller and younger than he actually is? The poem's final removal of these riddles to the glass at the end—why do we naturally suppose it is empty?—invites us to feel the burden of deciding too quickly which representation precisely fits, and ponder instead the responsibility of our mental enclosures and containments, both for what they hold in, but equally as important, for what they keep out. The fragile nature of representation that so transparently meshes container and thing contained, like the beer-glass teetering on the edge of that word "True," too often elides for us the configurable distance in between that opens up to challenge, if not defer, their apparently seamless relationship. That this distance—the space "in which meaning remains fascinated by what escapes and exceeds it"[34]—is not at all easily composed or willingly constrained, we have ample testimony for in several other of Hughes' poems: in "Strange Hurt," for example, where a female experiencing "queer pain" that "cozy houses hold," feels the need to "break down doors / To wander naked / In the cold" (*HCP*, 63); or, in "Desire," whose "unknown strange perfume" dies swiftly between a self and its other "In a naked / Room" (*HCP*, 105); or, again, in "Kid in the Park," in which the child, as a "little question mark," seems intuitively to know that "Home's just around / the corner / there— / *but not / really anywhere*" (*HCP*, 376), and so forth. Given how easily Hughes' own subjectivity could suffer the fatal elisions of spectatorial regulation and normative reference, there, thus, does seem to be considerable point in his asking elsewhere: "Waiting for nothingness. / Do you understand the *stillness* / Of this house / In Taos / Under the thunder of the Rain God?" ("A House in Taos" [*HCP*, 80], emphasis added).

The final text of Hughes' *Montage of a Dream Deferred* speaks of an "Island": "Between two rivers, / North of the park, / Like darker rivers / The streets are dark" (*HCP*, 429). No man is an island, it is true. But the poem foregrounds an approach to experience that makes this image fit perfectly the kind of subjectivity that, conceived in terms of the alterable flow of processual change, that is to say, in terms of "the *ongoing reality* of racial difference,"[35] puts it in touch with, rather

1990s," in *Lesbian Texts and Contexts: Radical Revisions*, ed. Karla Jay and Joanne Glasgow (New York, 1990), 381.

34. Stuart Alan Clarke, "Fear of a Black Planet," *Socialist Review* 21 (summer-fall 1991): 40; Eve Kosofsky Sedgwick, "How to Bring Your Kids Up Gay," in *Fear of a Queer Planet*, ed. Michael Warner (Minneapolis, 1993), 78, 79; Minh-Ha, "Documentary Is/Not a Name," 96 (further on 77, 85).

35. Winant, "Postmodern Racial Politics in the United States," 137, emphasis added. Similarly, Chauncey speaks about "a variety of ways to be gay," and hence "the plasticity of gender assignment." Chauncey, *Gay New York*, 278, 62. Hence, Posnock's characterization of dramatist Adrienne Kenne-

than shelters it from, the ever-growing prospect of otherness in America, and in the modern world: "Black and white, / Gold and brown— / Chocolate-custard / Pie of a town" (*HCP*, 429). In fact, constituted in the space of a "between" that serves both to draw the rivers of reality together, as well as hold them apart, Hughes' island-subject *becomes* the very image of that otherness itself. As such, it puts its own being beyond the conventional separations of the logical dualism that would channel subjectivity into either the landlocked liberalism of social pluralism, or that of cultural relativism.

Neither the vision of bourgeois transcendence in Europe, then, nor that of melting-pot indifferentism in the American dream, Hughes' going the distance of his dissident subjectivity works another variation perhaps on Caliban's "triple-play" in its "largesse as signifier." For in this new, third space, in what Hughes calls the *"Dream within a dream, / Our dream deferred"* (*HCP*, 429), what can only mean more to us than any island of definitive representation and achieved truth would be its yielding, once more, to the darkness of the streets within, and to the darkness of the rivers without.[36] And in the perpetual confluence of inner and outer, likeness and unlikeness, center and margin, this process of yielding makes promise of the dream-within-a-dream forever renewable. Less an answer, then, to the day-old question of the "essential" or "true" identity in, and of, America, dreaming subjectivity in Langston Hughes' Modernist poetic texts readies us for a whole new dawning in desiring forthrightly to be otherwise. And no more forthrightly put than by the author of "Island" himself: "Good morning, daddy! / Ain't you heard?" (*HCP*, 429).

---

dy's approach to a "ceaselessly shifting" selfhood as "helpless plasticity under the impress of heterogeneous cultural commodities." Posnock, *Color and Culture*, 272.

36. Houston A. Baker, Jr., "Caliban's Triple Play," in *"Race," Writing, and Difference*, ed. Henry Louis Gates, Jr. (Chicago, 1986), 392; Damon, *The Dark End of the Street*, passim.

Chapter 4

"Vanilla Hemorrhages":
The Queer Perversities of Frank O'Hara

The center of myself is never silent.

— Frank O'Hara, The Collected Poems

The self only becomes a self on the condition that it has suffered a separation
. . . a loss which is suspended and provisionally resolved through a melan-
cholic incorporation of some "Other." That "Other" installed in the self thus
establishes the permanent incapacity of that "self" to achieve self-identity.
. . . [Yet] the disruption of the Other at the heart of the self is the very
condition of that self's possibility.

— Judith Butler, "Imitation and Gender Insubordination"

There's nothing metaphysical about it.

— Frank O'Hara, "Personism: A Manifesto"

I N the early morning of July 24, 1966, American poet Frank O'Hara, at the age of forty, stepped out in front of a beach buggy on Fire Island, New York, and was fatally injured. By nightfall of the following day, he was dead. Since then, only the rare commentator on O'Hara's work fails to be moved by the pathos of the poet's bizarre demise—one of the most prolific writers of the so-called New York School tragically snuffed out midway through, apparently, an already extraordinarily accomplished career. Indeed, as far as tragic endings go, this one might even strike the reader as somewhat perverse. "He was coming towards me, that's all I could see," the driver of the fatal vehicle alleges in a sworn affidavit recounting the details of the strange accident. "He didn't try to move, he just kept on walking."[1]

1. Brad Gooch, *City Poet: The Life and Times of Frank O'Hara* (New York, 1993), 459.

I will have more to say later about the "reading" of O'Hara's final actions as a possible death-wish—a brutal ending in the larger context of the collision between the "abstractionism" of New York School art predominant in the 1950s, and the "neo-realism" of Pop Cult art ascendant through the 1960s. At the very beginning of this chapter, I want to make inaugural to a meditation on the "queer perversities" of Frank O'Hara surrounding, and ultimately leading up to that inevitable collision, another kind of clash. This second type of collision, although seemingly more academic and up-to-the-minute, nonetheless strikes me as entirely related to the first. It has to do with a certain kind of violence, so some would contend, that may be done to an author whose life and work is recovered from the near or distant past, when the primary act of historical retrieval is perceived to be chiefly guided by what, in the contemporary parlance of cultural studies, has popularly come to be known as "queer theory." Thus, while from one direction—the historical past—the lifework of a writer like O'Hara seems prematurely to have been cut short by certain social and cultural forces arguably outside his artistic control, from another direction—the scholarly present—he appears to be mowed down all over again, and perhaps even more against his will, by the ultra-chic engines of queer discourse motored by the likes of Judith Butler, Jonathan Dollimore, or Eve Sedgwick.

While the original form of this chapter somewhat guilelessly made promise of an attempt to reread Frank O'Hara—an insistently "perverse" Frank O'Hara—with the help of a number of contemporary queer theorists, like those just mentioned, who might be able to illuminate that "perversity" *within* its proper historical context, the essay has since generated new thematic contours in view of the highly contestatory climate supervening current, queer-critical inquiry. Central to what I have now come to perceive as an overarching paracritical dimension to my original investigation is a highly incendiary debate concerning the use and status of texts in queer theory as sites of reference for the interpretation of writers like O'Hara (and to anticipate, Elizabeth Bishop in the next chapter). Perhaps even more to the point, the debate concerns precisely what those texts and that theory necessarily may be implying about an author and/or a body of work in which they, wittingly or no, happen to be taken up.

An early anonymous reader of this chapter, for instance, though generally pleased with the effort to bring together "some of the most elusive dimensions of O'Hara with a range of recent theory," was nonetheless insistent on registering "some qualms" about the inferential claim of an argument "in which queerness and poststructuralism appear to converge." A second nameless reader was less temperate about what my deployment of contemporary discourses endeavored to

achieve—an effort, purportedly, "to enlist O'Hara as a nineties-styled queer theorist . . . [and] as a post-structuralist before the term." Hence, by "squeezing the
poet into pants that make him look sexy," my chapter was perceived to be nothing
more than a futile exercise in castration—one which indelicately "cuts off
O'Hara's balls in order to zip up his fly." More rigorous, more searching, and
more precise, however, than either of these, a third respondent to my argument
masterfully crystallized what seemed to lie at the very heart of the whole debate
this way:

> I'm not objecting to your interpretations of individual passages in O'Hara; rather,
> I'm questioning the wisdom of the critical practice of recuperating O'Hara's texts
> by bringing them into conformity with what is quickly becoming a kind of theoret-
> ical orthodoxy in queer cultural studies. Not only does that practice patronize
> O'Hara, in effect by finding him interesting only insofar as he can be seen to have
> anticipated or prefigured more recent critical doctrines, but it makes his contribu-
> tion to contemporary thinking less interesting than it could be by claiming that he
> merely discovered early on what we now think we "know" about the politics of
> identity. . . . For that reason I think it is a tactical as well as an interpretative mis-
> take to treat O'Hara's texts as a kind of allegory of queer theory . . . or to attempt
> to enhance O'Hara's canonical status by arranging to have queer theory pay him
> the compliment of finding him in accord with its tenets.

Beleaguered by such critical disgruntlement, my insistence nonetheless on keeping the argument (most of which follows in the next two sections) in circulation,
has forced it to share, several times over, those dreadful moments of heedless
abandon that conceivably may have been the poet's last. And it persists to the
light of day only by standing the poet's ground even more fearlessly, more provoc-
atively, perhaps more perversely: "He didn't try to move, he just kept on walking."
    In this opening, therefore, I must concede one point, and make promise of a
much fuller and more highly qualified amplification of the idea in the chapter's
concluding section, once my argument proper has had a chance to play itself out.
For as should be clear even now, I'm not at all averse to disclosing much (or little)
that might be considered "allegorical" between a poet's (or any other writer's)
texts and queer theory.[2] But unlike my essay's respondents, I'm not always sure

---

2. Two fairly recent examples, randomly at hand, that perhaps also might stand accused of perverting the literary record for the sake of allegorizing the queer theory agenda are Sandra Runzo's
"Dickinson, Performance, and the Homoerotic Lyric," *American Literature* 68 (June 1996): 347–63,
where Sue-Ellen Case, Judith Butler, and Esther Newton (among others) are all given a prominent
place in this recuperative reading of the Belle of Amherst; and, more egregiously, Richard Rambuss'

precisely *what* that allegorical relation would require us to understand every time, either about the poet in particular, or about queer theory more generally: a convergence with "poststructuralism"? a nineties-styled "sexy" theorist? a "theoretical orthodoxy" in cultural studies? If *there is* such a thing as a queer "theoretical orthodoxy," to pick up just this last point, that the allegory may be pointing us toward, I honestly cannot say what that could possibly look like. As with most queer academics, one tends to feel, for most of one's adult (sexual) life, that a "critical orthodoxy" was something that the *other* guy was constantly trying to back a gay person into (and no doubt, still is). And that for each, his or her first genuine moment of sexual manumission would almost certainly have had something of the tear in the doctrinal fabric about it, although what shape the garment finally took might have been anyone's guess (and no doubt, still is). As Wallace Stevens says about the "disassociated abundance of being" in "The Woman in Sunshine," the "form . . . is empty" (*SCP*, 445).

Yet precisely on this note of orthodox uncertainty, I'm tempted to make one of those tactical moves of interpretation that I've been warned against, and endeavor to establish an "allegorical" relation between theory and text that I can't help thinking would be of considerable advantage to both. For isn't "Abstract Expressionism," according to Frank O'Hara, very much like the queer theory that, in the very first instance, would spirit us past anything resembling a doctrine, a code, or a creed, when he writes: "[Its artists] are serious because they are *not* isolated. So out of this populated cavern of self come brilliant, uncomfortable works, works that don't reflect you or your life, though you can know them. Art is not *your* life, it is someone else's. Something very difficult for the acquisitive spirit to understand, and for that matter the spirit of joinership that animates communism. But it's there" (*AC*, 6). I'm sure I'm not the first to suspect that queer theory more and more continues to attract a burgeoning number of readers and writers not for anything it manages to say with any degree of consistency or predictability or regularity or sometimes even clarity, in an already hypernormative social and collective life. The gay Cold War poet, yesterday, who at last found a mode of expression that could break the cycle of reproductive sameness within heteronormative culture—"Art is not *your* life, it is someone else's"—strikes me

"Homodevotion," in *Cruising the Performative: Interventions into the Representation of Ethnicity, Nationality, and Sexuality*, ed. Sue-Ellen Case, Philip Brett, and Susan Leigh Foster (Bloomington, 1995), 71–89, where the Anglocatholic devotional lyrics of Richard Crawshaw, for instance, stand cheek-by-jowl with the hardcore videoporn of Jerry Douglas "because at the juncture of these admittedly disparate cultural sites—one high, the other low, one early modern and the other contemporary—the prayer closet might be rendered at its most pellucid" (79).

as the very type of the queer theorist, today, who is pleased *only* to know that an acquisitive orthodoxy of self-perpetuating reflection is the only thing standing between her and the words that Frank O'Hara, as we shall see later, would carry to his grave: "Grace to be born and live as variously as possible." Championing a greater critical distance by establishing an allegorical relation between yesterday and today, I'm thus given to think we're in a much *better* position to understand why it might not be very useful, according to Lauren Berlant and Michael Warner, "to consider queer theory a thing," since so many of its possible extrapolations in the form of "queer commentary," in the end, "cannot be assimilated to a single discourse let alone a propositional program." Hence, if the spirit of Abstract Expressionism, both in the visual and the verbal arts, resides mainly in its being "out," as O'Hara contends ("*out*—beyond beauty, beyond composition, beyond the old-fashioned kind of pictorial ambition" [*AC*, 10]), would it really be a tactical or interpretive error to point to a similar kind of spirit informing so many of the discourses living possibly and variously under the rubrical grace of queer difference? And what *better* word than "out" to contrast with the "danger of the queer theory label," one "that makes its queer and nonqueer audiences forget these differences," and as with the former pictorial ambition, for lack of distance "imagine a context (theory) in which *queer* has a stable referential content and pragmatic force."[3]

Calling severely into question any kind of stable referentiality, particularly in the era of the Cold War in which such old-fashioned ambitions were perhaps policed more than most, delivers us up to at least one dimension of Frank O'Hara's perversity as an artist. At this point, therefore, I think it time that I finally make good on my claim as to the soundness of hypothesizing an allegorical relation between queer theory and historical practice by turning to the life and work of the poet himself. If the next two sections of my argument might be seen to function as an analogue to the debate outlined thus far, my concluding apologue, I hope, will serve to provide some further justification for maintaining that the intercalation of present and past discourses, in what immediately follows, should continue to have considerable point, and merit.

    3. Berlant and Warner, "What Does Queer Theory Teach Us About *X*?" 343, 344. In his essay "Robert Motherwell" later in *Art Chronicles*, O'Hara clarifies the subversion of "pictorial ambition" as follows: "The Abstract Expressionists decided, instead of imitating the style of European moderns, to do instead what they had done, to venture into the unknown, to give up looking at reproductions in *Verve* and *Cahiers d'Art* and to replace them with first-hand experimentation. This was the great anguish of the American artists. . . . They shot off in every direction, risking everything. They were never afraid of having a serious idea, and the serious idea was never self-referential" (*AC*, 69–70).

* * *

An extraordinary paradox stands at the center of the poetic achievement of Frank O'Hara (1926–1966). Avowedly, unashamedly, unrepentantly gay, O'Hara rose to prominence as a poet—a leader in the New York School—in one of the most virulently homophobic decades this century, during the Cold War years spanning the Eisenhower administration of the 1950s. Three out of a total of five collections of O'Hara's poetry were published through this period: *A City Winter and Other Poems* (1952), *Meditations in an Emergency* (1957), and *Odes* (1960). And yet an era wracked by an anti-Communist paranoia that would witness the trial of Judith Coplon for espionage, the conviction of Alger Hiss for perjury, and the execution of Ethel and Julius Rosenberg for treason as Russian spies could hardly be thought receptive, let alone encouraging, to the counter-cultural gay artist. More especially might this be the case, given the fact that "[t]he pens of right-wing ideologues," searching for political scapegoats, could so easily convert homosexuality, according to John D'Emilio, "into an epidemic infecting the nation, actively spread by Communists to sap the strength of the next generation." Throughout the 1950s, as D'Emilio goes on to document, "the web of oppression tightened around homosexuals and lesbians. An executive order barred them from all federal jobs, and dismissals from government service rose sharply. The military intensified its purges of gay men and lesbians. The Post Office tampered with their mail, the FBI initiated widespread surveillance of homosexual meeting places and activities, and urban police forces stepped up their harassment."[4]

4. John D'Emilio, "The Homosexual Menace: The Politics of Sexuality in Cold War America," in *Making Trouble: Essays on Gay History, Politics, and the University* (New York, 1992), 60. Particularly on the issue of harassment, D'Emilio further records that during the 1950s, "lesbians and gay men suffered from unpredictable, brutal crackdowns. Women generally encountered the police in and around lesbian bars while men also faced arrest in public cruising areas, but even the homes of gay men and women lacked immunity from vice squads. Newspaper headlines would strike fear into the heart of the gay population by announcing that the police were combing the city for nests of deviates. Editors often printed names, addresses, and places of employment of men and women arrested in bar raids" (62). Thus "[s]hunted to the margins of American society, harassed because of their sexuality," as D'Emilio writes in "The Bonds of Oppression," "many gay men and women internalized the negative descriptions and came to embody the stereotypes . . . the homosexual or lesbian [as] a flawed individual, not a victim of injustice." John D'Emilio, "The Bonds of Oppression: Gay Life in the 1950s," in *Sexual Politics, Sexual Communities: The Making of a Homosexual Minority in the United States, 1940–1970* (Chicago, 1983), 53. Additional historical background on "the Cold War image of homosexuals as dangerous sexual psychopaths" is provided by Allan Bérubé, *Coming Out under Fire: The History of Gay Men and Women in World War Two* (New York, 1990), 263ff. See also David Savran's introduction to *Communists, Cowboys, and Queers: The Politics of Masculinity in the Work of Arthur Miller and Tennessee Williams* (Minneapolis, 1992), 4–6.

The widely accepted linkage, from this time, between sexual and political de-
viance, as D'Emilio further points out, "made the scapegoating of gay men and
women a simple matter": "the effete men of the eastern establishment lost China
and Eastern Europe to the enemy" while "'mannish' women mocked the ideals
of marriage and motherhood." O'Hara's continuing to maintain a quite visible
profile as an arguably "effete" poet—"all cruisy and nelly" in the "pursuit of the
purple vices" (*OCP*, 97, 86)—in addition to more regular hours spent as a curator
at MoMA and critic for *Art News*, might strike us as somewhat perverse in face
of such egregious stereotyping. For while Cold War anxieties, heightened by the
Korean War and the McCarthy witch hunts, might silence other notable New
York School writers like John Ashbery for a time, Frank O'Hara, paradoxically,
appeared to thrive amidst the panic. And he did so well into the 1960s, when the
final crackdowns on New York's homosexual population in advance of the Stonewall riots, around the time of the World's Fair in 1964, perhaps signaled the waning of an excruciatingly beleaguered era. "I wonder," he sneeringly writes to
fellow artist and sometime lover Larry Rivers, "what they think people are *really*
coming to NYC for, anyway?"[5]

Even more paradoxical is the fact that the queer perversity of Frank O'Hara
was apparently belied by the visible quantity of his own published output through
the fifties. "That *The Collected Poems of Frank O'Hara* should turn out to be a
volume of the present dimensions," John Ashbery is given to speculate in his introduction to the edition from 1971, "will surprise those who knew him," and
still more incredulously adds, "and would have surprised Frank even more" (*OCP*,
vii). But O'Hara himself was perhaps more waywardly knowing. Immediately
following his untimely death due to internal injuries sustained from the freak au-
tomobile accident described earlier, his longtime friend Kenneth Koch performed

---

5. D'Emilio, "The Homosexual Menace," 68, 64; Gooch, *City Poet*, 424. "Lots of committees,"
O'Hara goes on to write, "are springing up to protest all this [persecution by police] . . . (Allen [Gins-
berg] and I read for . . . one), and one Diane [di Prima] has started[,] to protest all this plus the new
zoning laws which are driving artists out of their lofts. . . . The fair itself, or its preparations are too
ridiculous and boring to go into." Gooch, *City Poet*, 424. Ashbery's "silence" from the early 1950s is
further cited by Gooch, *City Poet*, 190, and by Catherine Imbriglio, "'Our Days Put on Such Reticence': The Rhetoric of the Closet in John Ashbery's *Some Trees*," *Contemporary Literature* 36 (spring
1995): 282n. 16); and Gooch also gives a parallel account of the more tragic Cold War victimization
of the secretly gay Harvard critic and Communist "fellow traveler," F. O. Mathiessen (*City Poet*,
129–30), which ended in suicide. For a much fuller account of Mathiessen in the context of this
intensely homophobic period, see Michael Cadden, "Engendering F. O. M.: The Private Life of
American Renaissance," in *Engendering Men: The Question of Male Feminist Criticism*, ed. Joseph A.
Boone and Michael Cadden (New York, 1990), 26–35.

a thorough search of O'Hara's apartment, worried that unpublished work might be prone to confiscation, since O'Hara had died intestate. As Koch divulges to the poet's biographer: "In the closet we found all of these manuscripts. Jesus, he'd written a lot that no one had ever seen. They were all dated. They were very organized, some of them revised. I went over those poems, crying all the time."[6]

The "closet" in Koch's seemingly guileless remark here perhaps provides a general insight into the kinds of perversity in the poetry of Frank O'Hara that I would like to engage in what follows in this chapter. Suggestive of a kind of "tact and discretion" in "a whole restrictive economy" having to do with the "policing of statements" and "the tightening up of the rules of decorum," O'Hara's Cold War closet, *at the same time*, functions paradoxically much like the imperceptibly constitutive (as opposed to the more visibly constraining) function of the Repressive Hypothesis, in Michel Foucault's well-known formulation. For within this paradoxical dynamic, the impasse of closeted repression, conventionally understood as "a hindrance [and] a stumbling-block," *simultaneously* serves the instrumental purpose as "a point of resistance and a starting point for an opposing strategy," thereby perversely *producing*, "as a countereffect, [the] valorization and intensification of indecent speech" coterminous with "the multiplication of discourses concerning sex in the field of exercise of power itself." This paradox of repressive power, moreover, represents a kind of perverse shift in the evolution of Foucault's own thought. Earlier, as John Caputo observes, "In an interview given in 1977 [Foucault] says that the repressive mechanisms of *Madness and Civilization* were 'adequate' to his own purposes in that book, revealing (in Foucault's words) that 'during the Classical age power over madness was, in its most important manifestations at least, exercised in the form of exclusion . . . in a great movement of rejection.'" However, it was "his investigations into the history of sexuality," Caputo continues, that led Foucault "to see another mechanism of power, the productive one, which proceeds not by repressing and saying no, but

6. Gooch, *City Poet*, 467. "My guess," Diane di Prima further speculates on O'Hara's Cold War output, "is that huge collected Frank O'Hara has only about one-third of his actual work." Diane di Prima, quoted in Marjorie Perloff, *Frank O'Hara: Poet among Painters* (New York, 1977), 115. Yet as Cold War homophobic tensions began to wane beginning in the 1960s, so did O'Hara's poetic output: "In the *Collected Poems*, the period from July 1961 to June 1966 is covered by a scant 84 of the total 491 pages, and most of the poems in this section date from 1961–62. The year 1963 is represented by only eleven poems, 1964 by thirteen, 1965 by three. We have only one published poem for 1966." Marjorie Perloff, "Frank O'Hara and the Aesthetics of Attention," in *Frank O'Hara: To Be True to a City*, ed. Jim Elledge (Ann Arbor, 1993), 216n. 1. Of course, O'Hara's chronic alcoholism ought not to be discounted as a factor in this overall pattern of artistic decline as well.

which 'traverses and produces things . . . induces pleasure, forms of knowledge, produces discourse.'"[7]

Later, Foucault would perhaps lay a greater claim to the constitutive rather than the constraining aspect of the "juridico-discursive" representation of power—"its productive effectiveness, its strategic resourcefulness, its positivity"—in the preface to the German edition of *La Volonté de savoir* (1983), where he observes: "I simply asked myself whether the analysis, as a whole, was obliged to be articulated around the concept of repression to decipher the relations among power, knowledge, and sex; or, indeed, whether one might not understand things better by inserting the taboos, the obstacles, the expulsions, and the dissimulations into a more complex, more global strategy *that would not be fixed on repression as its principal and essential focus.*" Despite the shift in focus, Foucault at the same time is careful to emphasize that he "never claimed that there had been no repression of sexuality." As he discloses in another interview from 1977, we start "with the apparatus of sexuality in the midst of which we're caught, and which make it function to the limit; but at the same time, [we] are in motion relative to it, disengaging [our]selves and surmounting it." This "motion," I would argue, seems precisely to configure the status of Frank O'Hara's Cold War closet, as it might be both literally and figuratively conceived through the decade that witnessed his most productive output. In such terms (in Foucault's words, once again, from yet another 1977 interview), "the interdiction, the refusal, the prohibition, far from being essential forms of power, are only its limits: the frustrated or extreme forms of power. The relations of power are, above all, productive."[8]

As an example of the kind of Cold War transvaluation effected by the figure of the closet, we might look to O'Hara's "Poem (Khrushchev is coming on the

7. Michel Foucault, *The History of Sexuality,*vol. 1, *An Introduction,* trans. Robert Hurley (New York, 1980), 18, 101, 18; further on 32, 33–34, 82–83, 105–106, 152, and 155–56; John Caputo, "On Not Knowing Who We Are: Madness, Hermeneutics, and the Night of Truth in Foucault," in *Foucault and the Critique of Institutions,* ed. John Caputo and Mark Yount (University Park, Pa., 1993), 245.

8. Foucault, *History of Sexuality,* 82, 86; Michel Foucault, preface to *La Volonté de savoir,* quoted in Didier Eribon, *Michel Foucault,* trans. Betsy Wing (Cambridge, Mass., 1991), 276, emphasis added; Michel Foucault, "Interview," in *Politics Philosophy Culture: Interviews and Other Writings, 1977–1984,* trans. Alan Sheridan et al. (New York, 1988), 114–15; Michel Foucault, "Interview," quoted in Butler, *Bodies That Matter,* 109. Thus, as Caputo concludes: "it would be a mistake to think that the repressive hypothesis is somehow inconsistent with productive power. In fact, the two are quite compatible and, indeed, produce a similar effect. I would even say that the hypothesis of a productive power is a continuation of the repressive hypothesis by another means." Caputo "On Not Knowing Who We Are," 245–46.

right day!)" (*OCP*, 340), from 1959, in which the Russian Communist leader's train bearing down irrevocably upon New York is felt to be not so much constricting as liberating: "so I go home to bed and names drift through my head / Purgatorio Merchado, Gerhard Schwartz and Gaspar Gonzales, all / unknown figures of the early morning as I go to work." What marks the conversion, what makes "New York seem blinding," is precisely the narrator's playful intensification of sexual discourse just as Foucault describes ("Khrushchev is coming," "my tie is blowing," "hard wind," etc.) that, by the end of the poem, mysteriously has the effect of transforming the highly repressive climate of the Cold War—"when September takes New York / and turns it into ozone stalagmites"—into its exact opposite:

> though [my tie] is cold and somewhat warms my neck
> as the train bears Khrushchev on to Pennsylvania Station
> and the light seems to be eternal
> and joy seems to be inexorable
> I am foolish enough always to find it in wind

In the most general terms, then, the controversion of discourse from ideological *repression* to a highly sexualized *expression* points to how we might begin to frame O'Hara's queer perversity—to "find it," as the airy-fairy poet himself avers, "in wind." Countering Cold War containments, for O'Hara, accordingly, was perhaps like using "judo" for Foucault, wherein "the best answer to the opponent's maneuver never is to step back, but to re-use it to your own advantage."[9]

The truly revolutionary character of Frank O'Hara's poetic project, as I shall argue in the next section of this essay, relates largely to matters of subjectivity, and to gay subjectivity in particular. In order to get there, however, in this section, I want to focus for the most part on O'Hara's intense preoccupation with the repressive aspects of mainstream culture which, in his mind, were merely writ large in the Cold War ideologies of his own day. Like Foucault's Repressive Hypothesis just scanned, the two parts of my argument, in the end, will begin to look very much like two sides of the same coin, for, as Judith Butler astutely inquires, "how do we pursue the question of sexuality and the law, where the law is not only that which represses sexuality, but a prohibition that *generates* sexuality, or, at least, compels its directionality?"[10]

9. David M. Halperin, *Saint Foucault: Towards a Gay Hagiography* (New York, 1995), 114.

10. Butler, *Bodies That Matter*, 95. In its most general nature, then, my argument thus shares considerable agreement with Rudy Kikel's searching rumination that "Without the fact of O'Hara's being gay held *strictly* in the forefront of a critic's and his or her reader's mind, I wonder, however, whether the fully subversive nature of the poet's contribution can be appreciated." Rudy Kikel, "The Gay Frank O'Hara," in *Frank O'Hara: To Be True to a City*, ed. Jim Elledge (Ann Arbor, 1993), 336.

To the extent that law and sexuality may be mutually dependent upon each other, as with repression and expression previously, or ideology and subjectivity in what follows—only with this realization are we then prepared to understand how the imbrication of self and other, in Butler's further insight, may so well constitute "the very condition of that self's possibility." Yet that further insight would merely represent only an additional means of gaining a purchase on O'Hara's queer perversity. For as Jonathan Dollimore argues, "the most extreme threat to the true form of something [like the self] comes not so much from its absolute opposite or its direct negation, but in the form of its perversion . . . [which is] inextricably rooted in the true and authentic . . . as at once utterly alien to what it threatens, and yet mysteriously *inherent* within it."[11] But first things first.

In his brief commentary on the French-Canadian Abstract Expressionist painter Jean-Paul Riopelle, O'Hara observes that "The artist who has an ideology!—that's worse than having a system! It has sense for him, and has no sense for anyone else" (*SS*, 152). In this brief remark, we take the word "system" to mean what is more conventionally understood to be so oppressive about ideologies in their less private and more general form, that is, the "sense" that *must* apply to everyone else rather than just to the single artist. "To put it very gently," O'Hara elsewhere writes, "I have a feeling that the philosophical reduction of reality to a dealable-with system so distorts life that one's 'reward' for this endeavor (a minor one, at that) is illness both from inside and outside" (*SS*, 37).

It is also in "an attempt to comment on and extend the interested struggles of gay people today" that Bruce Boone "raise[s] the historical question of Frank O'Hara's sexuality." Bruce Boone, "Gay Language as Political Praxis: The Poetry of Frank O'Hara," *Social Text* 1 (1979): 63, 77.

11. Judith Butler, "Imitation and Gender Insubordination," in *Inside/out: Lesbian Theories, Gay Theories*, ed. Diana Fuss (New York, 1991), 27; Dollimore, *Sexual Dissidence*, 121, emphasis added. The variations which Dollimore plays upon what he describes here, and throughout much of *Sexual Dissidence*, as "the paradoxical perverse," include "antagonistic interdependence" (122), "originating, antithetical proximity" (123), and "internal deviation" (124), and they all converge within this somewhat "perverse" prediction: "The paradoxical perverse, activated by the perverse dynamic, reveals the potential for transformations inherent in all social orders as a consequence of their own structure and developmental logic; transformations which dominant factions seek to repress or disavow because contrary to their interests, and which are usually identified as external, or the internal counterparts of what is fundamentally external. So perversion is doubly insurgent—a threat from outside in, and from inside out" (125). On this last point, one is reminded especially of how "[t]he anti-homosexual campaigns of the 1950s represented but one front in a widespread effort to reconstruct patterns of sexuality and gender relations shaken by depression and war," since, for better or worse, "[t]he labeling of sexual deviants helped to define the norm for men and women." D'Emilio, "The Homosexual Menace," 68.

Whether private, or more generally public—"inside" or "outside"—ideology, then, as a "dealable-with system," threatens life with "illness" if either of ideology's forms aims to reduce "reality" to any kind of systematic representation. For O'Hara, "reality" is thus unassimilable to ideology, and in this ultimately Kantian formulation (according to Slavoj Žižek), "is never given in its totality [since] there is always a void gaping in its midst, filled out by monstrous apparitions."[12] "Being essentially mysterious, 'nature,' where it does not imply naturalism" (i.e., another kind of ideological reduction), in O'Hara's mind, would be synonymous with reality in the foregoing Kantian sense. And O'Hara can only stand in awe of Jean-Paul Riopelle's unabating artistic approximation of that reality's mysterious "nature": "the thoroughness and completeness with which spontaneous energies seek and achieve their aims and the unendingness of the process which bears the forces of continuation" (*SS*, 153).

Spontaneity, energy, force, unending continuation—"process", in a word—these are all the terms central to O'Hara's conception of reality, what he also refers to, in his unpublished "Journal" from 1949, as "being," and like reality with respect to private ideology or public system, what he uses to set against the opprobrious "pattern" (a term borrowed from Mary McCarthy). Hence, "the most harrowing experience of man [is] the failure to feel steadily, to be able to compose a continuous pattern."[13]

It is the rare individual, indeed, who can "feel steadily" in the *absence* of pattern or system—the poet, say, who draws emotional sustenance from a love for the limitless *process* of creativity. For most others, however, in getting us to "feel

12. Slavoj Žižek, *Tarrying with the Negative: Kant, Hegel, and the Critique of Ideology* (Durham, 1993), 105. The "void" in Žižek's Kantian formulation here thus suggests an important intersection with Abstract Expressionism and the New York School poets, who "struggled to expose the sense of something infinite at the heart of sensation, nothing beyond human experience, but something indescribable within it," according to Anthony Libby, "O'Hara on the Silver Range," in *Frank O'Hara: To Be True to a City*, ed. Jim Elledge (Ann Arbor, 1993), 153. "My sister, life, is in flood today," a line from Pasternak, was consequently one that had an especial appeal to O'Hara (*OCP*, 503).

13. Gooch, *City Poet*, 131. Gooch's additional clarification is useful: "O'Hara opposed amorphous 'being' to McCarthy's imposed 'pattern.' 'I feel steadily but there is no pattern, there can be no pattern, there is only being,' he argued. 'The artist *is* and always loves and always creates and cannot help but love and create; I do not mean that only the artist achieves being; I am not metaphysical, quite vulgarly I mean realization of personality'" (131). This last point O'Hara repeats in his "Personism" manifesto (*SS*, 110), and I'll return to it when I deal with O'Hara's realization of subjectivity later in the next section. On "process" mentioned earlier, see James E. B. Breslin, "Frank O'Hara," in *Frank O'Hara: To Be True to a City*, ed. James Elledge (Ann Arbor, 1993), 254, 261, and in the same volume, Marjorie Perloff, "Frank O'Hara and the Aesthetics of Attention," 112.

steadily" about experience, patterns, like ideologies, severely foreshorten our "being" in the world, whose natural mysteries should be full of "complexity" and "aleatory happenings." To this extent, O'Hara's notion of "pattern" (or "system") would, again, very much corroborate Slavoj Žižek's conception of the "function of ideology," whose mass construction "is not to offer us an escape from our reality but to offer us the social reality itself as an escape from some traumatic, real kernel"—a "traumatic point" or Lacanian "Real" (much like O'Hara's natural "mystery") as "that which resists symbolization."[14]

In O'Hara's "Meditations in an Emergency" (1954), "heterosexuality," as mainstream culture's default sexual ideology, is presented as a social reality that will brook no traumatic mysteries: "Heterosexuality! you are inexorably approaching" (*OCP*, 197). One thinks, perhaps, of Khrushchev's irrevocable train from the previous poem bearing down on New York in like terms. And a gay poet in the Cold War climate of 1954 is, no doubt, a sufficiently monstrous apparition lodged in the void of human experience inadvertently to help increase that ideology's heedless acceleration. "How discourage her?" is, therefore, the narrator's most pressing response in such an emergency (*OCP*, 197). O'Hara's Foucaultian strategy, then, is *to intensify* the narrator's mystery:

> St. Serapion, I wrap myself in the robes of your whiteness which is like mid-night in Dostoevsky. How am I to become a legend, my dear? I've tried love, but that hides you in the bosom of another and I am always springing forth from it like the lotus—the ecstasy of always bursting forth! . . . "to keep the filth of life away," yes, there, even in the heart, where the filth is pumped in and slanders and pollutes and determines. I will my will, though I may become famous for a mysterious vacancy in that department, that greenhouse.
>
> (*OCP*, 197)

Affecting "a mysterious vacancy" may be the appropriate strategy for resisting heteronormative ideology's totalizing symbolizations—"filth," in this case, which is slandering and polluting only because all-determining. "Mysterious vacancy" may thus suggest a further variation on the dissident subjects' distance examined previously in this study whose "identification at a distance from the self," according to Kaja Silverman (following Lacan), endeavors to maintain "the object [O'Hara's "being"] at an uncrossable distance" in order to "open up identifications which would otherwise be foreclosed by the imperatives of normative representa-

14. Gooch, *City Poet*, 131; Slavoj Žižek, *The Sublime Object of Ideology* (New York, 1989), 45, 69, and further on 161–62, 169–71, 180–81, and passim. Cf. Boone, "Gay Language as Political Praxis," 91.

tion and the ego." But the pose of "vacancy" we should note in this particular case has the ironical effect of *disclosing* rather than disguising its narrator's purported absence or distance—flaunting it, we might say, in "the ecstasy of always bursting forth" (*OCP*, 197).[15] And in this perverse turning between absence and presence, the narrator appears to have found a way of emerging from the prison house of systematically dealable ideology: "Turning, I spit in the lock and the knob turns" (*OCP*, 198).

One need not necessarily have to be to gay in the 1950s, however, in order to experience the crushing effects of ideological pattern or system. In "Jane Awake" (1951), the female persona is fully alive to life's mysteries only by night:

> as you sleep, as you ride ponies
> mysteriously, spring to bloom
> like the blue flowers of autumn
>
> each nine o'clock.
>
> (*OCP*, 72)

By day, in contrast, she respectfully defers to the patriarchal ideology of reserved feminine comportment imposed upon her by mainstream culture's disciplinary gaze:

> he is day's guardian saint,
>
> that policeman, and leaning
> from your open window you ask
> him what dress to wear and how
> to comb your hair modestly,
>
> for that is now your mode.
>
> (*OCP*, 72)[16]

15. Kaja Silverman, *The Threshold of the Visible World* (New York, 1996), 77, 41–42. According to John Champagne, therefore, for gay writers "any act of hiding is necessarily also an act of revelation," but can only maintain that linkage through an understanding of the constitutively creative notion of cultural constraint that Foucault would hang on O'Hara's Cold War closet, since "'social taboos' do not simply cause gay writers to hide, erase, universalize, or invalidate homosexual desire, but rather provide the very conditions of possiblity for the articulation—'self' or otherwise—of that desire." In precisely these terms, absence paradoxically converts to presence given the further understanding that "the alterity represented by homosexuality is not 'outside' of a normal that seeks to repress it, but rather is made possible by the deployment of that normality, set into motion by the play of power and resistance." Champagne, *The Ethics of Marginality*, 63.

16. "For a woman to pursue wealth overtly," Alan Nadel observes in "God's Law and the Wide

Discovering herself in an impasse between two diametrically opposed worlds, impossibly "pressing all that / riotous black sleep into / the quiet form of daylight" (*OCP*, 72), Jane might feel compelled by the overwhelming force of the patriarchy's waking mind to make a rational choice between the two, thereby upholding the Western mind's traditional law of non-contradiction. "Pain always produces logic," O'Hara tells us in the "Personism" manifesto, "so you have to take your chances and try to avoid being logical" (*SS*, 110).[17] Jane thus escapes her conundrum by refusing the choice, and by persisting to indulge her "luminous volutions," the poet tells us, "Only by chance tripping on stairs" (*OCP*, 72), the stairway, presumably, of patriarchal culture's hierarchically sexist order. In her recuperation of "the nightly savage" by the end of the poem (*OCP*, 73), ideological subversion is not inversion—merely doing the opposite—but rather perversion: even though "subdued, impeccably disguised," nonetheless, "repeat[ing] the dance" in all of its "perfect variety" (*OCP*, 72).

The repetitions near the end of "Jane Awake" are instructive. "That there is a

Screen: *The Ten Commandments* as Cold War 'Epic,'" *PMLA* 108 (May 1993), "or to make a man her acquisition instead of trying to be his violates the gender rules of the 1950s," and offers the prescription of Freudian sexologists Marynia Farnham and Ferdinand Lundberg (*Modern Woman: The Lost Sex* [1947]) as a case in point: "'The rule [is]: The less a woman's desire to have children, and the greater her desire to emulate the male in seeking a sense of personal value by objective exploit, the less will be her enjoyment of the sex act and the greater her general neuroticism.'" "The authors are adamant," Nadel further notes, "that every aspect of a woman's psychological and sexual health depends on her desire and ability to have and raise children" (422). Thus, through the 1950s, as David Savran further observes in *Communists, Cowboys, and Queers*, "The ideology of familialism and the theory of 'sex roles' conceived the distinction between men and women as a binary opposition that set the aggressive, 'go-getting' businessman and father against the 'warm, giving,' and 'expressive' housewife and mother whose responsibility it was to embrace domesticity and contain her sexuality" (8).

17. Hence, in the related dissident contexts of a restive feminism, postcolonialism, and pedagogy, Gayatri Spivak's injunction "to take a distance from the continuing project of reason," quoted in Young, *White Mythologies*, 169. Elsewhere, Young (following the ethics of Levinas) attributes to the "distance" of "dialogue language" a "relation of sociality, whereby the self instead of assimilating the other, opens itself to it through a relation with it" (14). In indulging his own intemperate "flaunting of logic," to use Perloff's phrase (Perloff, *Frank O'Hara*, 80), O'Hara here perhaps reveals his indebtedness to the influence of Surrealism on his work, and to the French post-Symbolists more generally. "It is helpful," Gregory Bredbeck reminds us, "to remember André Breton's definition of surrealism—'thought's dictation, in the absence of all control exercised by reason and outside all aesthetic or moral preoccupations.'" Gregory Bredbeck, "B/O—Barthe's Text/O'Hara's Trick," *PMLA*, 108 (March 1993): 277. See also Perloff, *Frank O'Hara*, 38–39, 41, 65–74, and Charles Molesworth, "'The Clear Architecture of the Nerves': The Poetry of Frank O'Hara," in *Frank O'Hara: To Be True to a City*, ed. James Elledge (Ann Arbor, 1993), 215.

need for a repetition at all," Butler observes, "is a sign that identity is not self-identical," and that if "[i]t requires to be instituted again and again," then "it runs the risk of becoming *de*-instituted at every interval." Jane's partial occlusion by night in luminous (re)volutions associated with some "nightly savage" casts some doubt upon her full identity, to be sure. But "the racing vertiginous waves" of uniformed policemen by day (*OCP,* 72) would seem to suggest that, for the forces of ideology, too, "repetition is the way in which power works to construct . . . the *illusion* of its own uniformity and identity."[18]

In both cases, what the compulsion to repeat brings us more compellingly back to, in O'Hara, is a certain mystery in the reality of being itself that seems sure to exceed every ideological attempt to secure it for the purpose of legitimating the individual's repeatedly depleted sense of selfhood. Thus, while Louis Althusser may describe how "the symbolic machine of ideology is 'internalized' into the ideological experience of Meaning and Truth," we can nevertheless, as Slavoj Žižek more pointedly views the case, "learn from Pascal that this 'internalization,' by structural necessity, never fully succeeds, that there is always a residue, a leftover, a stain of traumatic irrationality and senselessness sticking to it, and that . . . it is precisely this non-integrated surplus of senseless traumatism which confers on the Law its unconditional authority . . . in so far as it escapes ideological sense."[19] In "Ann Arbor Variations" (1951), O'Hara characterizes this traumatic irrationality in response to the surplus of experience as an "excess of affection" that one is likely to grasp only fleetingly "near an open window," or more tellingly, "a Bauhaus / fire escape" (*OCP,* 66). Thus,

> Workmen loiter before urinals, stare
> out windows at girders tightly strapped to clouds.
> And in the morning we whimper as we cook
> an egg, so far from fluttering sands and azure!
>
> (*OCP,* 66)

In a reminiscence of the previous poem, it is "The violent No! of the sun" which seems most resistant to this excess of ideological unsettlement in Ann Arbor. But along with Jane,

18. Butler, *Bodies That Matter,* 24, emphasis added. Some tripping up on the staircase of sexist culture we can now anticipate from the quarter of patriarchal hegemony. For if identifications "are never fully and finally made," then "they are incessantly reconstituted and, as such, are subject to the volatile logic of iterability. They are that which is constantly marshaled, consolidated, retrenched, contested, and, on occasion, compelled to give way." Butler, *Bodies That Matter,* 105.

19. Žižek, *The Sublime Object of Ideology,* 43.

We dance in the dark,
[and] forget the anger of what we blame

on the day even though, as in the final line, "we die upon the sun"
(*OCP*, 66)

Similarly, in "Commercial Variations," composed a year later (1952), "the glassy fencing of sunrise" is the adversarial posture of a Cold War "Americanism" that "jingoes and jolts daily / over . . . icebergs" to make war with that which exceeds its ideological sense of self-propriety: "The American Boy / from Sodom-on-Hudson (non-resident membership / in The Museum of Modern Art" (*OCP*, 86, 85). From that highly defensive perspective—the perspective of "the least common denominator" (*OCP*, 86)—there can be "no bushing around the truth, whatever that is" (*OCP*, 86). But Dame Art, "Belle of Old New York" (*OCP*, 86), whose province is mystery, cannot be constrained by such a restrictive economy as Truth:

"Never may the dame claim to be warm to the exact,
nor the suburban community amount to anything in any way
that is not a pursuit of the purple vices artsy-craftsy,
the loom in the sitting room where reading is only aloud
and illustrative of campfire meetings beside the Out Doors
where everyone feels as ill at ease as sea-food."
(*OCP*, 86)

"Sea-food" here, gay slang for sailors as sex objects, picks up on much of the camp tenor of this artsy-craftsy passage (purple vices, campfire, Out Doors) to frustrate a monolithically straight culture's dedication to ideological common sense. Answering their fixation on straight-talk with such perverse indirection only serves to reinforce, once again, the uncontrollable nature of processual experience that will always mean "more than the poem which embodies it"—embodied, indeed, in the very twistings and turnings of language itself.[20] And the more "luminous

20. Chauncey, *Gay New York*, 53 (on "sea-food"); Kevin Stein, "'Everything the Opposite': A Literary Basis for the Anti-Literary in Frank O'Hara's *Lunch Poems*," in *Frank O'Hara: To Be True to a City*, ed. James Elledge (Ann Arbor, 1993), 365. From the same volume, "Each poem is in some part excessive," Bill Berkson also observes, "and each has an element of joy." Bill Berkson, "Frank O'Hara and His Poems," in *Frank O'Hara: To Be True to a City*, ed. James Elledge (Ann Arbor, 1993), 233. Thus, it will be "the infinite preciousness of the real world, perpetually threatened by fantasy, self-loathing and conformism [that] will galvanize O'Hara's energies throughout his ca-

volutions," or in this case, variations, the better, as in "Commerical Variations'" revolving the earlier "Meditations'" conclusion in its own final line: "I'm turning in today for a little freedom to travel" (*OCP*, 87).

The camp lingo in the above citation may keep art from warming up too much "to the exact." But it also speaks to two further ideological issues. One has to do with a certain kind of poetry writing, prevalent in American universities by the early fifties that, thanks to the proliferation of the New Criticism particularly after the war, was allowing art, in fact, to accommodate itself to an intellectual establishment's preference for the elegance of closed forms and appropriately rarefied content, in the wake of canonical High Modernists like Ezra Pound, but especially T. S. Eliot—work of contemporary master craftsmen such as Robert Lowell, Delmore Schwartz, Karl Shapiro, and Richard Wilbur, among others.[21] O'Hara's notorious disdain for the niceties of poetic style and technique ("if you're going to buy a pair of pants[,] you want them to be tight enough so everyone will want to go to bed with you," he acerbically posits in "Personism" [*SS*, 110]), his endless experimentation with free-form structures, but most especially, his often baffling and enigmatic semantic opacity or obliqueness—all of this indirection, no doubt, was calculated to hold art free of Cold War ideologues, intellectual or otherwise.

As his biographer effectively puts the case, O'Hara's

personal puzzle was somehow to combine the dissociations of language practiced by his favorite post-Symbolist French poets with the free verse and local voice of the American poets descended from Walt Whitman, the poet whom William Carlos Williams claimed had "broken the dominance of the iambic pentameter in English prosody." . . . By exhibiting a taste for French poetry, and for such nonliterary models as Schoenberg's "Serenade" or the early paintings of Mondrian— with a natural temperamental inclination toward openness and spontaneity and

---

reer"—so Richard Howard contends also from the same volume, and "will goad him to recognitions and recollections of 'whatever is the case' that he can trust." Richard Howard, "Frank O'Hara: 'Since Once We Are We Always Will Be in This Life Come What May,'" in *Frank O'Hara: To Be True to a City*, ed. James Elledge (Ann Arbor, 1993), 115.

21. Gooch, *City Poet*, 183; see also Boone, "Gay Language as Political Praxis," 67, 68, 71. Though O'Hara's respect for Pound was measured, from whom, as "the father of modern poets," he discerns a tradition in contemporary poetry extending through Auden, Stevens, Crane, and the early Thomas, in a talk given in 1952, it was Eliot whom he viewed as his sworn enemy, "for his 'deadening and obscuring and precious effect.'" Gooch, *City Poet*, 216, and further on 138 and 172. See also Perloff, *Frank O'Hara*, 9–12, 45, 53, and 202n. 26. "Lord! spare us from any more Fisher Kings!" he lashes out elsewhere (*SS*, 162).

away from serious meaning—O'Hara was largely ignoring the Berryman-Lowell-Shapiro generation.

The campiness of O'Hara's style previously noted, therefore, is perhaps better understood within the much larger project of refusing to direct art toward "serious meaning," and thereby, in specifically ideological terms, preventing that art, in O'Hara's words, from making any "exact" claim to the Christianizing liberal humanist agenda of the well-established New Criticism patriarchy in America, and any number of its contemporary scions. This is not to suggest, however, that art ought to be *devoid* of meaning or intellectual commitment entirely. Quite the contrary. To be "camp," as Mark Booth argues, is "to present oneself as being committed to the marginal with a commitment greater than the marginal merits." In more bracing, anti-ideological terms, camp, through its signifying "a *relationship between* things, people, and activities or qualities, and homosexuality," ought ideally to be viewed as "a philosophy of transformations," hence a stay against artistic and cultural conformity.[22]

On this second issue of ideological transformation, we are brought back to the problematic of a surplus reality in O'Hara's work, once again. We don't want to confuse this reality, as an open-ended artistic matrix of spontaneous force and continuous creation, with "realism"—in Žižek's words, "a naive belief that, behind the curtain of representations, some full, substantial reality actually exists." With realism, then, we *do* get offered serious meaning, and it becomes a popular bourgeois discursive form or practice from the nineteenth century onwards mainly because, on the analogy of bourgeois culture itself, it (re)produces its exactnesses of meaning in quite predictable, controllable, and ultimately stable and finite ways.[23]

22. Mark Booth, quoted in Esther Newton, *Cherry Grove, Fire Island: Sixty Years in America's First Gay and Lesbian Town* (Boston, 1993), 74; Newton, *Cherry Grove, Fire Island,* 73.

23. Žižek, *Tarrying with the Negative,* 103. According to Roland Barthes, therefore, "realism," in this sense, works counter to the "modernity" of a perverse writer like O'Hara, since modernity "tries to resist the market for works (by excluding itself from mass communication), the sign (by exemption from meaning, by madness), sanctioned sexuality (by perversion, which shields bliss from the finality of reproduction). . . . In other words, society lives according to a cleavage . . . [but] has no notion of this split: *it is ignorant of its own perversion.*" Roland Barthes, *The Pleasure of the Text,* trans. Richard Miller (New York, 1975), 23–24, emphases retained. On the other hand, Alan Nadel reverses the analogy: "sex does not serve diversion—an 'art'—but reproduction—'life.'" Alan Nadel, "God's Law and the Wide Screen," 422. Michael Davitt Bell further imputes a sexist and possibly homophobic bias to "realism" when he observes that "a prominent function of claiming to be a realist or naturalist . . . was to provide assurance to one's society and oneself that one was a 'real' man rather than

A late-nineteenth-century homosexual novelist and dramatist like Oscar
Wilde, therefore, as Sue-Ellen Case points out (following Michael Bronski), is
sure to have invented a counter-hegemonic discourse like camp, not only to call
attention, through its obtuse use of irony, to the oppression of homosexuals in
such a closed and unforgiving culture, but more importantly, to win for art a
liberation from "the ruling powers of heterosexist realist modes." Thus, closer to
home, and closer to the time when Frank O'Hara would begin to think seriously
about writing, another gay novelist and dramatist, Tennessee Williams, would
compose one of his first serious works for the stage, *Me, Vashya* (1937), and according to Williams' biographer, would maintain "that his play was intended as
a melodramatic fantasy and not meant to be realistic." "I must remember that my
method of survival has always been a very oblique method," Williams confides in
an unpublished journal from 1939, and observes later that year that "by distor-
tion, by outrageous exaggeration [William Faulkner] seems to get an effect closer
to reality (or my idea of it) than strict realists get in their exact representation."
Williams' concept of "sculptural drama," therefore, would introduce to the stage
during the war a "non-realistic" dramatic form of "short cumulative scenes," "reduced mobility," and "statuesque attitudes or tableaux" that was intended to strike
at the very heart of the bourgeois American theater—"comparable to nothing but
the vomit of a hyena," the playwright once spat—and its most sacred convention
of the three-act play based upon "realistic action." More appropriately labeled
"surrealist," in contrast to that of the commercial theater, Williams' revolutionary
writing, then, reveals a kind of abstraction *away* from realism's documentary hold
on an arguably elusive reality as demonstrated in previous chapters of this study
that would find its precise strategic counterpart in the highly experimental
writing of New York School poets like Frank O'Hara, and their own unique surrealist extrapolations from the parallel world of postwar Abstract Expressionist
art.[24]

With the dissolution of the New York School and abstract art in the late '50s
and early '60s, camp discourse would obviously become more vital to the survival

---

an effeminate 'artist.'" Michael Davitt Bell, *The Problem of American Realism: Studies in the Cultural
History of a Literary Idea* (Chicago, 1993), 6. Hence, Helen Vendler's claim that O'Hara's "radical
and dismissive logic flouts the whole male world and its relentless demand for ideologies, causes, and
systems of significance." Helen Vendler, "Frank O'Hara: The Virtue of the Alterable," *Frank O'Hara:
To Be True to a City*, ed. James Elledge (Ann Arbor, 1993), 238.

24. Sue-Ellen Case, "Toward a Butch-Femme Aesthetic," 297–98; Lyle Leverich, *TOM: The
Unknown Tennessee Williams* (New York, 1995), 216, 331, 333, 446, 484, 446; Savran, *Communists,
Cowboys, and Queers*, 92 (on "surrealist").

of gay writing in American culture. Even more especially today, so Case argues, the artifice of camp qua artifice, through "its constantly changing, mobile quality," provides "the only reasonable modus operandi in the American Literalist Terror of Straight Reality" by "ironizing and distancing [its] regime . . . mounted by heterosexist forces." In opening up a space between reader and text in this ironical way—going the distance, under the general rubric of dissidence foregrounded throughout this study—camp discourse thus subverts all correspondent relationships to experience so privileged in the mode of realism, and playfully (and usually quite humorously) *transforms* that experience into a field of infinite interpretation. In playing *on* rather than *to* the phallic economy, camp thus installs an excess of "reality" in place of a finite "realism," perverting that economy sufficiently in order that one now might be allowed "to be constructed from outside ideology, with a gender role that makes [one] appear as if [s/he] is inside of it" at the same time. "[A] strategy of appearances replaces a claim to truth," so Case concludes, which, in O'Hara's particular instance, becomes another way to gauge the queer perversity of his poetry in face of a Cold War climate of ideological entrenchment.[25]

Sue-Ellen Case also makes the point in her essay that "[t]he identification with movie idols is part of the camp assimilation of dominant culture," and offers James Dean as one such example.[26] I would like to round out this first part of my argument, however, by looking briefly at one of the four elegies O'Hara composed to commemorate the death of James Dean, in order to reveal how the bourgeois realism of the movie star's iconographic representation in modern culture

25. Case, "Toward a Butch-Femme Aesthetic," 298 (citing Esther Newton), 300, 301, 304. See also Bredbeck, "B/O," 274. An interesting sideline to this whole realism/reality debate concerns its entanglement with the poet's own tragic demise. The considerable degree of speculation that, to this day, surrounds Frank O'Hara's death—"Living beyond forty," was his greatest fear apparently—such speculation pursues one line of argument that suggests that the poet may have felt no overriding reason to go on living once the ethos of Abstract Expressionism, in which the New York School of writers was so completely invested, had run its course in the later years of the Cold War. And one of the contributing factors, of course, to the death of the abstractionist movement in America in the early sixties was the Pop artist Andy Warhol, and the rise of "Neo-Realism" in his wake. See Gooch, *City Poet*, 451, 399. The poet's biographer claims that O'Hara completely detested Warhol, and for good reason (396–97), but the Lucie-Smith "Interview" from 1965 offers a more balanced and generous opinion of Warhol and what he represented (*SS*, 19–20). Neal Bowers, however, makes a case for a more realist sensibility overtaking American poetry at a much later time, in "The City Limits: Frank O'Hara's Poetry," in *Frank O'Hara: To Be True to a City*, ed. James Elledge (Ann Arbor, 1993), 332–33.

26. Case, "Towards a Butch-Femme Aesthetic," 302.

is what most disturbs the poet, that is to say, an ideological construction of the movie idol that all but empties his potentiality for camp assimilation, and by implication, may have been one of the contributing causes to Dean's early tragic demise. Not that the film icon in "For James Dean" (1955) does not hold out the prospect of perversely camping up his image, and so displacing his reception outside the bounds of mainstream culture. Yet in leaning heavily on Dean's iconic film status, O'Hara allows camp's distancing displacement to occur from within the identificatory realism driving the belief-system of that culture itself:

> you take up
> the thread of my life between your teeth,
> tin thread and tarnished with abuse,
>
> . . . .
>
> . . . and my loins move yet
> in the ennobling pursuit of all the worlds
> you have left me alone in, and would be
> the dolorous distraction from
>   (OCP, 229)

As the quintessential "Rebel without a Cause," James Dean would appear to be a perfect emblem for "the ennobling pursuit of all the worlds" besides a straight one. And he puts us in mind of the workmen back in Ann Arbor loitering before their urinals in prospect of such experiential alterity, when the poet places Dean drolly in the company of those whose "dreams / are their own, as are the toilets / of a great railway terminal" (OCP, 228–29). But where the film star, "smoldering quietly in the perception / of hopelessness and scandal" (OCP, 228), begins to lose his credibility as a source for the potentiality to pursue other worlds and live other dreams is just at that moment when, pressured no doubt by the movie-moguls from within and an adoring public without, James Dean stakes his claim for ultimate truth—his Cause: the rebel-without-cause—and in that "final impertinence to rebel," enslaves himself along with all the other

> starlets and . . .
> glittering things in the hog-wallow,
> lunging mireward in their inane
> mothlike adoration of niggardly
> cares and stagnant respects
>   (OCP, 229)

With his eye firmly fixed, now, on a single goal, he succumbs to the monocular ideology of the Hollywood star-system:

> He has banged into your wall
> of air, your hubris, racing
> towards your heights and you
> have cut him from your table
> which is built, how unfairly
> for us! not on trees, but on clouds.
>   (*OCP*, 228)

Mangled ideologically by Hollywood's dream factory, "without swish / without camp," to cite O'Hara in a related context, James Dean is now fit to be served up to "an army of young married couples' vanilla hemorrhages" (from "Easter" [1952; *OCP*, 97, 98]). As a "bleeding" (as opposed to "leading") man within mainstream cinema's tabloid lust for spectacles of normatizing (heterosexist) pathos, the matinee movie idol now plays it straight—at least, straight to the hearts (and minds) of middle-class "vanilla" America.[27] So that if there is any irony at all left by the end of "For James Dean," it's certainly of a kind that we're not likely to associate with camp. More likely, it's the further sense of pathos we feel in the narrator's realistic identification with his movie star in the final stanza:

> "Men cry from the grave while they still live
> and now I am this dead man's voice,
> stammering, a little in the earth"
>   (*OCP*, 230)

For in taking up the single cause of another in death, he diminishes not "a little" of his own self in life. Nonetheless, the egregious prospect of the ambisexual James Dean lodged in the bourgeois hearts of mainstream America ought to strike us here as not a little perverse, and at least alert us to the fact that the Cold War's disciplinary ideologies of hearth and home may bloody well have been imperiled as well. That O'Hara's "vanilla hemorrhages," therefore, might potentially be read as *openings* within American culture, as well as closings, thus adds a final

---

27. For the ideological import of "vanilla"—"heterosexual, marital, monogamous, reproductive, and non-commercial"—within a "charmed circle" of sexuality coded as "'good,' 'normal,' and 'natural,'" see Rubin, "Thinking Sex," 280–81. "I don't give a fuck for families," O'Hara once wrote to his brother, in a letter vowing never to return to his home town in 1952 following the death of his father. "I think that people should treat each other as they feel." Gooch, *City Poet*, 13.

dimension to their irony. And it's to a fuller expansion of this more open possibility buried in my title that I now propose to turn.

In *Art in America* (1975), Elaine de Kooning, artist and longtime friend of Frank O'Hara, relates a curious anecdote about painting the poet's portrait in the mid-fifties: "When I painted Frank O'Hara, Frank was standing there. First I painted the whole structure of his face; then I wiped out the face, and when the face was gone, it was more Frank than when the face was there." This rather interesting paradox—that we are likely to suggest *more* about a subject the *less* we are able to represent him accurately or definitively—expresses the kind of human predicament that ideological systems are likely to have the least tolerance for, and as in the case of James Dean, are happy to reduce to its simplest and most basic form, if not eliminate entirely. With O'Hara, the situation was obviously not quite so "dealable-with." "It always amuses me," he once wrote in a letter to his family while attending Harvard after the war, "when someone remarks how well they know me; throughout my life[,] my most cherished wishes have been my most secret (simply because to share is to spoil in many cases) ones."[28]

Secrecy might be one word to characterize O'Hara's life, particularly his efforts while a youth in Grafton, Massachusetts, and a seaman aboard the USS *Nicholas* during the waning years of World War Two "to deflect attention from his own hidden sexual identity." But later, O'Hara's own self-characterization as a "rococo self," or his characterization by others as "chameleonlike"[29] and "a dream of contradictions"—this last noticeably with respect to his especial attraction to straight men, and even his falling in love with straight women from time to time—such psychic and emotional complexity can at least lend credence to the poet's curt dismissal of any kind of "mythology of the Ur-self" bandied about by various Confessional poets, a notion of subjectivity that Oscar Wilde himself had demolished several generations ago: Dorian Gray "used to wonder at the shallow psychology of those who conceived the Ego in man as a thing simple, permanent, reliable, and of one essence. To him man was a being with myriad lives and myr-

28. Citations from Gooch, *City Poet*, 398ff, 106.
29. Gooch, *City Poet*, 114, 61, 117, 134, 413. Giles Gunn's linking of the New York School poets to the tradition of Pragmatism in American thought ("Religion and the Recent Revial of Pragmatism," 417n. 16) referenced in previous chapters is thus given especial point in this self-characterization of O'Hara in view of a similar remark that Dewey casts on his own person: "I seem to be unstable, chameleon-like, yielding one after another to many diverse and even incompatible influences; struggling to assimilate something from each." Dewey, "From Absolutism to Experimentalism," 9.

iad sensations, a complex, multiform creature.[30] And as I shall attempt to show in what follows, there can be no accident in the fact that O'Hara gave up his ambition to become a concert pianist and composer, and began to write poetry, both around the time of his coming out fully to his classmates at Harvard after the war—a time when it must have seemed to him that, once beyond the closet, man indeed was a myriad and multiform creature.

The argument, therefore, for what James Breslin refers to as the "protean self" in Frank O'Hara, a subjectivity that is at once "mobile, shifting, multiple . . . contradictory, elusive, and incomplete"—"the ecstasy of always bursting forth!" we recall from "Meditations in an Emergency" (*OCP*, 197)—this argument helps to refine our thinking about his poetry in a number of respects. In the first place, it steers us clear of various claims of essentialism with respect to O'Hara's handling of subjectivity—"the dead center of self" (Bowers), the "changeless, irreducible, yet contingent [?] self" (Molesworth), etc.—that tend to fit it so well to representation within the fixed modes of realism, and hence as we've seen, to the methodologies of ideological manipulation and cultural appropriation.[31]

30. Gooch, *City Poet*, 10, 227, 229, 212, 217; Wilde, quoted in Dollimore, *Sexual Dissidence*, 16. Thus, within the same year that *The Picture of Dorian Gray* was published (1890–91), William James would observe in *The Principles of Psychology* (1890) that "a man has as many social selves as there are individuals who recognize him and carry an image of him in their mind"—a view, according to Henry B. Wonham, that may have been anticipated a decade earlier by Henry James in *The Portrait of a Lady* (1881): "What shall we call our 'self'? Where does it begin? Where does it end? It overflows into everything that belongs to us—and then it flows back again . . . one's house, one's furniture, one's garments, the books one reads, the company one keeps—these things are all expressive." Henry James, quoted in Henry B. Wonham, "Writing Realism, Policing Conciousness: Howells and the Black Body," *American Literature* 67 (fall 1995): 701. After Wilde, the brothers James, and now O'Hara, Michel Foucault thus becomes merely one further writer in a series "to treat . . . human beings as a kind of pure *hyle* capable of taking on indefinitely many forms, of being historically constituted in an indefinite multiplicity of forms, no one of which is any better or worse than another." Indeed, all would appear to corroborate the idea Foucault was especially insistent upon in his later writings: "that there is always something other than or different from the various historical constitutions of human beings, some 'freedom' or resistance that is irreducible to the several enframing historical forms of life, some power-to-be-otherwise, some being-otherwise-than-the-present that radically, irreducibly, irrepressibly belongs to us, to what we are (not)." Caputo, "On Not Knowing Who We Are," 253–54, 256.

31. Breslin, "Frank O'Hara," 293, 268; Bowers, "The City Limits," 333; Molesworth, "'The Clear Architecture of the Nerves,'" 213. "The absence of any totalizing form," Breslin further elaborates, "allows [O'Hara] to explore the self fully, its insecurities, transparencies, defenses, evasions, yearnings, obsessions," and for which "[h]e adopts, variously, a dazzling range of roles, styles, tones, [and] 'selves'" (293; additionally on 275, 276, 283, 287, 292, and 294). And since our "selves" are "multiple and contestatory," Judith Butler hypothesizes that "it may be that we desire most strongly

Secondly, therefore, the many arguments for the privileging of "surface" effects in his writing we should perhaps now appreciate for their contributing to problematize rather severely the verticality of various depth models of psychic structure on which essentialist claims for selfhood are so often based, and hence for their underwriting a more politically astute approach to subjectivity in O'Hara's work, allowing us to take into account, alternatively, the more horizontal "discursive and institutional intersections of race, class, gender, and sexuality . . . that make 'identity' irreducible to consciousness."[32]

Thirdly, and perhaps most importantly, we cannot lose sight, as I have already endeavored to show, of the historical and social forces within which O'Hara's project is set. For it is these very Cold War constraints that function in a perversely vital way as the dynamic provocation for his exploring the highly nuanced and richly textured alternatives to an ideologically grounded identity that such constraints were so poised to foreclose and erase. As an instance of the Foucaultian "productive power of prohibition," paradoxically, O'Hara's Cold War culture demonstrates not a little of its own perversion in a way, and perhaps in the end, forcefully shows "how inappropriate it is," as Freud famously contends, "to use the word perversion as a term of reproach." In thus establishing this quite improbable intersection with its time, the poetry of Frank O'Hara reveals the most complex aspect of its perversity, disclosing as it does, in Jonathan Dollimore's words, "not an underlying unity in the name of which social division can be transcended, but a radical interconnectedness which has been and remains the unstable ground of both repression and liberation; the ground from which division and discrimination are both produced and contested." On this last point, I want to remain firm in resisting the temptation to view O'Hara's queer perversities as an

---

those individuals who reflect in a dense or saturated way the possibilities of multiple and simultaneous substitutions," and would argue even further that to the degree that such substitutions "can come to constitute and saturate a site of desire, it follows that we are not in the position of *either* identifying with a given sex *or* desiring someone else of that sex." Butler, *Bodies That Matter*, 99. Perhaps to this extent, "one is not always in command of oneself," O'Hara remarks, ". . . and as one sees longer it becomes apparent that an unknown quantity of perception is available to one's flagging powers, as in nature the hidden secret is partially revealed" (*SS*, 50).

32. Biddy Martin, "Lesbian Identity and Autobiographical Difference[s]," in *The Lesbian and Gay Studies Reader*, ed. Henry Abelove, Michèle Aina Barale, and David M. Halperin (New York, 1993), 282. Cf. Breslin, "Frank O'Hara," 283, 287. For arguments on O'Hara's "surface" effects, see Perloff, *Frank O'Hara*, 23–24; Charles Altieri, "'Varieties of Immanentist Expression,'" in *Frank O'Hara: To Be True to a City*, ed. James Elledge (Ann Arbor, 1993), 195; and Mutlu Konuk Blasing, *American Poetry: The Rhetoric of Its Forms* (New Haven, 1987), 160–61. For arguments on "essentialist claims" for selfhood, see Edward Stein, *Forms of Desire*, passim.

artful dodge in response to a punishingly homophobic period in American history, and the equal temptation to read his at times maddening thematic tendentiousness and frequent stylistic density as the lubriciously transcendent gestures of political and cultural quietism, coincident with "culturally imposed silences," or "the threat of dominant group penetrations." "[T]he center of [his self] is never silent," as we shall discover in a moment (*OCP*, 293). So that if there *are* silences in his work, we are better disposed to view them as "vanilla hemorrhages" in the more "open" and doubly ironic sense alluded to at the close of the previous section, that is to say, as sites of perverse *possibility* redounding to heterosexist culture, incipient and available within a multiply expansive discourse for alternative subjective construction and, by implication, relentless social engagement.[33]

In Frank O'Hara's "Ode to Michael Goldberg ('s Birth and Other Births)" (1958), a text that he always considered his best poem,[34] we are presented with a couple of these perverse sites. As such, in a poem memorably rooted for O'Hara in the experience of coming to terms with his gay identity, they function rather as markers in the transition between two distinct sexual economies: the ideologically normative, on the one hand, characterized by (re)productive sameness, stability, and truth, all played out discursively within the closure of realism; and on the other hand, the semiologically perverse, characterized by processual difference, volatility, and artifice, that we tend discursively to associate with the openness of reality, as that term was rehearsed in the previous section. Hence, early in the poem, we are presented with this juxtaposition: on the one hand, "at the clattering cutter-bar / of the mower ridden by Jimmy Whitney / 'I'd like to put my rolling-pin to her' his brother Bailey / leaning on his pitchfork, watching / 'you shove it in and nine months later / it comes out a kid' / Ha ha" (*OCP*, 291); on the other hand, "I'd like to stay / in this field forever / and think of nothing / but these sounds, / these smells and the tickling grasses / 'up your ass, Sport'" (*OCP*, 291–92). Later in the poem, the two economies are even more clearly contraposed with the lines: "the doubts / . . . from does she love me to do I love him, / sempiternal farewell to hearths / and the gods who don't live there" (*OCP*, 294).

Now the narrator of the poem, whom we might take to be gay from the foregoing, in the former normative case suffers from "ideological mystification, and

33. Butler, *Bodies That Matter*, 55; Freud, quoted in Diana Fuss, "Pink Freud," *GLQ* 2, no. 1–2 (1995): 2 (Cf. Mandy Merck, *Perversions: Deviant Readings* [New York, 1993], 7–8); Dollimore, *Sexual Dissidence*, 229 (Cf. Boone, "Gay Language as Political Praxis," 65); Imbriglio, "'Our Days Put on Such Reticence,'" 255; Boone, "Gay Language as Political Praxis," 66 (and further on 65, 87, 90).

34. Gooch, *City Poet*, 354, 384.

the subjective internalization of ideology, as well as of outright coercion":[35] "but unhappiness, like Mercury, transfixed me / there, un repaire de vipères / and had I known the strength and durability / of those invisible bonds I would have leaped from rafters onto prongs / then" (*OCP*, 292–93). Yet there seems to be no possibility for him to construct an alternative subject position for himself—an "other birth," as in the title—outside of holding fast, within that highly stratified economy, to the "crowds of intimacies and no distance / the various cries / and rounds . . . smiling in our confused way, darkly" (*OCP*, 296). For only by persisting in "the absence of desire" and in what must seem like "centuries of useless aspiration towards artifice" (*OCP*, 294, 296) can the narrator see his way clear through the "no distance" of ideological mystification to that perverse site of possibility where,

> there is a glistening
> blackness in the center
> if you seek it
> here . . . it's capable of bursting
> into flame or merely
> gleaming profoundly in
> the platinum setting
> of your ornamental
> human ties and hates
> hanging between breasts
> or, crosslike, on a chest of hairs
> (*OCP*, 293)

Within the "distance" that now opens up here at the join—"crosslike"—between two contrastingly coded gendered fields, we see how prohibition becomes powerfully transformed into production when it seems possible to round upon subjectivity not necessarily in the same old way. At another site, we discover even more promise: "a flickering light for us, but the glare of the dark / too much endlessness / stored up, and in store: / 'the exquisite prayer / to be new each day / brings to the artist / only a certain kneeness'" (*OCP*, 297). In either case, "to be new each day" suggests that the transition *can* be made from the sedimentations of normative in-dividuality to the optionality and potency of a more fluid and protean identity. Accordingly, "the center of myself is never silent" (*OCP*, 293). And this prospect must hold out as much promise for mainstream community—"a foreign land / toward whom I have been selected to bear / the gift of fire"—as for marginal community alike:

35. Dollimore, *Sexual Dissidence*, 7.

down where a flame illumines gravity and means warmth and insight,
where air is flesh, where speed is darkness, and
things can suddenly be reached, held, dropped and known,

where a not totally imaginary ascent can begin all over again in tears
(*OCP*, 293)

Within this perspective, both communities, like both O'Hara's discursive economies, seem destined for each other. For as the poem makes emphatic at the close,
"one alone will speak of being / born in pain / [so that] he will be the wings of
an extraordinary liberty" (*OCP*, 298). The fact that *both* mainstream and marginal
positionalities stand to gain in this mutual confrontation is perhaps the one imperative lesson that Frank O'Hara at mid-century can impart to queer theory in
our own day, so endlessly mired does it so often seem in the self-reflexive toils of
its *own* identity politics.

This "extraordinary liberty" that O'Hara locates in the "other" semiological
birth that doubles the biological birth in his ode's title lends considerable point
to Judith Butler's "Imitation and Gender Insubordination," wherein we understand that a self only achieves an identity through loss (O'Hara's "born in pain"
here, and "the endless originality of loss" elsewhere [*OCP*, 331]), which, as Butler
astutely observes, can only be "provisionally resolved" through the "incorporation
of some 'Other.'" Once installed, that "other birth" inscribed in O'Hara's text,
and in the self, as that "blackness in the center," breaks apart forever the ideological mystifications of an achieved self-identity, and replaces it with the semiological "endlessness" of constructing identity "new each day," thereby imbuing the
self with perverse possibility—"the gift of fire," as O'Hara writes. Moreover, if
we can recall O'Hara's narrator lying in this new discursive field ruminating about
"nothing" (*OCP*, 291), we might perhaps gain a further berth, so to speak, on
such perversity, following Žižek again, by thinking about it in terms of Lacan's
Real, which, like O'Hara's black center (and not too removed from his Reality),
is "*nothing but* [the] impossibility of its inscription," since that Real "is not a transcendent positive entity . . . in itself it is nothing at all, just a void, an emptiness
in a symbolic structure marking some central impossibility." As Žižek elaborates,
"[W]e can inscribe, encircle the void place of the subject through the failure of
. . . symbolization, because the subject is nothing but the failure point of the
process of . . . symbolic representation . . . we can *overtake* it, leave it behind us,
but we cannot *reach* it." Hence, O'Hara's "absence of desire" (*OCP*, 294), which,
for the "other" self, had highlighted the word *after* the preposition initially, now

switches to the one *before*—absence, or lack. For "[t]he subject of the signifier is \
precisely this lack," Žižek tells us, "this impossibility of finding a signifier which
would be 'its own,'" and as Silverman further affirms in O'Hara's own corroborating rhetoric, it is arguably "distance which consolidates lack and renders desire
fundamentally unfillable." Yet in line with the perverse prodigality of subjectivity
in the previous ode's concluding "extraordinary liberty," it is precisely "the failure
of its representation [which constitutes] its positive condition."[36]

"How many selves are there in a war hero asleep in names? under / a blanket
of platoon and fleet, orderly" (*OCP*, 255). Frank O'Hara asks that question in a
poem which, published the same year, might almost function as the companion
piece to the previous ode. Though composed two years earlier, "In Memory of
My Feelings" (1958) incorporates a much shorter text from 1955 which offers a
rather bizarre answer to the poet's question, and reads in part:

> I am a Hittite in love with a horse. I don't know what blood's
> in me I feel like an African prince I am a girl walking downstairs
> in a red pleated dress with heels I am a champion taking a fall
> I am a jockey with a sprained ass-hole I am the light mist
>   in which a face appears
> and it is another face of blonde . . .
>
> . . . .
> What land is this so free?
>
>   (*OCP*, 256)

If the "endless" construction of subjectivity reveals, as in the previous poem, how
"things," such as identities, "can suddenly be reached, held, dropped and known"
(*OCP*, 293), "In Memory of My Feelings" appears to want to push that insight
as far as it can go, consecrating the "Grace / to be born and live as variously as
possible," in perhaps O'Hara's most famous lines (*OCP*, 256)—pushing that insight, indeed, to the poet's very grave (and beyond) with the commemoration of
these lines on his tombstone. But just how much of a departure is O'Hara's an-

36. Butler, "Imitation and Gender Insubordination," 26 (and further in *Bodies That Matter*, 75); Žižek, *The Sublime Object of Ideology*, 173 (emphases retained), 75; Silverman, *The Threshold of the Visible World*, 95; Žižek, *The Sublime Object of Ideology*, 75. In thinking about O'Hara's counter-ideo-logical "reality," earlier, as a discursive excess or surplus, we find Žižek in the same text advancing our thinking about subjectivity in precisely these terms, as well, for: "there is always a certain remnant, a certain leftover escaping the circle of subjectivation, of subjective appropriation-mediation, and the subject is precisely correlative to this leftover. . . . The leftover which resists 'subjectivation' embodies the impossibility which 'is' the subject . . . [and yet] its limit is its positive condition" (209).

swer above from his war hero, or from any number of enlisted men for that matter, to whom it is thought O'Hara might have initially come out?[37]

Consider, for example, the following from a letter written by a gay infantry-
man ("Jerry Watson") to a friend, in 1944:

> I have not two personalities, but many. I can act the young, friendly, palsy walsy
> kid . . . who would not object to perverse advances made by my buddies . . . or I
> can be the quiet, thoughtful individual, with . . . closed mouth (sometimes very
> necessary) with sad, or mysterious eyes, and sometimes with a twinkle, or the
> scholar, interested in nothing but the consuming of book material and the like, or
> the flippant ageless fairy, tho with some dignity and reserve. Then again, I can be
> the sportsman, who usually commits himself to perversity if the conditions warrant,
> or the young man who seems to be like the others in his crowd, drinking jammily,
> and ending up the party with more liquor [sic] at someone's country retreat. Well,
> they all center around the great nucleus of pleasure.

The intense role-playing in this excerpt, perverse at times, artfully staged about
some "great nucleus of pleasure" so strikingly reminiscent of O'Hara's dark center
or Žižek's encircled void—the sublime "objects" of ideology, as it were—such
theatricalization no doubt also puts us in mind of that strategy of appearances
that replaces all claims to truth in our earlier dissection of camp reality, or what
O'Hara might call "the literary curse": "making everything known." In the present
text of O'Hara, "every seaman / with one eye closed in fear . . . at a sigh for
Lord Nelson" (OCP, 255) stakes such an ontologically phallic claim. And because
O'Hara intends nothing "metaphysical" in what he writes—"Abstraction (in
poetry, not in painting) involves personal removal by the poet," he proclaims (SS,
110–11, emphasis added; also Gooch 131), such a personage "is all dead" (OCP,
255). In his place, O'Hara offers "a meek subaltern" quite like "Jerry Watson" in
the above letter who "writhes in his bedclothes / with the fury of a thousand,
violating an insane mistress," located presumably within the heteronormative
dyad, "who has only herself to offer his multitudes" (OCP, 255).[38]

37. On O'Hara's tombstone, see Bill Berkson and Joe LeSueur, eds., *Homage to Frank O'Hara*
(Berkeley, 1980), 43; and on O'Hara's coming out in the navy, Gooch, *City Poet*, 64, 91.

38. "Jerry Watson," quoted in Bérubé, *Coming Out Under Fire*, 53; Gooch, *City Poet*, 254 (further
on 162–63 and 282; cf. Breslin, "Frank O'Hara," 275); Gooch, *City Poet*, 131 (on "abstraction"). In
sum, "Identities are always relational," George Chauncey asserts, and are "produced by the ways people affiliate themselves with or differentiate themselves from others," and goes on further to provide
a quite similar example of a gay man who, during a single evening, "might adopt several different
personas," as he makes his way from work to home. Chauncey, *Gay New York*, 273, 276; 163, 191,
and 274 are related.

The "writhing" in this furious portrait brings forward O'Hara's favorite gesture of "turning" noted earlier, and dealt with extensively in the Pragmatist context in the preceding chapter. The emphasis on strenuous movement in both actions can only intensify O'Hara's animus against metaphysics, since the "[f]ear of aberrant movement finds its counterpart in the affirmation of stasis as a metaphysical ideal," the loss of which, for humankind, "can only be regained in transcendence, the move through death to eternal rest." The "grace" to live variously marking the grave site of our own poet's eternal rest would thus appear to be a perverse parody of such idealism, as is the manifestation of that sacred virtue in the several allusions to snakes throughout the poem, a trope obviously not for Evil, but rather for plurality or "demoniacal texture . . . in areas where monologism appears to be the Law." Hence,

> My transparent selves
> flail about like vipers in a pail, writhing and hissing
> without panic, with a certain justice of response
> and presently the aquiline serpent comes to resemble the Medusa.
>
> (*OCP,* 253)

The separation, in this passage, between the narrator's viperous subjectivity—elsewhere, his "several likenesses," his "number of naked selves," his beautiful "lives," and so forth (*OCP,* 252, 253, 256)—and the Medusa-like serpent, restates, once again, the excess of distance impossibly opened up between subjectivity's achievement and its reality for O'Hara. "I am not quite you," he has his narrator address the serpent in the poem's final section, "but almost, the opposite of a visionary" (*OCP,* 256). Until he can actually *be* the serpent, he has only his "love of the serpent" (*OCP,* 253), the absence of desire once again, but in any case, "to move is to love" (*OCP,* 256). The ever present danger, of course, is that we can often weary of renewing our "selves" each day, and that an idolatrous "cancerous statue" can so easily come to take the place of the nucleus of pleasure, that is "[u]ntil we discover under the rubble of those ideological structures," observes Julia Kristeva, ". . . that they were extravagant and shy attempts intended to quench a thirst for love." In which case, the statue must be torn down, in the "scene of my selves" that concludes the poem, in order wantonly "to save the serpent in their midst" (*OCP,* 257).[39]

39. Dollimore, *Sexual Dissidence,* 118; Roland Barthes, *Image-music-text,* ed. and trans. Stephen Heath (New York, 1977), 160; Julia Kristeva, *Tales of Love,* trans. Leon S. Roudiez (New York, 1987), 5. As in O'Hara, "the whole pleasure of love is in changing," for Kristeva, and writing is "an emptying

The collocation of serpent and statue at the end of "In Memory of My Feelings" raises a final issue with respect to O'Hara's perverse distanciation of subjectivity that increases its political valence within the specific historical and social context of America: for "now it is the serpent's turn"—America's "aquiline serpent," previously—"which is our democracy" (*OCP*, 253, 256). The dilemma might be stated thus: In the land that "is so free" alluded to earlier, it is the hemorrhaging of the ideological economy that delivers us up to "The Word" and "what wit . . . we compound in an / eye[/I]" and "in excess" ("A Postcard from John Ashbery" [*OCP*, 56])—delivers us up, in other words, to the semiological economy. If America *is* the last Word within that economy, its restive serpent-like guile tempts us to "take a helicopter into the 'eye' of the storm" where "we'll be so happy in the center of things at last" ("Biotherm" [*OCP*, 444]), which represents approximately the impasse with the statue just described. Yet that centering of the pleasure-circle cannot explain an earlier moment in "Biotherm" when,

> . . . the other day I was walking through a train
> with my suitcase and I overheard someone say "speaking of faggots"
> now isn't life difficult enough without that
>
> . . . .
>
> well everything can't be perfect
> you said it
>
>   (*OCP*, 441–42)

What seems to come unraveled, therefore, in this "Americanization" of subjectivity is the precise function it had served in O'Hara's "Ode": as a vital space for opening up opposing fields of discourse to each other in the "crosslike" mutual relations of prohibition as well as production that constitute its own dynamic construction. At the join between—hence, imbricated within—each, but identi-

---

out—or infinitization, or indefinitization—of perversion." Kristeva, *Tales of Love*, 195, 340. "[M]y force is in mobility," the poet remarks elsewhere (*OCP*, 345). This whole set of issues, namely, a serpent-form "gulping after formlessness," a capitol or statue "just / collapsed" and linked to "a single man contained," and their mediation by "the velocities of change," are conceivably all borrowings from Wallace Stevens' "Auroras of Autumn" (1947 [*SCP*, 411, 416, 414]). Gooch writes that both O'Hara and John Ashbery "agreed on the importance of Wallace Stevens, whose *The Auroras of Autumn* would be published in 1950, while mutually downplaying T. S. Eliot." Gooch, *City Poet*, 138; also on 446 and *SS*, 23, but refuted by Perloff, *Frank O'Hara*, 62, 191. Gooch further observes that one of O'Hara's favorite self-stylizations was as a snake after reading Sacher-Masoch's *The Serpent in Paradise* in college: "His weaving together of sexuality and apostasy resulted in a curious blend of exhibitionistic liberation and more hidden pessimism." Gooch, *City Poet*, 197.

fiable with neither, "Lucky Pierre style," so to speak (*SS*, 111), this rather perverse notion of subjectivity bears considerable relation to the "*point de capiton*" in Laclau and Mouffe's theory of radical democracy. As Slavoj Žižek explains,

> [This complex designator] is not a point of supreme density of Meaning, a kind of Guarantee which, by being excepted from the differential interplay of elements, would serve as a fixed point of reference. On the contrary, it is the element which represents the agency of the signifier within the field of the signified. In itself it is nothing but a 'pure difference' . . . the element through which the signifier's non-sense erupts in the midst of meaning . . . [and] is perceived as a point of extreme saturation of meaning, as the point which "gives meaning" to all the others and thus totalizes the field of (ideological meaning) . . . as *ideological anamorphosis*.

Hence, we should not find O'Hara's political contextualization of the serpent's "turn" in relation to "democracy" necessarily problematic, provided it's an *articulatory* rather than an *identificatory* relation that we are in touch with: a semiotic relation as opposed to a mimetic one. "When you turn your head / can you feel yours heels, undulating? that's what it is / *to be* a serpent" (*OCP*, 256). As Judith Butler would say, "the copula is empty."[40] Let me conclude this section of the chapter with an illustration.

Earlier, we spoke of the space in the camp text opened up between reader and reality as one in excess of all possible determinate identification, and therefore, a site for the interpretive (per)versions of experience. What happens if that reality becomes the experience of subjectivity itself? More precisely, what if the subject position were masculine? In the ironization of experience that we can anticipate to uncover at this excessive site of differential articulation, there can be no representations of guaranteed meanings and no imitations of ultimate truths, but effectively, the construction of identity as a cultural registration of contest and negotiation. Here is an example from within the approximate time period in which O'Hara did most of his writing:

---

40. Žižek, *The Sublime Object of Ideology*, 99; Butler, "Imitation and Gender Insubordination," 16. In Ernesto Laclau and Chantal Mouffe, *Hegemony and Socialist Strategy: Towards a Radical Democratic Politics* (New York, 1995), the specific "construction of nodal points which partially fix meaning" is the effect of "the constant overflowing of every discourse by the infinitude of the field of discursivity," which, similar to O'Hara's reality, is equivalent to a "surplus [as] the necessary terrain for the constitution of every social practice" (113, 111). Bredbeck, following Diana Fuss' deployment of feminist rather than radical democratic theory, arrives at a similar formulation: "For signification for O'Hara is not a space marked off by difference but is the difference itself, the phenomenon that erases truth and reserve and that 'means' only in the present tense, depriviging the totalizing inscriptions of tradition." Bredbeck, "B/O," 279.

As much as the code of personal behavior for dress and mannerisms was modeled on heterosexual society, it was not simply imitative. Butches of the 1940s and 1950s actively worked to create a unique image. Their goal was not to pass as men. Although many of them knew passing women or might even have passed as men for short periods in their lives, as part of the lesbian community they were recognized on the streets as women who looked "different" and therefore challenged mainstream mores and made it possible for lesbians to find one another. . . . Untouchability expressed difference from the fem, control over one's life, and ambivalence about one's female body, all characteristics of the butch persona. [Thus,] the strong concern for role-appropriate eroticism developed in creative tension with the culture's validation of female sexuality and emphasis on learning about and exploring new sexual practices. . . . In reaction to the dominant ideas about women needing men for sexual satisfaction, these butches projected themselves as better in bed than any man. . . . Ironically, the rigidification of roles and the openness about sexuality interacted to create an erotic system predicated above all on the sexual satisfaction of women.

The masculine subjectivity, specifically the lesbian positionality of the "butch," that materializes at the intersection between straight and gay communities, is "not simply imitative," it is true, resistant as it is to the heteronormative ideology of "women needing men." Yet in challenging mainstream sexual mores and in exploring new ones, "the sexual satisfaction of women" for a change, we're still not any closer to identifying precisely what women looking "different" might actually be. The force of that concluding "Ironically" that we *do* seem most clear about with respect to the deployment of masculine subjectivity described here directs our attention, instead, more to the "creative tension" and to the "interaction" between two kinds of discrete though not completely antithetical sexual performance. So that if the articulation of a perverse masculine subjectivity is ironical in this instance, it's only because the idea of ironic meaning, like the serpentine subjectivity of Frank O'Hara as we've been exploring it, is relational, "the result of the bringing—even the rubbing—together of the said and the unsaid, each of which takes on meaning only in relation to the other." In Linda Hutcheon's further expansion of this ironical point, "it is not the two 'poles' themselves that are important; it is the idea of a kind of rapid perceptual or hermeneutic *movement between* them that makes this [rabbit/duck] image a possibly suggestive and productive one for thinking about irony . . . as something in flux, and not fixed." And for thinking about queer perversion as well, I would add, given the possible social context of an ironized subjectivity as in the above example.[41]

41. Elizabeth Lapovsky Kennedy and Madeline D. Davis, *Boots of Leather, Slippers of Gold: The*

The "additive oscillation" in the perversion of subjectivity will thus underscore, once again, its manifestation as pure difference in Žižek's previous formulation, or the "blackness in the center" of a dialectical turning in O'Hara's, given only to us as the blind intimation of a serpentine undulation. To repeat those extraordinary lines: "When you turn your head / can you feel your heels, undulating? that's what it is / to be a serpent" (OCP, 256). Thus, in "Poem (I don't know as I get what D. H. Lawrence is driving at)," from the next year (1959), we read:

> of light we can never have enough
> but how would we find it
> unless the darkness urged us on and into it
> and I am dark
> except when now and then it all comes clear
> and I can see myself
> as others luckily sometimes see me
> in a good light
>
> (OCP, 335)

In commenting on a similar "light of illumination that never arrives" ultimately, Butler is given to ask: "Is this infinite postponement of the disclosure of 'gayness,' produced by the very act of 'coming out' to be lamented? Or is this very deferral of the signified to be valued, a site for the production of values, precisely because the term now takes on a life that cannot be, can never be, permanently controlled?" André Gide once saw in the forces of permanent control the "sphinxes of conformity," whom he thought it was his first duty to attack. To O'Hara, such outright opposition would have appeared too much like "faithlessness / apologizing to the Sphinx" ("Invincibility" [OCP, 123]). If anything was to be valued, it was, ironically, the presentiment of control itself, which like the image of the Berlin Wall in the Cold War climate of his own day, could always be imagined to "drift back and forth according to the temperament of the artist and the temper of the time" (SS, 164), so like the undulation of subjectivity that egregiously comes to parody it. In that scandalous solicitation of proscription—solicit, here, in the sense of both "to importune" and "to disturb"—we fleetingly catch sight in the distance, for a final time, the queer perversions of the poet's own proliferating inscription, whose extraordinary wisdom it is to find in the sphinxes of conform-

History of a Lesbian Community (New York, 1993), 167, 214; Linda Hutcheon, Irony's Edge: The Theory and Politics of Irony (New York, 1994), 59–60; further on 66, 81, 88, and 209n. 49.

ity "the wistful sphinx of myself" ("Hatred" [*OCP*, 118]). Better yet, the wisdom in fellow seaman "Jerry Watson's" very own words, once again: the "perversion [that] is our destiny."[42]

The various intersections that I have endeavored to tease out between a New York School poet of the '50s and two or three queer theorists in the '90s, in the end, continue to provoke us to wonder whether Frank O'Hara becomes *diminished* as a writer in the face of the trendy discourses that some would argue he anticipates. Can "forerunners" ever be interesting in their own right? To answer this question, much, I suppose, would depend on what we imagine the poet to be a forerunner *of.* The claim, according to one of my respondents earlier, that O'Hara becomes less interesting for us today because he "merely discovered early on what we now think we 'know' about the politics of identity," and so forth, could certainly be a defensible one in terms of a whiggish narrative of progress. Yet it is precisely the extravagant investment of O'Hara's project in *not knowing,* as I previously attempted to show in some detail, that draws us to the very heart of his queer perversity, such as it is, and gathers us up into its great nucleus of pleasure. In an essay on "Franz Kline," O'Hara contextualizes the point in terms of Abstract Expressionist "style": "Like with Jackson [Pollock]: you don't paint the way someone, by observing your life, thinks you *have* to paint, you paint the way you have to in order to *give,* that's life itself, and someone will look and say it is the product of knowing, but it has nothing to do with knowing, it has to do with giving. *The question about knowing will naturally be wrong.* When you've finished giving, the look surprises you as well as anyone else" (*AC,* 52, terminal emphasis added). And it is for this privilege of not knowing, as it were, for this "unsettlement rather than systematization," that I think his stature as a writer enlarges for us rather than diminishes, and that he becomes *more* interesting rather than *less.*[43]

42. Hutcheon, *Irony's Edge,* 66; Butler, "Imitation and Gender Insubordination," 216; Dollimore, *Sexual Dissidence,* 12; Bérubé, *Coming Out Under Fire,* 252.

43. Berlant and Warner, "What Does Queer Theory Teach Us About *X*?" 348. A further comment from "Helen Frankenthaler" in O'Hara's *Art Chronicles* is related: "For in the reception of this psychic meaning [i.e., "the act of 'receiving' lyrical insight"], the artist, *as if unknowingly or subconsciously,* retains identification with the simultaneous art-experience" (*AC,* 125, emphasis added). The "exhilaration of uncertainty's openness" (the phrase is Kimberly Benston's ["'I Yam What I Am,'" 162]) contained in such a "remark" perhaps leads John Caputo to conclude that Foucault, like O'Hara, has "an entirely negative idea of the individual." Caputo elaborates: "He struggles against any 'positive' theory of the individual that takes itself seriously, that thinks it has the truth of truth, that thinks it can affirmatively say or positively identify who we are. He opposes all 'cataphatic' discourse about the individual, discourse that tries to say what the individual is or should be, and he does so in the name of a kind of 'apophatic' discourse, of preserving a purely apophatic freedom. . . .

But doesn't O'Hara's elective ignorance also point to what is most provocative and compelling about today's queer theorist? Isn't David Halperin, for instance, more rather than less interesting when, like O'Hara, he adjures his reader "to make use of the vacancy left by the evacuation of the contradictory and incoherent definitional content of the 'homosexual' in order to take up instead a position that is (and always has been) defined . . . by its distance to and difference from the normative"? And doesn't Halperin's distancing theory become even *more* interesting for us in view of the deployment of a similar line of argument in O'Hara's own work—one which I could hardly avoid citing earlier in my argument, to wit: "I may become famous for a *mysterious vacancy* in that department, that greenhouse" (*OCP*, 197, emphasis added).[44] Is either queer theory or poetic practice at all diminished by the admirably counter-intuitive epistemological agreements they secure between themselves, even ones so separated as these are by time and place and vocation and temperament? If so, I'm frankly at a loss to imagine how.

The various allegorical alignments between past and present queer discourses that, throughout this chapter, I find both legitimate and useful to honor will continue, no doubt, to strike some as yet another argument for privileging theory at the expense of practice. The view that theory, in such terms, will always patronize practice, in effect indenture the slave-poet to some master-theorist(s)—such a view, to my mind, is largely a matter of perception, and there's really very little one can do to counter it. O'Hara, I think, would bemoan the argument's lopsidedness. "Such criticism is panoramic and non-specific," he would argue. "It tends to sum up, not divulge. This is a very useful method if the truth is one, but where there is a multiplicity of truths it is delimiting and misleading, most often involving a preference for one truth above another, and thus contributing to the avoidance of cultural acknowledgement" (*AC*, 13).

The avoidance of "cultural acknowledgement"—selling a Cold War poet considerably short, in this instance—is the impasse to which queer theory itself may have brought us, where even an argument *against* theory can only be yet another "theoretical" argument. But the irony of "cultural avoidance" by a discourse thought to be one of the jewels in the cultural studies crown is perhaps one of the more ghastly effects resulting from the enormous avalanche of material on

[Ultimately,] Foucault wants to keep open the negative space of what the individual is *not*, of what we *cannot* say the individual is, to preserve the space of a certain negativity that refuses all positivity, all identification, that is always in the end a historical trap." Caputo, "On Not Knowing Who We Are," 251, emphases retained.

44. Halperin, *Saint Foucault*, 61.

gay-related topics that academic presses having been pouring out in the last few years. Considering its sheer vastness, one wonders if, today, we haven't been too easily lulled into thinking that not very much of any earth-shaking value could possibly have gone on yesterday, or the day before, by comparison. In the scramble to keep up, it's so easy to become seduced by the narrative of progress, once again—the story that as far as "theoretical" thinking goes, the 1969 Stonewall riot in New York City was the floodgate, and up to then, in a desert dotted with a few oases, it's been pretty much catch-as-catch can. Writers like Frank O'Hara go a fair distance to problematize that myth. But it hardly seems possible to mount that case convincingly unless we can find him standing his own ground with as much critical insight, theoretical sophistication, and political savvy— maybe even more—than the radical chic of more recent times induces us to think that we can find *only* in the "sexiness" of a Butler or a Dollimore or a Case.

At the end of the day, I would like to think it still possible to defer to a multiplicity of truths, as O'Hara mentions, rather than delimiting our cultural acknowledgments to one panoramic view or one summative (and ultimately misleading) perception. In the poet's own case, one might imagine his canonical status becoming enhanced in the way he contributes to bolster and flatter today's queer theory platform. But the reverse can quite conceivably be true, taking into account a certain determinate resistance to theory that most students in an undergraduate English program are likely to manifest. So that when Butler or Dollimore or Case are enlisted to illuminate the otherwise sexually eviscerated or institutionally vitiated canonical text, rather than paying queer compliments to the author, in the highly charged negotiation between theory and praxis, the author actually gets to pay *them* the compliment by showing, through the means of *literary* discourse, precisely the extent to which queer theory can (and does) perform important cultural, social, and politically viable work. My real point about multiplicity, here, is to acknowledge that there's enough of a mutual investment from *both* sides of the queer cultural-studies divide to make the ongoing negotiation between theory and practice always *more* beneficial and interesting for each, rather than less. For that reason, both theory and practice become self-affirming and self-authenticating for everyone concerned, despite sometimes what the vast separations by time looming in the middle distance often condition texts to say (or us not say).

Much of what I have attempted to clarify in the previous three sections of this chapter about the use and status of queer texts in the act of literary interpretation, in retrospect, I had originally thought ought to have been self-evident in the various readings performed on a highly selected number of poems drawn from Frank

O'Hara's extensive canon. In defense of those first efforts, I'm tempted to fall back on Theodor Adorno's remark about such undertakings: "The pleasures which rhetoric wants to provide to its audience are sublimated in the essay into the idea of the pleasure of freedom vis-à-vis the object, freedom that gives the object more of itself than if it were mercilessly incorporated into the order of ideas."[45] If, after having ventured several further clarifications of that original effort, the final "form" of my chapter-essay has sacrificed some of its initial "pleasure of freedom"—giving "less" of O'Hara by incorporating "more" of his poetry into queer theory's "order of ideas"—I feel the sacrifice would have been worth it if an actual *argument* for methodological interpretation has come to take the place of its mere *exemplification*. Nonetheless, the queer perversities of O'Hara have conditioned me sufficiently, I hope, to retain some of my original naïveté about the pleasure of his poetry, and the "more" that that object might still continue to give "of itself."

At this point, I'm reminded of something "more" that post-Stonewall pundits think they ought to be able to say, now, about that "great mystery" and the "one great trauma" that allegedly beset Walt Whitman in young adulthood, almost one hundred years earlier. Was it an act of sodomy or child abuse, or was it just a puritanical shame about "the kind of same-sex passion that was common among both men and women in nineteenth-century America"? According to his most recent biographer, David Reynolds, one of Whitman's responses to this dark event was to write the eighth number of his "Sun-Down Papers":

> In this almost pre-Melvillian piece, the protagonist dreams he searches for truth in all corners of the earth but cannot find it. The meaning of his fruitless quest is revealed to him by an angel, who shows him an allegorical vista of a huge mist-covered mountain viewed from a distance by throngs of people, all wearing different kinds of glasses. The mountain is truth, and the colored lenses are the purely subjective interpretations people of different creeds impose upon this always hidden truth.

According to Reynolds, Whitman has provided us here with "a gloomy tale," writing in what Reynolds has elsewhere anatomized as a "dark visionary mode," full of enervating skepticism and a kind of pointless relativism. The crowds of people "all wearing different kinds of glasses" are the key to such a reading, and in terms of Whitman's own sexually embattled state of mind at the time, it seems

45. Adorno, "The Essay as Form," 168.

fairly convincing.[46] Contrary to his biographer, however, I'm persuaded to feel that Whitman derived considerably *more* pleasure, and maybe even a sense of freedom, from this little narrative—pleasure and freedom of the sort just alluded to by Adorno. For it's the "huge mist-covered mountain" towards which the protagonist's attention is directed by the angel, and not the disparate and fractious and (for me) awfully "knowing" looking multitudes teeming below. And in a perverse sort of way, I'm sure Frank O'Hara, at sundown, would have found that allegorical vista viewed, significantly, "from a distance," more pleasurable as well.

46. David S. Reynolds, *Walt Whitman's America: A Cultural Biography* (New York, 1995), 69, 73, 72, 62, 62, 61.

"O Canada!":
The Spectral Lesbian Poetics of Elizabeth Bishop

> *What I tire of quickly in Wallace Stevens is the self-consciousness—poetry so aware lacks depth. Poetry should have more of the unconscious spots left in.*
>
> —ELIZABETH BISHOP, "KEY WEST NOTEBOOKS"

> *The lowest ebb, the point of true horror, is the moment of* Versagung *[Denial] when the subject finds himself face to face with the groundless abyss of his lack of being.*
>
> —SLAVOJ ŽIŽEK, *Enjoy Your Symptom!*

> *There has never been The Subject for anyone. . . . The subject is a fable . . . but to concentrate on the elements of speech and conventional fiction that such a fable presupposes is not to stop taking it seriously.*
>
> —JACQUES DERRIDA, "'EATING WELL,' OR THE CALCULATION OF THE SUBJECT: AN INTERVIEW"

D ESPITE the great increase in awareness that the writing of Elizabeth Bishop (1911–1979) has provoked in the last few years, literary critics are still generally reluctant to talk about her sexuality. Concerning a recent collection of feminist essays on the poet (Marilyn May Lombardi, ed., *Elizabeth Bishop: The Geography of Gender* [1993]), for instance, Alicia Ostriker draws notable attention to one surprised reviewer's response to the volume: that it "has almost nothing concrete to say about [Bishop's] lesbianism." Undoubtedly, critics are respecting the poet's own longstanding reticence in dealing with her homosexuality. That Bishop had several same-sex lovers throughout her lifetime—her biographer documents at least eight such relationships—is well known, especially her sixteen-year partnership in Brazil with Lota de Macedo Soares begun at age forty, when it first seemed possible for her to start "contemplating . . . questions of lifestyle and identity, specifically of a lesbian lifestyle as it might relate to her public and private identity."[1]

Yet as I remark elsewhere in a review of Bishop's selected letters (*One Art* [1994]), hardly a word about any of these involvements is whispered throughout hundreds of pages of voluminous correspondence. And if the very last word of her "Collected Poems"—"gay," from a text entitled "Sonnet"—is a playful attempt to set the record straight, so to speak, it's an effort which Bishop undertook "only cautiously, cryptically, and belatedly, as it turned out, from beyond the grave." On this side of the grave, as gay poet Frank Bidart attests, her watchword was more likely to be "closets, closets, and more closets." "I can't quote her words exactly," Bidart continues, "but she felt that certain kinds of directness and ambition . . . had been impossible. Out of her distrust of the straight world [therefore] she didn't want people to know she was gay. She certainly didn't want people to talk about it. The irony, of course, is that everyone at least in the literary world *did* know, and didn't care; but she could never believe that this was the case." One can easily imagine, then, Bishop's infamous objection to confessional poets being directed especially at the more sexually candid among them: "You just wish they'd keep some of these things to themselves."[2]

1. Alicia Ostriker, "I Am (Not) This: Erotic Discourse in Bishop, Olds, and Stevens," *Wallace Stevens Journal* 19 (fall 1995): 254 n. 2; Brett Millier, *Elizabeth Bishop: Life and the Memory of It* (Los Angeles, 1993), 237. Ostriker's essay itself appears in a collection of ten articles on the subject of "Stevens and Elizabeth Bishop" in an issue of *The Wallace Stevens Journal* from 1995, and only her contribution, not unexpectedly, makes specific reference to Bishop's lesbianism. Three of the most recent critical monographs on the poet's work, however, help to offset the discreet silence on this important aspect of Bishop's life; namely, Victoria Harrison, *Elizabeth Bishop's Poetics of Intimacy* (New York, 1993), Susan McCabe, *Elizabeth Bishop: Her Poetics of Loss* (University Park, Pa., 1994), and most purposively, Marilyn May Lombardi, *The Body and the Song: Elizabeth Bishop's Poetics* (Carbondale, Ill., 1995), esp. Ch. 2: "'The Queer Land of Kissing': Sexuality and Representation."

2. David Jarraway, "Saint Elizabeth," review of *Elizabeth Bishop: One Art: Letters*, ed. Robert Giroux, *MLA Lesbian and Gay Studies Newsletter* 20 (summer 1995): 31; Millier, *Elizabeth Bishop*, 547; Frank Bidart, quoted in Gary Fountain and Peter Brazeau, *Remembering Elizabeth Bishop: An Oral Biography* (Amherst, 1994), 327; Elizabeth Bishop, quoted in Ashley Brown, "An Interview with Elizabeth Bishop," in *Elizabeth Bishop and Her Art*, ed. Lloyd Schwartz and Sybil P. Estess (Ann Arbor, 1983), 303. See also Millier, *Elizabeth Bishop*, 323, and *OA*, 562, 565. Harrison also notes that although "[Bishop] and [May] Swenson were living with women, they never addressed the subject of lesbianism in their letters to each other," and observes further that "Bishop did not write explicitly about sex . . . intend[ing] to jolt no reader with her bursts of sexuality." Harrison, *Elizabeth Bishop's Poetics of Intimacy*, 72, 205. "Elizabeth and I belonged to a generation of women who were

While it may be that Elizabeth Bishop was reluctant to take up the issue of her lesbian identity *explicitly* throughout her writing career, in this chapter, I want to entertain the argument that the exploration of dissident subjectivity constitutes a quite vital part of her poetic project nonetheless, particularly in the early work with which I shall be mostly concerned in the next section—a project, therefore, that we have to undertake to begin rereading in a decidedly non-referential, non-descriptive, hence more *implicitly* eroticized, libidinized, and ultimately, sexualized way. Her rather cryptic remark to Robert Lowell, that "I've always felt that I've written poetry more by *not* writing it than writing it," can thus start to foreground that "experience profoundly felt and obliquely expressed" that I shall more and more be alluding to as a certain *unspoken* dimension of thought in the Bishop canon that continues even in her later poetry, and that I shall address briefly in the chapter's final section. But particularly in the early work, I shall contend, we might locate the more implicit exploration of same-sex identity that Bishop obviously felt considerably frustrated or anxious to revolve in the referentially descriptive terms that could only suffer severe ideological curtailments on the more demonstrative level of public scrutiny. Yet to recapture the unspoken and unwritten dimension of Bishop's highly secretive but no less vital identity, as I shall further argue, requires that we travel with the poet not to the Key West and Paris of her initial lesbian attachments in the '30s and '40s, nor to the Brazil and San Francisco of her more settled domestic partnerships in the '50s and '60s. Rather than move forward in time, we have to move backward, to Bishop's childhood and early youth, to that place in Canada—Great Village in the Maritime province of Nova Scotia—whose influence was so profoundly formative of her primordial sense of selfhood that its loss must surely constitute the "decisive shock of her early life . . . when she had to give [it] up," and in one version or another, must surely express "perhaps an almost unstateable premise to all her poems" in the life, or better, the lives that followed.[3]

---

terrified by the idea of being known as lesbians," Canadian artist and writer Mary Meigs reveals, "and for Elizabeth as poet, the lesbian label would have been particularly dangerous . . . so that a kind of caution was exercised (certainly it was by Elizabeth) that no longer seems necessary today." Meigs, quoted in Fountain and Brazeau, *Remembering Elizabeth Bishop*, 86. Thus, Lombardi, *The Body and the Song*, aptly speaks of "a woman and a lesbian bound to leading a life of surface conformity and concealed depths" (34).

3. Elizabeth Bishop, quoted in McCabe, *Elizabeth Bishop*, 194; Joanne Feit Diehl, *Women Poets and the American Sublime* (Bloomington, 1990), 93; David Kalstone, *Becoming a Poet: Elizabeth Bishop with Marianne Moore and Robert Lowell*, ed. with a preface by David Hemenway and an afterword by James Merrill (New York, 1989), 26; Peter Sanger, "Elizabeth Bishop and Nova Scotia," *Antigonish Review* 60 (1985): 21.

Elizabeth Bishop, of course, was not Canadian herself. She was brought to Canada by her maternal grandparents in her first year as a consequence of her mother's nervous breakdown and sequestration in a Boston sanatorium, perhaps resulting from the premature death of her husband from Bright's disease in 1911. After five relatively happy years shared among doting grandparents and several loving aunts "in a child's beautiful dream of life," Elizabeth was reunited with her mother in Nova Scotia in 1916, whereupon the mother fell into an incurable insanity, and Elizabeth was removed once again. This time she was taken by her paternal grandparents back to her birthplace in Worcester, Massachusetts, in 1917, "for the one awful winter," as she recalls it, "that was almost the end of me." Sent to live permanently with a matronly aunt the following year, Bishop began writing poetry at the age of eight, and apparently never stopped. She never saw her mother again.[4]

In a quite general way, then, the writing of Elizabeth Bishop stands on guard as a kind of national anthem—a hymn of praise, in the generic sense foregrounded by my title—for a country to which, despite her own citizenship, she would remain fiercely loyal from her earliest years. In her autobiographical prose reminiscence "The Country Mouse," mostly recollecting the childhood year of her fateful return to the States, she recounts that "most of all I hated saluting the [American] flag":

> I would have refused if I had dared. In my Canadian schooling the year before, we had started every day with "God Save the King" and "The Maple Leaf Forever." Now I felt like a traitor. I wanted to win the War, of course, but I didn't want to be an American. When I went home to lunch, I said so. Grandma was horrified; she almost wept. Shortly after, I was presented with a white card with an American flag in color at the top. All the stanzas of "Oh, say, can you see" were printed on it in dark blue letters. Every day I sat at Grandma's feet and attempted to recite this endless poem. . . . Most of the words made no sense at all.
>
> (*BCPr*, 26–27)

The extraordinary sense of self-division in this vivid portrait of the hapless child stationed reluctantly at her paternal grandmother's feet perhaps underscores most of all the paradoxical significance that Canada represents to this modern American poet—a significance that oddly appears to resonate at a distance—more from

4. Lombardi, *The Body and the Song*, 209 (see also 41); Elizabeth Bishop, quoted in Kalstone, *Becoming a Poet*, 27.

the side of the foreign than from the native, from the unstatable rather than the articulable, from loss rather than gain.[5]

From this irreducible paradox, moreover, we come most to understand that, in much of her writing, the importance of place for Bishop invariably resides in a world elsewhere: if in Key West, "with the village pieties and simplicities that recalled Nova Scotia," as David Kalstone points out, or if in Brazil, with "her Nova Scotia childhood [that Brazil] helped her recapitulate and reclaim," and so forth. One wonders somewhat fancifully, indeed, if Aunt Consuelo's "*oh!* of pain," so memorably recounted in the later "In the Waiting Room" (1971), and set in Worcester, Massachusetts, in her final book of poetry (*BCP*, 160), is but another anthemic variation on the "O Canada!" underscoring so much of the hurtful feeling of displacement throughout Bishop's work.[6]

Critics of Bishop's poetry who tactfully manage to avoid saying very much about her lesbianism are perhaps for the most part also looking at an *American* poet. And, no doubt, an important overarching theme like displacement can be usefully understood precisely to the degree that it returns us to the greatness of a modern American writer that Elizabeth Bishop by now has generally come to be acclaimed. "Canada" in Bishop's life and work, however, should at least tell us that what we are confronted with in her case is not just one identity, but two. To begin to separate the *explicit* from the *implicit* identity in Bishop,[7] and as I men-

---

5. "I didn't even know," Joseph Frank admits candidly, "if Elizabeth was American or not. I wasn't quite clear because she spoke so much about Nova Scotia. I had the feeling that she didn't feel at home in this country somehow, that she was rather alien from that point of view because [these] early years had shaped her sensibility in such a way. She wasn't a regular fellow—she was more Canadian and more English than she was American." Frank, quoted in Fountain and Brazeau, *Remembering Elizabeth Bishop*, 116.

6. Kalstone, *Becoming a Poet*, 68, 196. Bishop's sense of "existential displacement" (Diehl, *Women Poets and the American Sublime*, 93) is also taken up by Barbara Page, "Elizabeth Bishop and Postmodernism," *Wallace Stevens Journal* 19 (fall 1995), 169; McCabe, *Elizabeth Bishop*, 25; and Lombardi, *The Body and the Song* 24 (Harrison, *Elizabeth Bishop's Poetics of Intimacy*, 22–23, is related). As Robert Dale Parker observes more generally, "The very act of imagination presupposes some displacement (*différance*) from an original that the same displacement defies." Robert Dale Parker, *The Unbeliever: The Poetry of Elizabeth Bishop* (Urbana, 1988), 71. For a specific enumeration and summary of all of the poems, essays, and stories based upon Bishop's life in Nova Scotia, see Sanger, "Elizabeth Bishop and Nova Scotia." For an extensive biographical recounting of Bishop's several returns to Maritime Canada throughout her life, see Millier, *Elizabeth Bishop*, passim, most of which is summarized in my review of *Elizabeth Bishop: Life and the Memory of It*, by Brett C. Millier, *Journal of Canadian Poetry* 10 (1995), 140–41.

7. As with previous poets in this study, the characterization here is not untypical of a certain Pragmatist predisposition as Ray Carney describes it: "inextricably embedded in the group, never to

tioned earlier, to undertake a much fuller understanding of the lesbian subject
developed and carried forward in her work primarily in terms of the latter, we
might do well to meditate further on the the significance to Bishop of the loss of
her mother outlined previously. But even here, we seem to be confronted with
two discrete types of loss rather than a single one.

Drucilla Cornell, in her Lacanian theorizing about "our radical cut from the
maternal body," observes how the primordial loss of the mother from birth can
be radically different for men and for women. Writes Cornell:

> Men are construed in relation to signifiers that are different from the ones to which
> women relate. The subjectivity of the masculine subject is guaranteed a fixed posi-
> tion in the realm reigned by phallic reference. But the price paid for this fixed posi-
> tion is still a form of symbolic castration. . . . Women, by contrast, because they
> are barred from the Mother and thus a primary signifier by which to organize their
> identity, cannot find "themselves" in the order of the symbolic. . . . [Accordingly,]
> [i]f the privilege of the phallus as the primary signifier of sexual difference fixes
> man in his subject position, it dislocates woman from any fixed position on which
> to ground her subjectivity. What is left over, for Lacan, is beyond expression. The
> feminine imaginary cannot be given form because it cannot find the symbolic
> "stuff" to register the diversification of feminine sexual difference.

Bishop's first real experience of mother-loss to mental illness following the death
of her father, thus prompting her "maternal" removal to Canada, uncannily seems
to rehearse a general stage of dislocation in the poet's early life which conceivably
might have had the effect, as described here, of freeing her "from any fixed position on which to ground her subjectivity." Bishop's own recollection from this
period of the image of the child that so "horrified" her paternal grandparents—
"the only child of their eldest son running about the village in bare feet, eating at
the table with the grown-ups and drinking tea," and so forth—this image seems
to parallel only too well "the figure of the Woman outside the system who slides
out from under its strictures and dictates," and whose "very lack of a fixed signi-

---

be released from its pressures or even able to want to turn [one's] back on it, but with this imaginative
movement [by which one] has also forevermore been propelled outside of it, at an *infinite distance*
from it, reflecting on it." Carney, *American Vision*, 435, emphasis added. As George Kateb further
observes (in "Hannah Arendt: Alienation and America"), "The key to [the individual's] stature is self-
consciousness carried to the point of what Emerson calls, with mixed feelings, the 'double-consciousness' in 'The Transcendentalist' and 'Fate' . . . There is no social identity worth holding on to. The
self is loose-fitting . . . There is restlessness, contradiction, bursting all confines. . . ." Kateb, quoted
in Carney, *American Vision*, 401; further on 156, 400–401, 424, and passim.

fied" makes "this sliding between the positionings of femininity . . . always possible." Hypothetically (and analogically), then, Bishop's own feminine positioning as a lesbian from a quite early age becomes one of the *possibilities* that accrue to her construction of sexuality by virtue of her sliding between two cultures, allowing her to avoid any fixed or normative gender assignment in the way that her national identity remains indeterminable. In this subject position's very ungroundedness—Is Bishop American, or is she Canadian?—the dissident poet thus stands "to endlessly challenge any interpretation of [Woman] as [her] ultimate truth."[8]

The precisely unlocatable and hence inexpressible subjectivity that we might only implicitly identify in Bishop as "Canadian" and "lesbian," therefore, points to the positive effects of mother-loss, especially in terms of the strong sense of independence, mobility, and free-spiritedness such separation inevitably instills in the young child. When Bishop, however, attributes to herself "a prize 'unhappy childhood,' almost good enough for the text-books," she gives voice to a second type of loss replete with negatives. Drucilla Cornell, once again, is instructive in characterizing these negatives, observing that with women, "identified as lack," and as "the castrated Other," the "hole [they] leave in reality" as the ultimate objects of desire "[becomes] filled with masculine fantasy" in their patriarchal designation and peremptory consignment within culture's symbolic order. In Elizabeth Bishop's case, we are thus reminded of her second experience with maternal loss following her mother's permanent incarceration in an insane asylum in Dartmouth, Nova Scotia, and Bishop's own enforced return to the States that, among other impositions, requires her dutifully to memorize verses in honor of Uncle Sam at the foot of her paternal grandmother. In this conscripted transition from one loss to the other in the apparent exchange between Bishop's implicit "Canadian" and her explicit "American" identity, the "hole" she and her mother both ultimately leave in reality is achieved not without significant sacrifice. For Bishop, an uncanny anticipation of this (w)hole transition apparently came early: "My own first ride on a swan boat occurred at the age of three and is chiefly memorable for the fact that one of the live swans paddling around us bit my mother's finger when she offered it a peanut. I remember the hole in the black kid glove and a drop of blood."[9]

8. Drucilla Cornell, "What Is Ethical Feminism?" in *Feminist Contentions: A Philosophical Exchange?* intro. Linda Nicholson (New York, 1995), 88, 89–90; Elizabeth Bishop, quoted in Kalstone, *Becoming a Poet,* 27; Cornell, "What Is Ethical Feminism?" 93, 97, 99.

9. Elizabeth Bishop, quoted in Kalstone, *Becoming a Poet,* 25; Cornell, "What Is Ethical Feminism?" 90; Elizabeth Bishop, quoted in Brown, "An Interview with Elizabeth Bishop," 282; *cf. BCPr,* ix.

The image of a bloody hole opening up painfully within a covering or containment of blackness is an extraordinarily powerful one for us as we find our own
selves struggling, much like Bishop, to see through the ideological constraints of
her Americanism, and peer into something more implicitly free-floating, uncontrollable, unsayable off in the distance: "O Canada!" In characterizing further the
relation between hole and glove here, we might find Slavoj Žižek's description of
the "asymmetry" between two "returns" of the repressed in Lacan quite useful:
namely, "that of the stain of the Real where the word fails[, and] that of the
signifier to fill out the void that gapes in the midst of representational reality"—
two repressive returns that may be schematically aligned with the two types of
maternal loss just described that would haunt Elizabeth Bishop since childbirth.[10]
    Žižek elaborates further on their asymmetry when he notes how strongly it is
dependent, following Lacan, "on the split between reality and the Real":

> "Reality" is the field of symbolically structured representations, the outcome of
> symbolic "gentrification" of the Real; yet a surplus of the Real always eludes the
> symbolic grasp and persists as a non-symbolized stain, a hole in reality which desig-
> nates the ultimate limit where "the word fails" . . . as an attempt to inscribe into
> the symbolic order the surplus that eludes the field of representation.

Now if Elizabeth Bishop's implicitly lesbian subjectivity becomes possible only as
a function of a Real that eludes symbolic articulation within reality's dark holes—
poetry with "the unconscious spots left in," as she puts it in one of her Key West
Notebooks—little wonder, then, that she has so little *programmatically* to say
about homosexuality in her work, and that we should find ourselves falling relatively silent on this issue as well.[11]

    10. Slavoj Žižek, "'In His Bold Gaze My Ruin Is Writ Large,'" in *Everything You Always Wanted
to Know about Lacan (But Were Afraid to Ask Hitchcock)*, ed. Slavoj Žižek (New York, 1992), 239.
Victoria Harrison offers the fascinating archival evidence of Bishop's various attempts to turn her
anecdote of the swan-bite into a poem on three separate occasions, wherein a "child faces a terrifying
thought: perhaps her mother's 'madness & death' began here in this bloody hole." Harrison, *Elizabeth
Bishop's Poetics of Intimacy*, 134–37. Elsewhere, she cites Chase Twichell's thesis that each poem of
Bishop's "has a hole at its heart, a hollow spot" that sets up a "complex tension between the thing
said and the thing unsaid." Twichell, quoted in Harrison, *Elizabeth Bishop's Poetics of Intimacy*, 109;
see also 120. Although Harrison finds Twichell's position to be a close approximation of Lacan's
theory of "metonymy," she apparently does not find this theory very useful herself in studying Bishop
225 n. 14, unlike McCabe, *Elizabeth Bishop*, 131, and Lombardi, *The Body and the Song*, 242 n. 4.
    11. Žižek, "'In His Bold Gaze My Ruin Is Writ Large,'" 239. Cf. Slavoj Žižek, *Enjoy Your
Symptom! Jacques Lacan in Hollywood and Out* (New York, 1992), 134, 136; Elizabeth Bishop, quoted
in George S. Lensing, "Wallace Stevens and Elizabeth Bishop: The Way a Poet Should See, The
Way a Poet Should Think," *Wallace Stevens Journal* 19 (fall 1995): 128. "Consciousness," on the other

What is more, if "The Western tradition codes the female body as negative and threatening," as Marilyn Farwell recently observes, "a body so excessive in its functions and sexuality that it must be controlled," how might it respond to the lesbian body as the Žižekian "ultimate limit" of that tradition—that is to say (in Farwell's concluding words), as "an extension of the excessive female body and therefore the ultimate threat to the dominant order"? In real life, Bishop knew only too well the price such a tradition exacted, recounted in detail by her biographer with the poet's long and tortured history of alcohol and substance abuse—in the poet's words, "Queer, drunk, and all the rest." In Bishop's art, however, the story is quite different. But here, once again, as Žižek adjures, we have to "distinguish strictly between *fiction* and *spectre*": "fiction is a symbolic formation that determines the structure of what we experience as reality, whereas spectres belong to the Real; their appearance is the price we pay for the gap that forever separates reality from the Real, for the fictional character of reality." Not surprisingly, "The gap between the observed world and the unknown, the psychic one," as David Kalstone cogently observes, "is something that disturbs Bishop in her early work, and something that only long experience helped her overcome." In foregrounding the *spectral* poetics of Elizabeth Bishop, therefore, my aim is directed towards taking stock of those dark holes where, unknown and unseen, her art, I would argue, is able to wrest control away from the tradition, and in that discursive distance interposed between reality and Real, thematize an empowered subjectivity within an "O Canada!" well beyond an "Oh, Say, Can You See."[12]

As a means of rounding out my general theoretical aim in the first part of this

---

hand for Bishop, would have a certain affinity with ideological normativity's symbolic articulation as "life's petrifying residue" (Kalstone, *Becoming a Poet*, 67); hence, her own asseveration (in an interview for *Christian Science Monitor*) that "Poetry should be as unconscious as possible" (quoted in Lombardi, *The Body and the Song*, 243 n. 1), that is to say, "separate from the conscious mind," as Bishop puts it in her essay on "Gerard Manley Hopkins" (quoted in Lorrie Goldensohn, *Elizabeth Bishop: The Biography of a Poetry* [New York, 1992], 92). For evidence of Bishop's abiding interest in psychoanalytic theories of the unconscious (Ernest Jones' three-volume study of Freud, and works by Karen Horney and Melanie Klein), see Harrison, *Elizabeth Bishop's Poetics of Intimacy*, 175, 224–25 n. 7; and also Lombardi, *The Body and the Song*, 231, for a notation of Bishop's that "Freud's theories should be carried a step further" (further on 47). But Bishop could also be dismissive of some forms of psychoanalysis, writing to Marianne Moore in 1937, for instance, that "everything I have read about it has made me think that psychologists misinterpret and very much underestimate all the workings of ART!" Bishop, quoted in Millier, *Elizabeth Bishop*, 126–27; cf. Lombardi, *The Body and the Song*, 3, 237 n. 2.

12. Marilyn R. Farwell, "The Lesbian Narrative: 'The Pursuit of the Inedible by the Unspeakable,'" in *Professions of Desire: Lesbian and Gay Studies in Literature*, ed. George E. Haggerty and Bonnie Zimmerman (New York, 1995), 157–58; Elizabeth Bishop, quoted in Millier, *Elizabeth*

chapter, and as a prelude to the transfer of theory into practice with the analysis of a specific trio of early poems in part two, we might take a brief look at one of Bishop's more well known stories just to see in fact the degree to which the spectral becomes foreshortened by the fictional in the structuring of subjective experience. In her fictional foray into the "spectral" in the highly poetical prose account of an emotionally unstable mother's Nova Scotian reunion with family and friends in "In the Village" (1953), Bishop appears to be revisiting her second traumatic encounter with maternal loss that we've been characterizing as entirely negative. For by the end of the story, it becomes clear that the visit has not been successful, and the mother, rather than being put away in a Dartmouth asylum as in real life, has had to be returned to a sanatorium in Boston. The moody opening of the story thus creates an indelible anticipation of its pathetic closing:

> A scream, the echo of a scream, hangs over that Nova Scotian village. No one hears it; it hangs there forever, a slight stain in those pure blue skies, skies that travelers compare to those of Switzerland, too dark, too blue, so that they seem to keep on darkening a little more around the horizon—or is it around the rims of the eyes? . . . something darkening over the woods and waters as well as the sky. The scream hangs like that, unheard in memory—in the past, in the present, and those years between. . . . Its pitch would be the pitch of the village. Flick the lightning rod on top of the church steeple with your fingernail and you will hear it.
>
> (BCPr, 251)

The darkening Maritime sky that suggestively threatens to close over the "unheard" scream in this remarkable passage becomes premonitory of the sanatorium that *will* eventually close around the scream's incurable source once back in Boston, the transition between one place and the other clearly marked by the mother's "being fitted again" for a purple dress while grandmother holds the young narrator "against her knees" (BCPr, 266).

In linking the sanatorium to the purple dress in this way—we notice also that "The address of the sanatorium is in my grandmother's hand-writing, in purple indelible pencil, on smoothed-out wrapping paper" (BCPr, 272)—with this linkage, we seem to have been ushered before another hole-in-glove arrangement, in other words, before another metaphorical standoff between some indiscernible feminine Real and the socio-symbolic order of reality attempting to control or curtail it. If the Real eludes the grasp of the symbolic in its persistence as "a non-

---

Bishop, 429, and see further 421–22, 439, 505–506; Slavoj Žižek, *The Metastases of Enjoyment: Six Essays on Women and Causality* (New York, 1994), 194; Kalstone, *Becoming a Poet*, 15.

symbolized stain" noted earlier, then Bishop's further connecting the mother's "unheard" scream to "a slight stain" in the village's "darkening" skies above would seem to suggest a means by which the feminine subject may still yet prevail over reality's paternalistic encroachments, much like mother's perfume later: "A bottle of perfume has leaked and made awful brown stains. Oh, marvelous scent, from somewhere else! It doesn't smell like that here; but there, somewhere, it does, still" (*BCPr*, 255).

Slavoj Žižek offers a parallel reading of "the scream that is not heard" in the paintings of Edvard Munch and the films of Alfred Hitchcock, but hastens to caution against our making a too-ready psychoanalytic "interpretation" of the maternal superego "as the 'secret' of the voice-stain":

> the point is not to interpret the unfathomable "*acousmatique*" voice as the maternal superego, but rather its opposite, *i.e.*, to explain the very logic of the maternal superego by means of this vocal stain—what we call "maternal superego" is *nothing but* such a voice which smears the picture and disturbs its transparency . . . a stain which blurs the field of vision. . . . Therein consists the most elementary formal definition of psychosis: the massive presence of some Real which fills out and blocks the perspective openness constitutive of "reality." This magnetic force which distorts the linear perspective on reality is of course enjoyment: Munch's *Scream* depicts the intrusion of enjoyment into reality.

Like the concluding "enjoyment" in this passage that can have both negative and positive connotations, so a certain transvaluation also overtakes the conventional associations attached to "psychosis," which, in Bishop's story, may be explained as follows. If the maternal superego in "In the Village" is psychotic in the manner Žižek describes, then she skews the reality of experience sufficiently enough— "blurs the field of vision"—to allow for the possibility of the child to imagine living outside of or alternative to the constraints of domestic normativity: to "entertain the idea of not going home today at all, of staying safely here in the pasture all day, playing in the brook and climbing on the squishy, moss-covered hummocks in the swampy part" (*BCPr*, 265). Similar to Lacan's characterization, then, of the "*objet petit a*" as "the bone which got stuck in the subject's throat," the mother's silent scream becomes "the voice *qua* object" Žižek might say, "what cannot burst out, unchain itself and thus enter the dimension of subjectivity" in any of its ideologically straitened forms. And the child, conceivably in the process of constructing a dissident (lesbian) subjectivity for herself, appears to have internalized her mother's silent lesson by holding a five-cent piece in her mouth "for

greater safety on the way home," and soon after, swallowing it. "Months later, as
far as I know," she avers, "it is still in me, transmuting all its precious metal into
my growing teeth and hair," since "I am struggling to free myself" (*BCPr*, 259,
270).[13]

Hence, "To this silent scream which [conventionally] bears out the horror-
stricken encounter with the real of enjoyment," Žižek further notes that one invariably "has to oppose the scream of release, of decision, of choice," and in this
final Lacanian extrapolation, he observes how "the opposition of silent and vocal-
ized screams coincides with that of enjoyment and Other": "the silent scream
attests to the subject's clinging to enjoyment, to his/her unreadiness to exchange
enjoyment (*i.e.*, the object which gives body to it) for the Other, for the Law, for
the paternal metaphor, whereas the vocalization as such corroborates that the
choice is already made and that the subject finds himself/herself within the community." Mysteriously, the young narrator's mother disappears from "In the Village," as mysteriously as she appeared. And the talk of the child's aunts making
plans to visit their sister in the Boston sanatorium would denote that mother still
clings to her "enjoyment," namely, that her ultimate capitulation to the disciplinary Law of community has been secured completely against her will. This realization of the negative effects of psychosis would thus appear to be hastening the
narrator to a climactic moment of choice in Bishop's structuring of events. But if
so, as Žižek rightly points out, the choice seems already to have been made for
the child. It comes early in the narrative with her visit to the blacksmith, Nate,
and signaled by his "*Clang.* The pure note: pure and angelic" (*BCPr*, 253). As a
result, "the external opposition of outbursts of noisy rage and of restrained silence" that the blacksmith sets in motion suggests that the child will always already have acceded to "the phallic dimension" by the end of the story:

> Clang. *Clang.* Nate is shaping a horseshoe. Oh, beautiful pure sound! . . . Now
> there is no scream. Once there was one and it settled slowly down to earth one hot
> summer afternoon; or did it float up, into that dark, too dark, blue sky? But surely
> it has gone away, forever . . . things damaged and lost, sickened or destroyed; even
> the frail almost-lost scream—are they too frail for us to hear their voices long, too
> mortal? Nate! Oh, beautiful sound, strike again!
>
> (*BCPr*, 274)

With the narrator's vociferous affirmation of the redoubtable Nate in these concluding lines, Bishop effectively reveals how fiction drives a wedge between the

---

13. Žižek, *Enjoy Your Symptom!* 117, 119, 117.

distant Real, and reality as the "structured" form of experience at its furthest remove from that Real's spectrally distanciated presentiment.[14]

By the same token, with the daughter's furthest remove from the mother,
Bishop also reveals that there can be no such thing as "The Subject," as Derrida
holds, namely, that the subject "only ex-ists as the void of a distance from the
Thing . . . the subject *qua* O, the mark of the absent, 'sacrificed' Thing." Clearly,
from "the void of a distance," it was the fabled "subject *qua* O" and not some
determinate or essentialized fictional "Subject" that was the more inspiring for
Elizabeth Bishop as a lesbian writer. And stories like "In the Village" more than
anything helped her to see that the greater promise for continuing to revolve that
"O Canada" fable of identity—go the distance, as it were—perhaps lay more with
poetry than with prose. "What I really like best," as Bishop herself once remarked, "is silence!"[15]

Elizabeth Bishop's biographer informs us that a proposed new (and quite likely
final) collection of poems the poet had been planning in her very last years was
to be entitled *Grandmother's Glass Eye*. This fascinating title, however, actually
goes back quite early in Bishop's work, to an incomplete notebook entry from the
1930s, as Barbara Page documents. And it was not until four decades later, in
her outline for a Guggenheim application, that Bishop finally took the trouble to
clarify the significance behind her rather bizarre trope:

14. Žižek, *Enjoy Your Symptom!* 129. Nate's affirmation in the story's conclusion perhaps may
help us to understand some of the "guilt" that Bishop herself felt concerning her relation to her
mother: "My life has been darkened always by guilt feelings, I think, about my mother," she writes in
a letter from 1970, "—somehow children get the idea it's their fault—or I did. And I could do nothing about that, and she lived on for twenty years more and it has been a nightmare to me always."
Bishop, quoted in Harrison, *Elizabeth Bishop's Poetics of Intimacy*, 131. On the same page, Harrison
comments that this letter is likely to be "Bishop's only written mention of her mother's incarceration
at the Nova Scotia hospital, where she remained, psychotic and without family contact, until her
death in 1934."

15. Jacques Derrida, "'Eating Well,' or the Calculation of the Subject: An Interview with Jacques
Derrida," trans. Peter Connor and Avital Ronell, in *Who Comes after the Subject?* ed. Eduardo Cadava
and Peter Connor (New York, 1991), 102; Žižek, *Enjoy Your Symptom!* 181; Elizabeth Bishop, quoted
in Brown, "An Interview with Elizabeth Bishop," 291, and see further Harrison, *Elizabeth Bishop's
Poetics of Intimacy*, 115. With poetry, arguably more than any other artistic medium, "intensities of
feeling and imagination are, in effect," according to Carney, "openings out of the world of ordinary
social and verbal life. They are escape hatches out of the traps and confinements of routine social
structures and institutional systems of discourse . . . [and] characters granted such momentary richness of consciousness stop participating practically in society and the world entirely and stare into the
distance in silent rapture." Carney, *American Vision*, 336–37.

Quite often the glass eye [of her maternal grandmother in Canada] looked heaven-
ward, or off at an angle, while the real eye looked at you. . . . The situation of my
grandmother strikes me as rather like the situation of the poet: the difficulty of
combining the real with the decidedly un-real; the natural with the unnatural; the
curious effect a poem produces of being as [canceled: "inevitable"] normal as sight
and yet as synthetic, as artificial, as a *glass eye*.[16]

The "difficulty" of combining the real with the unreal, the natural with the unnatural, the normal (or inevitable) with the artificial (or hypothetical)—so much
of this difficulty we have already witnessed in the analogous Lacanian separation
between the fictional and the spectral in the previous section, particularly when
we attempt to think these combinations through the specific terms of gender and
sexuality. What interests me now, however, when we turn to some of Bishop's
early poetry from the 1930s and '40s that arguably may have been informed by
her initial thinking about "Grandmother's Glass Eye," is the *way* this "difficulty"
may be accommodated from the point of view of the dissident lesbian poet.
"Point of view" is not quite the right phrase at this stage, for what we're *really*
being presented in these poems cannot be properly seen at all (taking the glass
eye literally), or at least only be seen "off at an angle" (taking the glass eye figuratively). And yet, paradoxically, the purest gauge of what ideally cannot be seen
(or seen readily) is what "the real eye," in fact, *does* see, and perhaps sees only too
well: the natural, the normal, the inevitable, and so forth. Reminiscences of Canada seemed to raise this crisis of vision most poignantly for Bishop precisely in
this paradoxical way: "I now see . . . a house in Nova Scotia on the bay, *exactly*
like my grandmother's," she once wrote Robert Lowell, then added, "—idiotic as
it is, and unbearable as the reality would be" (*OA*, 388).

Lacan, of course, would characterize this paradoxical crisis in vision as "enjoyment," a kind of "pleasure in pain" coincident with "the circular movement which
finds satisfaction in failing again and again to attain the object"—in this case, the
"*objet petit a*" once more, which is "not a positive entity existing in space," but is
"ultimately nothing but a certain *curvature of space itself* [pressing Bishop's angular
perspective to its limit] which causes us to make a bend precisely when we want
to get directly at the object." "Tell all the Truth, but tell it slant— / Success in
Circuit lies," as Emily Dickinson might say; "And of the curveship," Hart Crane
adds, "lend a myth to God" ("To Brooklyn Bridge"). In exactly these terms, who

16. Millier, *Elizabeth Bishop*, 538; Page, "Elizabeth Bishop and Postmodernism," 171; Elizabeth
Bishop, quoted in Page, "Elizabeth Bishop and Postmodernism," 171–72 (see also Harrison, *Elizabeth Bishop's Poetics of Intimacy*, 224 n. 6).

could have "enjoyed" himself *more* than Charles Darwin, in Bishop's well-known description, unless it was the reader of Darwin herself?

[In] reading Darwin one admires the beautiful solid case being built up out of his endless, heroic observations, almost unconscious or automatic—and then comes a sudden relaxation, a forgetful phrase, and one feels that strangeness of his undertaking, sees the lonely young man, his eyes fixed on facts and minute details, sinking or sliding giddily off into the unknown. What one seems to want in art, in experiencing it, is the same thing that is necessary for its creation, a self-forgetful, perfectly useless concentration.

Or perhaps more than either Darwin or Bishop, the poet's own "Sandpiper," in his hysterical "state of controlled panic":

> As he runs,
> he stares at the dragging grains.
>
> The world is a mist. And then the world is
>
> minute and vast and clear
>
> . . . .
> His beak is focused; he is preoccupied,
>
> looking for something, something, something.
> Poor bird, he is obsessed!
> (*BCP*, 131).[17]

17. Žižek, *Enjoy Your Symptom!* 48–49; Dickinson, *The Complete Poems*, 506–507; Hart Crane, *The Complete Poems and Selected Letters and Prose of Hart Crane*, ed. Brom Weber (Garden City, N.Y., 1966), 46; Elizabeth Bishop, "The 'Darwin' Letter," cited in Lloyd Schwartz and Sybil P. Estess, *Elizabeth Bishop and Her Art* (Ann Arbor, 1983), 288. And just as it is part of Lacan's thesis "that *objet a* serves as a support to reality: access to what we call 'reality' is open to the subject *via* the embarrassing intruder in its midst [viz., the Real]" (Žižek, *Enjoy Your Symptom!* 49), so would the same relation hold in the theory of Bishop, only run the opposite way: "There is no split [between the role of consciousness and subconsciousness in art]. Dreams, works of art (some) glimpses of the always-more-successful surrealism of everyday life, unexpected moments of empathy (is it?), catch a peripheral vision of whatever it is one can never really see full-face but that seems enormously important." Bishop, "The 'Darwin' Letter," 288. The legion of commentators, therefore, who champion Bishop for her extraordinary and impeccable "reading in detail" (in Naomi Schor's feminist phrase in *Reading in Detail: Aesthetics and the Feminine* [New York, 1987]—see e.g., Fountain and Brazeau, *Remembering Elizabeth Bishop*, 198, 208, 288, 325, 355, and passim) need to think further about the "perfectly useless" direction into which her powers of concentration may perhaps be sinking or sliding (see Lombardi, *The Body and the Song*, 96, 97). "Oh dear I hate that picture of myself, and that

As with most aspects of Bishop's work, the late David Kalstone expresses precisely the epistemological conundrum at root in the relation between the seen and the unseen when he early observes that "[s]he sees with such a rooted, piercing vision, so realistically, because she has never taken our presence in the world as totally real," and later, that with Bishop, "[o]ne only *approached* [the] truth; one never statically possessed it." But as with the preceding poets in this study (wittingly or not) writing in the shadow of American Pragmatism, it's perhaps William James who states Bishop's (and their) conundrum precisely here:

> Philosophers are after all like poets. They are pathfinders. What everyone can feel, what everyone can know in the bone and marrow of him, they sometimes can find words for and express. . . . [Yet] the poets and the philosophers themselves know as no one else knows that what their formulas express leaves unexpressed almost everything that they organically divine and feel. So I feel that there is a center in truth's forest where I have never been . . . there is a gleam of the end, a sense of certainty, but always there comes still another ridge, so my blazes merely circle towards the true direction. . . . Truth's fulness is elusive; ever not quite, not quite! So we fall back on the preliminary blazes—a few formulas, a few technical conceptions, a few verbal pointers. . . . And that to my sorrow, is all that I can do. . . . Inconclusive I must be, and merely suggestive.[18]

Accordingly, therefore, the wide range of opinion concerning the truth about Bishop's sexualized presence in the world, from the "silent and secretive" (Mc-

---

insistence on my 'coldness and precision,' etc.," Bishop remarks in a letter of 1953. "I think that's just some sort of cliché always used of women poets, at least I don't *feel* as if I wrote that way" (*OA*, 262); and, in in a letter the following year (to Marianne Moore), Bishop confesses: "I think my approach is so much vaguer and less defined and certainly more old-fashioned—sometimes I'm amazed at people's comparing me to you when all I'm doing is some kind of blank verse—can't they *see* how different it is? But they can't, apparently." Bishop, quoted in Kalstone, *Becoming a Poet*, 4. As Anne Stevenson remarks with considerable hindsight, "She preferred the iceberg to the ship every time." Stevenson, cited in Fountain and Brazeau, *Remembering Elizabeth Bishop*, 189.

18. David Kalstone, *Five Temperaments: Elizabeth Bishop, Robert Lowell, James Merrill, Adrienne Rich, John Ashbery* (New York, 1977), 32; Kalstone, *Becoming a Poet*, 96, emphasis added; William James, "Philosophical Conceptions and Practical Results," in *William James, Writings: 1878–1899*, comp. and ed. Gerald E. Myers (New York, 1992), 1078–79. These observations help us to understand further Kalstone's contention elsewhere in *Becoming a Poet* regarding Bishop's "desire to see the world by withdrawing from it." As Kalstone explains, "Bishop gives us an odd troped version of what separates us from natural experience—odd because her tropes, a simile and a metaphor, dramatize what is hidden in terms of humanizing activity, creations, a primitive alphabet, song . . . repetitions *that for a moment* tease us into some sense of plain identity between human speech and things." Kalstone, *Becoming a Poet*, 60, 120, last emphasis added; cf. Parker, *The Unbeliever*, 67.

Cabe), through "confusion" (Parker), to the deliberately "unsaid" (Harrison)—
the range is likely *all* true, if the unseen expressed as a function of the seen can
only be *an approach* to the truth of lesbian identity—the ultimate "limit" of truth,
or (w)hole truth, once again, where, as James points out, formulas and conceptions and verbal pointers finally fail. Hence, Bonnie Costello's suggestion "that
the self is amorphous in an amorphous world" can perhaps give us our best purchase on the "Glass Eye" in Bishop's early work, if the "inward eye [which] is
that blank center around which all questions are formed" is given to us punningly
by Bishop as a highly refractional Glass "I." So that if "the question is the final
form" no less concerning "Grandmother's Glass Eye/I" than so much else in
Bishop, it's only because it is the poet herself who writes: "I think myself that my
best poems seem rather *distant*."[19] As in the case of the several other dissident
subjects in this study, therefore, the American Modernist text provides the legitimate occasion for enlarging upon for the purpose of cultivating the distance underwriting the expansionary possibilities of self-construction.

    With the death of her mother following hard upon the poet's graduation from
Vassar and move to New York City in 1934, Elizabeth Bishop's vocation as a
writer began apace. And for all that we have said thus far about her ambiguous
response to mother-loss, and the openings and the closings it brought significantly to bear on the state of her psychic and emotional life, it's hard to imagine
that issues of gender and sexuality could not have been on Bishop's mind in her
early work, despite how removed from the "tangible reality of physical fact and
emotional risk"[20] this writing often strikes so many of her readers, in comparison
to the later. Indeed, if angularity and curvature are likely to be rhetorically condu-
cive to affording us the proper "slant" on gay as opposed to so-called straight
culture, then the general obliquity of the address in the texts of Bishop's first
book, *North and South* (first published in 1946), is perhaps the very kind of presentation one would understandably assume might be appropriate for the treatment of dissident subjectivities and sexualities, which is why I choose initially to
dwell upon these early texts rather than those from her three later collections.

    Slavoj Žižek's concise historical summation of posthumanist subjectivity (a
history I shall return to anon) rendered in the Lacanian *aperçu*, to wit, "Yet as

    19. McCabe, *Elizabeth Bishop*, 41; Parker, *The Unbeliever*, 49; Harrison, *Elizabeth Bishop's Poet-
ics of Intimacy*, 64; Bonnie Costello, "One Art: The Poetry of Elizabeth Bishop, 1971–1976," in *Elizabeth Bishop and Her Art*, ed. Lloyd Schwartz and Sybil P. Estess (Ann Arbor, 1983), 117, 123, 132
(cf. Parker, *The Unbeliever*, 25–26); Elizabeth Bishop, quoted in Harrison, *Elizabeth Bishop's Poetics
of Intimacy*, 29, emphasis added.
    20. Thomas Travisano, *Elizabeth Bishop: Her Artistic Development* (Charlottesville, 1989), 28.

soon as the Thing [the Real] in itself is posited as unattainable, *every universality is potentially suspended*"—this statement also sums up fairly the epistemological project Bishop proposes for herself in her earliest writing, and subsumed under the figure of "Grandmother's Glass Eye." In essence, she purposes to turn a blind eye to universalist (i.e., natural, normal) notions of selfhood, constructing in their place hypothetical (i.e., synthetic, artificial) versions, the endlessly rhetorical prospect of which makes true selfhood—even a genuine "lesbian" selfhood—generally unattainable, hence "spectral." But the "Canadian" opening in Bishop's rhetoric can just as quickly convert itself to something like an "American" closing of the mind, in face of the enormous risks that "this kind of porosity or disloyalty to fixed ideological definitions—running stubbornly contrary to the notion of unchanging cores of personal identity" can often incur: humiliation, discrimination, rejection, ostracism, abandonment, perhaps even madness. Bishop's ocular figure can thus equally mark, as Žižek puts it, "the lowest ebb, the point of true horror" for human identity, by turning a blind eye/I in that moment of denial "when the subject finds himself face to face with the groundless abyss of his lack of being."[21]

This latter prospect appears to be roughly the situation of "The Unbeliever" (1938), a text which provides a convenient entry-point into Bishop's treatment of dissident subjectivity in some of her earliest writing:

> He sleeps on the top of a mast
> with his eyes fast closed.
> The sails fall away below him
> like the sheets of his bed,
> leaving out in the air of the night the sleeper's head.
>
> . . . .
>
> But he sleeps on the top of his mast
> with his eyes closed tight.
> The gull inquired into his dream,
> which was, "I must not fall.
> The spangled sea below wants me to fall.
> It is hard as diamonds; it wants to destroy us all."
>
> (*BCP*, 22)

The tightly closed "eyes," repeated in both the opening and closing stanzas cited here from the text, underscores the protagonist's strict aversion to the experience

21. Žižek, *Enjoy Your Symptom!* 182, emphasis retained; Debbora Battaglia, "Problematizing the Self: A Thematic Introduction," in *Rhetorics of Self-Making*, ed. Debbora Battaglia (Berkeley, 1995), 7; Žižek, *Enjoy Your Symptom!* 169.

of subjectivities (eyes/I's) in any other form but their ideologically mandated samenesses, which we might have assumed in the epigraph provided for the poem from Bunyan, and repeated in the final stanza's first line. Why the "spangled sea" is the most sinister prospect in this regard ("wants me to fall"), prompting the unbeliever to turn a blind eye to its "hard as diamonds" threat of destruction, is provided in what may be taken to be a rather useful gloss on this passage by Elizabeth Grosz, in a context not unrelated to Bishop's own from her early period:

> [(Their) own tenuous hold over the multiplicity of sexual impulses and possibilities that characterize all human sexuality] is both the power and danger posed by lesbian and gay sexual relations: that what one does, how one does it, with whom and with what effects, are ontologically open questions, that sexuality in and for all of us is fundamentally provisional, tenuous, mobile, even volatile, igniting in unpredictable contexts with often unsettling effects: its power, attraction and danger the fundamental fluidity and transformability or liquidity of sexuality and its enactment in sexed bodies.[22]

Fluidity, transformability, liquidity—these are definitely *not* the features of the sea the unbeliever, "Secure in introspection" (*BCP*, 22), expects to complicate his eye when he "peers at the watery pillars [for] his reflection" (*BCP*, 22). His obsessive need, therefore, to convert all the contingent elements of marine experience into marmoreal extensions of his decidedly fixed sense of being—"air . . . 'like marble,'" "marble wings," "marble pillars," and so forth—ultimately comes itself to reflect an identity that can ignore, and so remain impervious to, the multiple possibilities of human sexuality just described: "I am founded. . . . I never move" (*BCP*, 22).

With Bishop's "The Man-Moth" from two years earlier (1936), however, we are presented with something quite different. The counterpoint between two opposed rhetorics of subjectivity that we have been loosely dividing between the poet's sense of an "American" (natural) and a "Canadian" (synthetic) identity gains considerably in its elaboration in terms of two distinct "voices," as in the last section of this chapter, and of two distinct "eyes" presently scanned in this section. Lacan's ultimate distinction between two fathers—the "anal" and the "symbolic"—will finally help to bring the tension of these binaries to a head, and in this second poem from *North and South*, to a "head" in a quite literal sense, as

---

22. Elizabeth Grosz, "Experimental Desire: Rethinking Queer Subjectivity," in *Supposing the Subject*, ed. Joan Copjec (New York, 1994), 152.

in the third stanza, where we find the protagonist, in the poet's rather surreal
rendering of the modern city, moving

> Up the façades,
> his shadow dragging like a photographer's cloth behind him,
> he climbs fearfully, thinking that this time he will manage
> to push his small head through that round clean opening
> and be forced through, as from a tube, in black scrolls on the light
> (Man, standing below him, has no such illusions.)
> But what the Man-Moth fears most he must do, although
> he fails, of course, and falls back scared but quite unhurt.
>
> (*BCP*, 14)

The socio-symbolic, fully acculturated subject—man standing below, in this passage, without any illusions—is given his phantasmatic or "spectral" projection in
this by-now familiar glove-and-hole scenario, with the Man-Moth's "shadow
dragging like a photographer's cloth behind him," as he literally heads for a "clean
round opening" in the darkening urban skyscape. In this attitude of shadowy
alienation, the Man-Moth is perhaps our Lacanian manifestation of "the 'anal
father' who definitely *does* enjoy":

> He is the subject's double who accompanies him like a shadow and gives body to a
> certain surplus, to what is "in the subject more than subject himself"; this surplus
> represents what the subject must renounce, sacrifice even, the part in himself that
> the subject must murder in order to start to live as a "normal" member of the com-
> munity.[23]

In tumbling back to earth, "of course," and into a regression of more and more
restriction and containment—"subways of cement," "artificial tunnels," "ties . . .
beneath his train," "hands in his pockets," and so forth—we witness the phantasmatic subject forsake the "queer light" emanating from the "small hole at the
top of the sky" (*BCP*, 14), which may (or may not) be the moon, since in Bishop's
keeping with the spectral motif of blindness, the Man-Moth can only feel "her
vast properties" on his hands.

Hence, by the final stanza of the poem, the "normal" part of the subject, in an
act of sacrificial self-constitution, will have renounced the "abnormal" part, the
superfluous insect-like "Thing" blindly attracted as moths are to some mysteriously fatal source of light. And we seem to be left with a subject in somewhat the

23. Žižek, *Enjoy Your Symptom!* 125.

same position as the narrator from "In the Village," swallowing for the sake of a
regulatory hegemonic continuity what Bishop in a much later text will call the
"O difference that kills, / or intimidates, much / of all our small shadowy / life!"
("Song for the Rainy Season" [1960; *BCP*, 102]):[24]

> If you catch him,
> hold up a flashlight to his eye. It's all dark pupil,
> an entire night itself, whose haired horizon tightens
> as he stares back, and closes up the eye. Then from the lids
> one tear, his only possession, like the bee's sting, slips.
> Slyly he palms it, and if you're not paying attention
> he'll swallow it. However, if you watch, he'll hand it over,
> cool as from underground springs and pure enough to drink.
>
> (*BCP*, 15)

In this concluding stanza, the overseeing "you," as a kind of pronominal marker
for the "sacrificial sociality" of culture-at-large in its "more profound project of
ideological reproduction," appears to have triumphed: the grounded self surren-
ders its tearful underground self—Grosz's "liquidity of sexuality," again—at the
point of a "flashlight," and with the threat of further disciplinary coercion, subjectivity closes up its eye/I once more.[25]

Yet the title of Bishop's text, footnoted with an asterisk further to read "News-

---

24. In Cary Wolfe and Jonathan Elder's brilliant essay "Subject to Sacrifice," which has much to
say about the speciesism of moths in Demme's 1991 film, particularly the death's-head totem "[b]los-
soming like an exotic *fleur du mal* from Jodie Foster's mouth . . . which rather conventionally fixes the
female icon at the point where her beauty and her helplessness converge," the authors work up to an
insight in many ways parallel to Bishop's: "If animals become sacrifical substitutes in the erection of
the humanist law of culture, so, too, does the feminine in the normative ontogenetic narrative of
patriarchal culture." Cary Wolfe and Jonathan Elder, "Subject to Sacrifice: Ideology, Psychoanalysis,
and the Discourse of Species in Jonathan Demme's *Silence of the Lambs,*" *Boundary* 22 (summer 1995),
141, 162. The position of both texts on the overpowering regulation of phallogocentric culture, however, may have been somewhat anticipated by Virginia Woolf several decades ago in her anecdote on
"The Death of the Moth": "when there was nobody to care or to know, this gigantic effort on the
part of an insignificant little moth, against a power of such magnitude, to retain what no one else
valued or desired to keep, moved one strangely. . . . As I looked at the dead moth, this minute wayside
triumph of so great a force over so mean an antagonist filled me with wonder." Virginia Woolf, *The
Death of the Moth, and Other Essays* (London, 1981), 11. I thank Shannon Ross, a student in my
graduate seminar on "Self-Confession in Contemporary American Poetry," for pointing out the latter
connection to me. On the act of swallowing here, and maybe elsewhere, McCabe detects the "partak-
ing of some secret, transgressive pleasure, marking, perhaps, the privacy and reticence of Bishop's
own lesbian identity and her possible fear of public opinion." McCabe, *Elizabeth Bishop*, 78.

25. Wolfe and Elmer, "Subject to Sacrifice," 164, 167. Also relevant are several other texts in the

paper misprint for 'mammoth'" (*BCP*, 14), suggests something quite opposite to this seeming triumph. "I've forgotten what it was that was supposed to be 'mammoth,'" the poet remarks on her choice of title, "But the misprint seemed meant for me. An oracle spoke from the page of the *New York Times*, kindly explaining New York City to me, at least for a moment." Could the "oracle" speaking through the regulatory institution of mass-print journalism, in fact, be speaking to its own institutional failure in the form of what Joan Copjec aptly calls a "misfire"—a failure, that is to say, "that slips from us whenever we disregard the nontransparency of subject to signifier," as in the rank disjunction between "man" and "moth," "whenever we make [i.e., coerce] the subject [to] coincide with the signifier"? If Bishop's mis-printed title is telling us anything at all, then, it's just that "*In* language and yet *more than* language, the subject is a cause for which no signifier can account. Not because she transcends the signifier, but because she inhabits it *as limit*," in other words, as "the deadlock of language's conflict with itself that produces this experience of the inexperienceable (which [in Bishop's very own testimony above] can neither be remembered nor spoken)."²⁶ Here, the utter silence of the Man-Moth is crucial to Bishop's radicalization of discourse once again.

Bishop canon in which the act of shedding tears invariably marks the restive capitulation to regnant culture's supervening ideologies, for example, in "Sestina" (from *Questions of Travel* [1965]), those symbolized by "the almanac" hovering "half open" above both grandmother and child:

> *I know what I know*, says the almanac.
>
> . . . .
>
> . . . secretly, while the grandmother
> busies herself about the stove,
> the little moons fall down like tears
> from between the pages of the almanac
> into the flower bed the child
> has carefully placed in the front of the house.
>
> *Time to plant tears*, says the almanac.
>
> (*BCP*, 123–24)

26. Elizabeth Bishop, "On 'The Man-Moth,'" cited in *Elizabeth Bishop and Her Art*, ed. Lloyd Schwartz and Sybil P. Estess (Ann Arbor, 1983), 286; Copjec, "Sex and the Euthanasia of Reason," 22, 22, 24. Cf. Bishop's "Mechanics of Pretence" from 1934 (an unpublished commentary on W. H. Auden): "One of the causes of poetry must be, we suppose, the feeling that the contemporary language is not equivalent to the contemporary fact; there is something out of proportion between them, and what is being said in words is not at all what is being said in 'things.' . . . But as the imaginary language is elaborated and is understood by more people, it begins to work two ways at once. . . . [So that] [t]o the initiate, the world actually manages to look like so-and-so's poems." Bishop, "Mechanics of Pretence," quoted in McCabe, *Elizabeth Bishop*, 54, 55.

. It's as if, at the moment of extrusion "through that round clean opening" by the Man-Moth's head, "the voice gets lost, as though it had leaked out through a hole in the discourse," as sometimes happens in the classic text, according to Roland Barthes, when its identifiable voices become "subject from time to time to a sudden *dissolve,* leaving a gap which enables the utterance to shift from one point of view to another, without warning . . . which in the modern text becomes atonality."[27] If the Man-Moth, therefore, is a monster or perversion at the limit of self-expression, it's only because what we actually *do catch,* by the end of the poem, is precisely this shift in Bishop's utterance from one point of view to the other. On this basis, the Man-Moth seems almost destined to pay yet again one of his "rare, although occasional, visits to the surface," and begin "to scale the faces" of his other life (or lives) all over (*BCP,* 14). The oracle thus spoken to Bishop that seemed "meant" to inaugurate her spectral lesbian poetics may have called to her from the pages of the *New York Times.* But in the "silent scream" of the Man-Moth in this poem, it is an oracle that her own double-consciousness quite likely had always already "answered" back in Canada, and would only belatedly come to confirm some fifteen years later in long-term partnership with her beloved Lota.

In working up to a look at a final text from the early Bishop, we ought to say a further word or two about the historical location of her spectral poetics that has perhaps already been hinted at by Roland Barthes, whom Bishop would come later to read, and his suggestion of a shift in point of view from Classic to Modernist discourse. Charles Taylor, whose *Sources of the Self* massively undertakes to chart this shift by way of a careful sifting through nearly all the great writers in the history of Western thought from ancient times to the present, propounds the thesis that this "shift can be thought of as a new subjectivism." With the "erosion of the sense of authority as something natural, something given in the order of things or the community," to "a conception which puts the autonomous individual at the centre of our system of law," Taylor foregrounds the modern evolution of the individual's "'poietic' powers," the key insight about which is the realization that "Knowledge comes not from connecting the mind to the order of things we find," but rather "in framing a representation of reality" by means of "the function of language . . . to aid the construction of thought." As Taylor further elaborates his history of the new subjectivism:

The centring on the constructive powers of language undergoes a further crucial development in the late eighteenth century. Language and in general our represen-

27. Roland Barthes, *S/Z,* trans. Richard Miller (New York, 1974), 41–42.

tational powers come to be seen not only or mainly as directed to the correct portrayal of an independent reality but also as our way of manifesting through expression what we are, and our place within things. And on the new understanding of ourselves as expressive beings, this manifestation is also seen as a self-completion.

Language, however, in the service of an "independent reality" like self-expression, to an extent still labors under the former discursive protocols of a mimetic Classicism. In the previous text, this would roughly be the position of the Man-Moth "seat[ing] himself facing the wrong way," while "the train starts at once at its full, terrible speed, / *without a shift* in gears or a gradation of any sort" (*BCP*, 14–15, emphasis added).[28]

Starting in the late nineteenth century, therefore, the "poietic powers" of language are required to take an even more inward turn—"the lines of modern poetry which flow from Baudelaire have detached themselves from the straightforwardly mimetic and expressive," Taylor instantiates—and post-Classical discourse begins to pull us in the direction of "something for which we have no words": the "nothingness" of Mallarmé, the "unattainable" in Schopenhauer, the "non-representable and indefinable" in Iris Murdoch, and so forth. As Novalis sums up the case, "Inward goes the way full of mystery," and Bishop's Man-Moth begins now to head forward, toward "that round clean opening" in the sky (*BCP*, 14). Thus, poetry in the modern age which attempts to be "accurate" will not just be "mimetic." It will be poetry, Taylor observes, "that makes something appear, brings it into our presence . . . [not] *in* the object or image or words presented; it would be better to say that it happens *between* them . . . a force field which can capture a more intense energy."[29]

28. Lombardi, *The Body and the Song*, 70, for Bishop's reading of Barthes; Charles Taylor, *Sources of the Self: The Making of the Modern Identity* (Chicago, 1993), 188, 195, 197, 198.

29. Taylor, *Sources of the Self*, 426, 473, 420, 442, 95, 427, 475. Readers of Bishop are fairly unanimous in identifying abundant "reserves of mystery" throughout her work, what Helen Vendler aptly anoints the "guerilla attack of the alien" in "Domestication, Domesticity, and the Otherworldly," *Elizabeth Bishop and Her Art*, ed. Lloyd Schwartz and Sybil P. Estess (Ann Arbor, 1983), 48, 37, and Lombardi tags "the primary source of pleasure," in *The Body and the Song*, 45. See further: Kalstone, *Five Temperaments*, 21; Travisano, *Elizabeth Bishop*, 21, 24, 122, 126, 154; McCabe, *Elizabeth Bishop*, 15; Parker, *The Unbeliever*, 83; and, Harrison, *Elizabeth Bishop's Poetics of Intimacy*, 5, 13, 39, 64, 69, 72, 125, 138, 157, 201. With respect to Bishop's creature "heading" in an otherly direction, Derrida remarks that "the heading of an other being [is] perhaps the first condition of an 'identity' that is *not* an egocentrism destructive of oneself and the other." Jacques Derrida, *The Other Heading: Reflections on Today's Europe* (Bloomington, 1992), 15, emphasis added, thus corroborating the necessity for enlarging the distance in this and other of Bishop's early Modernist texts.

Yet here is Elizabeth Bishop in 1929 (at an astonishingly precocious eighteen years of age) expatiating on precisely these issues:

> How very boring the world would be were it not for the rebellious and uncontrolled lava within it that does queer and violent things whenever it feels like it. . . . We have in ourselves, not the boiling lava of the earth, but a kind of burning, unceasing energy of some sort that will not let us be finished off and live in the world like the china people on the mantlepiece [sic]. This energy, this fire, is always there, ready to explode or to burn fretfully, to show itself surprisingly in our work, our games, our looks and actions. It is the part of us that the Blue Pencil [her student journal] uses for its stories and poems—and editorials.

With this foregrounding of a "betweenness" of force or energy in modern "poiesis"—the "space," the "gap," but more particularly the "distance" registering an "alterity . . . between sign and signified" where Bishop is inclined to locate "queer and violent things"—Taylor is finally able to gain a purchase on the formulation of his Modernist subjectivism:

> The recognition that we live on many levels has to be won against the presumptions of the unified self, controlling or expressive. And this means a reflexive turn, something which intensifies our sense of inwardness and depth, which we have seen building up through the whole modern period. . . . The reflexive move comes first in the fact that we unveil the power of language by turning back onto it from our ordinary unthinking focus on things. We have to stop seeing language as simply an inert instrument whereby we can deal more effectively with things. It involves becoming aware of what we do with words. . . . The modernist multi-levelled consciousness is thus frequently "decentred": aware of living on a transpersonal rhythm which is mutually irreducible in relation to the personal. But for all that it remains inward; and is the first only through being the second. The two features are inseparable.

The spectral lesbian poetics of Elizabeth Bishop similarly may be thought to be a constituted effect of a "transpersonal rhythm" locatable in the "spaces between" things—her example comes from a "fragile net-work" of flying birds—"interspaces mov[ing] in pulsation," actually, which are not to be thought "a blankness[,] but a space as musical as all the sound." In this way, her most famous bird, "The Sandpiper," is perhaps panicked by the loss of a controlled self not through the ceaseless movement of his toes, but by "the spaces of sand between them" (BCP, 131). He therefore enters into Taylor's weighty lexicon of theorists of modern decenterment, "looking for something, something, something" (*BCP*, 131), which in the "O Canada!" context of lesbian sexuality, becomes for an "American" poet the "epiphany . . . of something only indirectly available, something the visible object can't say itself but only nudges us towards."[30]

When we come, finally, to "The Gentleman of Shalott" from 1936, not only do we discover a Modernist text that looks back to the travail of dissident subjectivity in the complex shift away from the discursive paradigms of Classical representation in the history of Western thought, already well under way in the original "The Lady of Shalott," when "The mirror cracked from side to side," and Tennyson's Lady leaves her room (III.v). But we also encounter a text that looks forward, one that for several decades sets the stage for Bishop's own personal travail in arranging a life in America (and elsewhere, as we shall see in the next section) to accord with an art filled with the possibility and promise she would always associate with her childhood in Canada:[31] "what we imagine knowledge to be . . . drawn from the cold hard mouth / of the world" (*BCP*, 66).

In order for Bishop to bring life into line with art, however, she knew that she would inevitably have to move past the closed mimetic economy of grand-

30. Elizabeth Bishop, quoted in Parker, *The Unbeliever*, 141; Taylor, *Sources of the Self*, 478, 479, 480, 481; Elizabeth Bishop, quoted in Millier, *Elizabeth Bishop*, 45; Taylor, *Sources of the Self*, 469. The inconclusiveness of subjectivity in Bishop's spectral poetics is perhaps best rendered by the mysterious status of "knowledge" at the conclusion of one of her most famous "Canadian" poems, "At the Fishhouses" (1948):

> It is like what we imagine knowledge to be:
> dark, salt, clear, moving, utterly free,
> drawn from the cold hard mouth
> of the world, derived from the rocky breasts
> forever, flowing and drawn, and since
> our knowledge is historical, flowing, and flown.
> (*BCP*, 66)

In locating this text in a Pragmatist context not unlike Taylor's argument for a discursive Modernism, Giles Gunn would view it as a moment "when those capacities that enable language to swerve away from its own inherited meanings . . . are seen as a source of empowerment that needs no sanctions, religious or otherwise, for the sense of personal enhancement that accompanies them," and attaches particular importance to "the way the writing calls attention to the performative presence of the self even in gestures of its own dissolution or self-effacement." Gunn, *Thinking Across the American Grain*, 149 (184 is related). Hence, "many of Bishop's characters lose themselves to find themselves," as Bonnie Costello remarks (Costello, "One Art," 113), since, as Parker concludes his study *The Unbeliever*, "The bare existentialism of identity exceeds the reach of [Bishop's] language" (143–44).

31. See esp Harrison, *Elizabeth Bishop's Poetics of Intimacy*, 184–85.

mother's replicative "real" eye, in order to cultivate the open semiotic economy of the more proliferant "glass" one. Yet because progress towards the latter can only be charted within a relation of dependence on the former, in this third text, Bishop brings the crisis of vision in her spectral poetics to a "head," so to speak, halfway between the Classicism of "The Unbeliever," on the one hand, and the Modernism of "The Man-Moth," on the other, reflected by the Gentleman's "doubt":

> But he's in doubt
> as to which side's in or out
> of the mirror.
> There's little margin for error,
> but there's no proof, either.
> And if half his head's reflected,
> thought, he thinks, might be affected.
> (*BCP*, 9)

With only half a head devoted to a self-replicating foundationalism, the Gentleman's unseen half steers us clearly in the direction of what Žižek would describe as "the opposition between a harmonious work of art and the queer remainder which sticks out," already anticipated by the sleeper's head left out "in the air of the night" in "The Unbeliever," and again by the "small head" attempting to thrust itself out of the urban enclosures of "The Man-Moth" (*BCP*, 22, 14).[32]

Yet the remarkable insight of Bishop's poem occurs when her Gentleman shows absolutely no inclination to efface the harmonious work of art for the sake of its unseen/obscene remainder, for "he's resigned / to such economical design" (*BCP*, 9). Here, the implication seems to be that the unseen supererogatory glass "I" takes form on the basis of what is seen to be a more naturally correspondent

32. Žižek, *Enjoy Your Symptom!* 179, and further on 78, 89, 100. "'Freedom is knowledge of necessity,'" Bishop has the narrator remark at the end of "In Prison." "I believe nothing as ardently as I do that" (*BCPr*, 191). In the context of Bishop's intense preoccupation with subjectivity, David Lehman's gloss on this passage is insightful: "It is almost as though he (or his author) were consciously designing a test for 'one' art—singular, definitive of the poet's identity—an art that feeds on what might otherwise consume it, that thrives on loss that welcomes limits in order to transcend them . . . [hence,] the mentality that yearns for fixed borders." David Lehman, "'In Prison': A Paradox Regained," in *Elizabeth Bishop and Her Art*, ed. Lloyd Schwartz and Sybil P. Estess (Ann Arbor, 1983), 68–69. Cf. Kalstone, *Five Temperaments*, 22, 32, and Travisano, *Elizabeth Bishop*, 25, 28. "The best way out, the only way out, is through," as Ray Carney remarks in the Pragmatist context. Carney, *American Vision*, 311.

true "I"—or, to reverse the terms slightly, on the basis of what is in language and
yet *more* than language. Judith Butler may be enlisted to gloss what appears to be
a mirror with two faces in this harmonious arrangement when she writes, "The
body in the mirror does not represent a body that is, as it were, before the mirror:
the mirror, even as it is instigated by that unrepresentable body 'before' the mirror, produces that body as its delirious effect—a delirium, by the way, which we
are compelled to live." Bishop's Gentleman could hardly be less delirious: "The
uncertainty / [the Gentleman] says he / finds exhilarating" (*BCP*, 10). Hence, if
what we are given by Bishop's lesbian spectral poetics in the dimorphism of this
"Gentleman" may be construed, in the end, as a kind of lesbian phallus, to speak
of such "as a possible site of desire," as Butler explains, "is not to refer to an
imaginary identification and/or desire that can be measured against a *real* one; on
the contrary, it is simply to promote an alternative *imaginary* to a hegemonic
imaginary and to show, through that assertion, the ways in which the hegemonic
imaginary constitutes itself through the naturalization of an exclusionary heterosexual morphology."[33] Elizabeth Bishop would still have a long way to go to reverse that sense of exclusion in her own life. But to the extent that we descry the
horizon of an alternative "Canadian" imaginary already firmly in place in her earliest art, it still remains possible for her "American" identity to work towards that
vanishing point—go the distance, as it were, in another Modernist American text
for the sake of what her Gentleman loves most: "that sense of constant re-adjust-
ment" (*BCP*, 10). And because both "Canada" and "America" would each remain
so instinct, so interanimate with the other, in the gender exploration that lay
ahead both in literature and in life, from the very beginning Bishop, like her
Gentleman of Shalott, no doubt also "wishes to be quoted as saying at present:
'Half is enough'" (*BCP*, 10).

In this wrap-up of the chapter, I want to move much further ahead in the Bishop
canon in order to take up another group of related poems that the poet went a
considerable distance, literally, to compose. The texts come from *Questions of
Travel* (1965), a gathering of verse published near the end of Bishop's lengthy
stay in Brazil alluded to previously. My aim, therefore, in this final section is to
provide a much rounder portrait of the dissident subject in Bishop's lifetime project, so that if a certain "spectral" lesbian poetics might be thought to be of some
concern in the poet's earlier work, a correspondingly "spectral" postcolonial poetics could conceivably be imagined taking shape in the later. The join between

---

33. Butler, *Bodies That Matter*, 91.

early and late Bishop, of course, would be the distance—that "sophisticated, privileged space," in Toni Morrison's words remarked upon in the Introduction— maintained and guarded at the heart of Modernist treatments of the rogue subject that have all along formed the central focus throughout this study of various twentieth-century American writers.

Now one of the questions in "Questions of Travel," the third poem in Elizabeth Bishop's third collection of verse bearing the same title, centers itself upon the image of home. "Think of the long trip home," the poet adjures (*BCP*, 93). Then comes: "Should we have stayed at home and thought of here? / Where should we be today?" (*BCP*, 93) Appearing in the "Brazil" section of *Questions of Travel* and ostensibly recounting her initial encounter with that country either in 1951 or 1952, the text's "here," designating a rich landscape of waterfalls, streams, mountaintops, and sunsets, suggests that the true "home" for Bishop was likely the United States. Bishop's biographer, however, complicates the sense of "home" by describing the poet's embarkation upon her seventeen-year South American sojourn in 1952 thus:

> [Bishop] would not live alone; she would not have to get a job (the income from her father's estate would keep her in Brazil as it could not in the United States) . . . and in the "timeless" Brazilian world she would be free at last from the pace of New York, which had seemed to her a dizzying plunge toward loss and death. The very impracticality and inefficiency of the Brazilian way of doing things charmed her thoroughly . . . [so that] [b]y the time [Bishop] returned to Rio on June 7 [1952], she was glad to be "home."

Where, then, is "home" for Elizabeth Bishop: the United Sates? South America? Or perhaps "Elsewhere"—the second section of *Questions of Travel*—Canada, for instance, as she intimates in a letter to Robert Lowell from 1958:

> There are wonderful birds now—one a blood-red, very quick, who perches on the very tops of trees and screams to his *two* mates—wife and mistress, I presume, again in the Brazilian manner. But oh dear—my aunt writes me long descriptions of the "fall colors" in Nova Scotia and I wonder if that's where I shouldn't be, after all.
>
> (*OA*, 366)

Indeed, Bishop's sense of "home" suffers a further complication when her Aunt Grace sends to her in the States "two family portraits from Nova Scotia" that Bishop is at last only able to view firsthand in her South American "home-away-

168   GOING THE DISTANCE

from-home": "how strange to see them in Brazil" (*OA,* 349). In the end, maybe "place doesn't matter so much to writers," as Bishop parenthetically remarks to Ilse and Kit Barker in an earlier letter from 1954 (*OA,* 292). In which case there really is *no place* like home, as only a "friend of Dorothy" (camp argot for "gay") with a queer sense of irony might understand.[34]

Still, the question of "home" persists in *Questions of Travel* that Bishop published a little over a decade later, particularly at the well-known close to the poem after which the volume is named:

> *"Is it lack of imagination that makes us come*
> *to imagined places, not just stay at home?*
> . . . .
> *And here, or there . . . No. Should we have stayed at home,*
> *wherever that may be?"*

(*BCP,* 94)

By 1965, of course, Brazil had completely reversed itself in Bishop's mind according to her biographer: "She had felt her strangeness all her life, had escaped it for a time in Brazil, but now that sense was back." Mother-loss, homosexuality, alcoholism, and artistic self-doubt are all postulated by Millier to round out that homeless sense of "strangeness"—one that, not uncoincidentally, Millier uses Bishop's "Strayed Crab" from her 1969 *Complete Poems* to frame: "This is not my home. . . . It must be over that way somewhere" (*BCP,* 140). If the later poetry of Elizabeth Bishop is any indication, therefore, it can hardly be doubted that "Home and the loss of home constitute a recurring motif of modernity," particu-

34. Millier, *Elizabeth Bishop,* 246. The phrase "no place like home" is also used by McClintock et al. to introduce their new gathering of "postcolonial studies" essays on behalf of the Social Text Collective: "'There's no place like home,' whispers a dislocated Dorothy as she and her lost dog, so far away from Kansas, hanker to get back home. Comforting words, written by Frank Baum in 1900 just as U.S. expansionism was yet again displacing Native America and denying its quest for a settled share of land, now met with a 'vanishing-world' nostalgia." Anne McClintock, Aamir Mufti, and Ella Shohat, introduction to *Dangerous Liaisons: Gender, Nation, and Postcolonial Perspectives* (Minneapolis, 1997), 1. Demetrio Yocum further observes that "Martin Heidegger, in *Return to the Native Land* on Hölderlin's poetry, argues that there is no primary original home; such a place will never be found. Like the traveller's journey, the poet is consumed in the separation from the lost homeland and *articulates its absence.* Only in this manner might the poet approach it. Therefore poetic writing delineates the impossibility of a 'return to a homeland,' of a final voyage home." Demetrio Yocum, "Some Troubled Homecomings," in *The Post-Colonial Question: Common Skies, Divided Horizons,* ed. Iain Chambers and Lidia Curti (London, 1996), 221, italics retained.

larly in view of the fact, as in Bishop's case, that "the loss of home and the struggle to reclaim and reimagine it are experiences fraught with tension." Accordingly, postcolonial theorists offer "the figure of the migrant" as modernity's "social type"—one for whom "home, that place and time outside place and time, appears to mingle promiscuously with its opposite—exile, the outside, elsewhere." That Bishop's own opposition between "Brazil" and "Elsewhere" in her *Questions of Travel* should so closely follow this dichotomous theoretical trajectory can thus set us before a kind of "double bind within which criticism is practiced today[,] in a context where 'home' is both a myth of belonging and the name of a state that criticism cannot avoid wanting to inhabit"—a double bind that may usefully be seen to inform what I shall here nominate as Elizabeth Bishop's "postcolonial poetics."[35]

Yet if "the idea of home appears locked within a fundamental ambivalence," another kind of double bind appears to shadow—double, if you will—the first. Here, the image of home in a more intensely conflicted sense is rent between "a Euro-American masculinist ideology of domesticity . . . of imperial gregariousness," on the one hand, and those "communities of mobilization against precisely that hegemonism,"[36] on the other hand, communities that I am tempted, following Bishop, to code as distinctively feminist in their contrapuntal resistance. The two poems preceding "Questions of Travel" might be thought to establish the

35. Millier, *Elizabeth Bishop*, 388, 387; McClintock, Mufti, and Shohat, introduction to *Dangerous Liaisons*, 2, 8, 8. In his indispensable essay "The World and the Home," Homi Bhabha similarly gives voice "to the unhomely condition of the modern world," and more particularly speaks to "the unhomely [as] a paradigmatic postcolonial experience." Homi Bhabha, "The World and the Home," in *Dangerous Liaisons: Gender, Nation, and Postcolonial Perspectives*, ed. Anne McClintock, Aamir Mufti, and Ella Shohat (Minneapolis), 448, 446. Similarly, Iain Chambers gives voice to "a modernity [that] is maintained not by the stable physicality of a permanent home but by the risky experience of travel and transit sustained by 'imaginary homelands' (Salman Rushdie) and disrupted patrimonies." Iain Chambers, "Signs of Silence, Lines of Listening," in *The Post-Colonial Question: Common Skies, Divided Horizons*, ed. Iain Chambers and Lidia Curti (London, 1996), 53. Thus, as Stuart Hall observes, "[Post-colonialism] is the retrospective re-phrasing of Modernity within the framework of 'globalisation' in all its various ruptural forms and moments. . . . Understood in its global and transcultural context, colonization has made ethnic absolutism an increasingly untenable cultural strategy. It made the 'colonies' themselves, and even more, large tracts of the 'post-colonial' world, always-already 'diasporic' in relation to what might be thought of as their cultures of origin. . . . [Hence,] what distinguishes modernity is this over-determined, sutured and *supplementary* character of its temporalities." Stuart Hall, "When Was the Post-Colonial? Thinking at the Limit," in *The Post-Colonial Question: Common Skies, Divided Horizons*, ed. Iain Chambers and Lidia Curti (London, 1996), 250, 251.

36. McClintock, Mufti, and Shohat, introduction to *Dangerous Liaisons*, 1.

limits of this more politically clamant double bind. In "Brazil, January 1, 1502,"
for instance, it's a group of very tough, very aggressive Christian soldiers—"hard
as nails, / tiny as nails, and glinting, / in creaking armor" (*BCP*, 92)—who present
the reader with the sense of a masculinist ideology of domesticity that is linked
to "an old dream of wealth and luxury . . . when they [leave] home" in one place,
and belligerently attempt to discover it "not unfamiliar" and "corresponding, nevertheless" in another. In Bishop's historical narrative,

> they ripped away into the hanging fabric,
> each out to catch an Indian for himself—
> those maddening little women who kept calling,
> calling to each other (or had the birds waked up?)
> and retreating, always retreating, behind it.
>   (*BCP*, 92)

As for the counter-hegemonic resistance to such masculinist aggression, Bishop
offers "Arrival at Santos" as an introduction to *Questions of Travel.*

Now Miss Breen in this introductory poem, "[Whose] home, when she is at
home, is in Glens Fall / s, New York" (*BCP*, 89), together with (one supposes)
her female fellow-traveler—both women can hardly be viewed as a counter-hegemonic "community" of mobilization. Nonetheless, the arguably agile manner
with which they manage successfully to negotiate their way past their menacingly
masculine surroundings—"Please, boy, do be more careful with that boat hook!"
and so forth (*BCP*, 89)—such deportment does suggest that these women very
well *might* form such a colony, and with the several repetitions of "we" near the
end of the poem, perhaps sooner rather than later:

> There. We are settled.
> The customs officials will speak English, we hope,
> and leave us our bourbon and cigarettes.
> . . . .
>   . . . We leave Santos at once;
> we are driving to the interior.
>   (*BCP*, 90)

With respect to this last text, Bishop's biographer helpfully informs the reader
that "Miss Breen" actually existed in real life, and that what the poet en route to
Brazil got from a brief acquaintance with this woman "was a vision of an accomplished and successful lesbian life, not at all secretive or ashamed, and at a time

when [Bishop] was herself at a major transition." Hence, with the doubling between virulently heterosexual and compliantly homosexual communities in the
aggression and resistance straddling these last two homebound poems, we are
perhaps afforded the clearest sense of what, in Walter Benjamin's apt phrasing,
"carr[ying] the incommensurable to extremes in the representation of human life
and in the midst of life's fullness" is perhaps most intended to convey: namely,
the sense that the "home" *can* be "refashioned . . . by cultural production as a
whole, once its violent and exclusionary function vis-à-vis women and other
minorities stands so unnervingly exposed," and allowed to "transcend the boundaries separating segregated disciplines, discourses, and communities of identification and mobilization."[37]
      The transvaluation of home coterminous with the transcendence of bound-
aries places otherwise segregated communities of women between Bishop's two
opening poems—native on the one hand and lesbian on the other—in an empowering alignment of identification and mobilization where, as Homi Bhabha
observes in a related context, "the limits of race and gender . . . are in a position
to translate the differences between them into a kind of solidarity." One achieves
that kind of solidarity, Bhabha scruples further to observe, "by living on the borderline between history and language," so that it's important to view both of these
referents steadily and in relation to each other. It does have to be acknowledged,
however, that Bishop not always could. Her biographer, once again, relates how
important it was for Bishop "to restrain her urge to impose a North American,
even a New England, standard of judgment" in order to sustain "her strongest
writings about Brazil."[38] But some of Bishop's ruminations on Brazilian life are
nasty enough to make a shambles of any kind of judgmental standard, North
American or otherwise:

> Now I know why poor children cry more than rich ones. It isn't that they don't
> have enough to eat or anything like that; it's just because their parents are so dumb
> the way they treat them. . . . I really do think that stupid or ignorant people *like* to
> be mean to babies unnecessarily . . . but there's not much we can do after a certain
> point, after all. . . .
>   I don't know how you feel about Indians . . . the most primitive people alive
> except for the pygmies. . . . It's only depressing to think about their future. They
> are quite naked, just a few beads; handsome, plump, behaving just like gentle chil-
> dren a little spoiled. . . .

37. Millier, *Elizabeth Bishop*, 239; Walter Benjamin, quoted in Bhabha, "The World and the
Home," 449; McClintock, Mufti, and Shohat, introduction to *Dangerous Liaisons*, 11.
      38. Homi Bhabha, *The Location of Culture* (London, 1994), 170; Millier, *Elizabeth Bishop*, 311.

But I am pessimistic about anything Brazilian, I'm afraid. I've never known such a bunch of uncooperative, self-indulgent, spoiled—and yes, *corrupted,* even the nice ones—people . . . but you know how true it is. . . . It is just something in the air.

(*OA,* 321, 362, 393)

Where in any of these various ruminations on race and gender and class, we might ask, is the sense of difference that, at the margins of culture, ought to bespeak political and social solidarity?

If there is to be a new cultural politics of difference, as Cornel West argues in a well-known essay, "[i]t will require all the imagination, intelligence, courage, sacrifice, care and laughter we can muster." For Bishop, imagination would undoubtedly have had the greatest appeal in this searching list—the very imagination whose lack, as we've seen, *"makes us come / to imagined places, not just stay at home"* (*BCP,* 94). And yet the more Bishop revolved the sense of place under the impress of her imagination, the less constrained she felt by the need for home, *"wherever that may be"* (*BCP,* 94). "I want an *old* farmhouse," she was once given to remark, "but I think it's better to . . . see from a distance—not be right there with the rocks and mud [since] this is all a day-dream." In that "distance" interposed between rocks and mud on one side and fertile day-dreams on the other we perhaps descry that borderline between history and language along which, according to Bhabha, social and cultural differences might at last come into their own. Bishop's "distance" thus bears an uncanny resemblance to "the disturbing distance in-between [the colonialist Self and the colonized Other] that," in Bhabha's further speculation, "constitutes the figure of colonial otherness."[39] And

39. Cornel West, "The New Cultural Politics of Difference," in *Beyond a Dream Deferred: Multicultural Education and the Poltics of Excellence,* ed. Becky W. Thompson and Sangeeta Tyagi (Minneapolis, 1993), 39; Elizabeth Bishop, quoted in Millier, *Elizabeth Bishop,* 348; Bhabha, *The Location of Culture,* 45. "It is in relation to this impossible object [the disturbing distance just noted]," Bhabha concludes, "that the liminal problem of colonial identity and its vicissitudes emerges" (45)—or indeed, the problem of dissident subjectivity more generally in Modernist discourse, as this study has been at pains to reveal throughout. In a related passage that illuminates further the "distance" that Bishop would imagine opening up in the dream-figures of house and home, Bhabha observes: "[The] spheres of [social experience] are linked through an 'in-between' temporality that takes the measure of dwelling at home, while producing an image of the world of history. This is the moment of aesthetic distance that provides the narrative with a double edge that . . . represents a hybridity, a difference 'within,' a subject that inhabits the rim on an 'in-between' reality . . . at the crossroads of history and literature, bridging the home and the world." Bhabha, "The World and the Home," 451. Arif Dirlik also remarks on a "'hybridness' or 'in-betweenness' of the postcolonial subject which is not to be contained within fixed categories or binary oppositions." Arif Dirlik, "The Postcolonial Aura: Third World Criticism in the Age of Global Capitalism," in *Dangerous Liaisons: Gender, Nation, and*

it perhaps comes as no accident that precisely in that impossible distanciation between history and language that Bishop herself should sense "[her] Anglo-Saxon blood . . . gradually relinquishing its seasonal cycle," and consequently, find herself "quite content to live in complete confusion, about seasons, fruits, languages, geography, everything [since] [t]here are hundreds of birds now, but nobody knows their names" (*OA*, 243). If there really is *no place* like home, for Bishop, as for Bhabha, it is the "impossible object" of colonial otherness—"the really lofty vagueness of Brazil" (*OA*, 237)—that makes it so.[40]

The three longest poems in the "Brazil" section of *Questions of Travel* published between 1956 and 1960 to which I now turn to round out this discussion of Bishop's distanciated poetics—all three poems in their separate ways take up the investigation of colonial subjectivity and its problematic relation to home that was undoubtedly provoked by the poet's own long-term Third World migrancy. In the longest of these texts, "The Burglar of Babylon," Bishop revolves the relation to home from the side of history, basing the forty-odd stanzas of her *faux naif* ballad on an actual event that took place in April of 1963 while "she watched idly from the balcony in Rio as police pursued a thief over the steep hills behind [her] building."[41]

> Micuçú was a burglar and killer,
>   An enemy of society.
> He had escaped three times
>   From the worst penitentiary.
>
> They don't know how many he murdered
>   (Though they say he never raped),

Postcolonial Perspectives, ed. Anne McClintock *et al.* (Minneapolis, 1997), 506. Thus, "[t]he concept of space," according to Paul Gilroy, "is itself transformed when it is seen less through outmoded notions of fixity and place and more in terms of the ex-centric communicative circuitry that has enabled dispersed populations to converse, interact and even synchronise" by means of "the constitutive asymmetry of the insubordinate political cultures nurtured in what Homi Bhabha calls 'the in between' [*sic*]." Paul Gilroy, "Route Work: The Black Atlantic and the Politics of Exile," *The Post-Colonial Question: Common Skies, Divided Horizons*, ed. Iain Chambers and Lidia Curti (London, 1996), 22, 23. See also Chambers, "Signs of Silence, Lines of Listening," 59.

40. Bhabha, *The Location of Culture*, 45. With reference to Bishop's willfully "complete confusion" here, Bhabha perhaps might say that the poet "displays the unhomely world" of colonial otherness, that is to say, "'the halfway between, *not defined*' world of the colored, as . . . an image of 'interstices,' the in-between hybridity of the history of sexuality and race." Bhabha "The World and the Home," 452, emphasis added.

41. Millier, *Elizabeth Bishop*, 345.

And he wounded two policemen
This last time he escaped.
                              (*BCP*, 112–13)

As it turns out, Micuçú isn't much of a burglar—"He got caught six times—or more" (*BCP*, 117)—and he ends up dead, shot "behind the ear" (*BCP*, 116), as he "dashed for shelter" among the caves in the hillside Babylon slum (*BCP*, 113).

In his important set of "Reflections on Exile," Edward Said elaborates briefly upon one possible issue at back of this first rendering of Bishop's migratory discourse. "Most people," Said tells us, "are principally aware of one culture, one setting, one home," but that "exiles are aware of at least two," and it is precisely this "contrapuntal" awareness that accounts for an exilic or postcolonial "plurality of vision." In Bishop's "Burglar," it's perhaps the act of "wound[ing] two policemen" just noticed that sets her protagonist completely outside the lawful regulation of the single setting or the unitive culture—a hypernormative extrusion, like Bishop's own sense of homelessness previously rehearsed, that in all likelihood produces in her homeless outlaw the contrapuntal crisis of vision when he observes:

There are caves up there, and hideouts,
    And an old fort, falling down.
They used to watch for Frenchmen
    From the hill of Babylon.

Below him was the ocean.
    It reached far up the sky,
Flat as a wall, and on it
    Were freighters passing by,

Or climbing the wall, and climbing
    Till each looked like a fly,
And then fell over and vanished;
    And he knew he was going to die.
                              (*BCP*, 113–14)

In the poetical presentation here of the colonial identity straddling a kind of bipolar location between subjective porosity ("caves," "hideouts,") and density ("freighters," "wall"), Bishop aims to render "a repertoire of conflictual positions that constitute the subject in colonial discourse [as] . . . the site of both fixity *and* fantasy." As Lota Soares, the poet's lover of some fifteen years, was given to remark in a parallel instance, "I always thought a strange trait in the human nature—the desire for the permanent, when in realité we are always changing—does not make sense" (*OA*, 367). Once again, dissident subjectivity finds itself on that impossible borderline between fact and fiction where, "[n]ot quite the Same, not quite Other, [it] stands in that undetermined threshold place . . . constantly drifting in and out." And by depicting the in-betweenness of Micuçú's demise as he "dashed *for* shelter" (*BCP*, 116), Bishop registers a certain resistance to any pat or "homey" resolution to the subjective drift of her "Burglar," since, as she remarks about "Faustina" in her previous collection *A Cold Spring* (1955), "it is hard to choose among the various versions [one] gives of [one's] life" (*OA*, 152).⁴²

Most critics of Bishop's work tend to remark on the discursive shift between her early and later writing, as Margaret Dickie recently observes: "from her surrealistic Paris poems to her realistic Brazilian writing." The second in the trio of longer "Brazil" poems, "The Riverman," can therefore present some difficulty to readers, since both its form ("magical fiction," according to her biographer) and much of its content (drawn from Charles Wagley's arcane *Amazon Town*) turn a conventional dramatic monologue into what Robert Lowell once described as "an effective fairy tale." Postcolonial critics, however, who target realism as a "tactic of nationalist legitimation," and thus are happy to begin nudging their own theoretical projects in the direction of what Kwame Anthony Appiah elects to call the "postrealist"—such critics can be very helpful in allowing us to see how Bishop perhaps reverses the rhetorical direction of her more realistic "Burglar," proposing in the postrealism of this second poem to revolve the colonial subject's relation to home from the side of language now rather than history.⁴³

42. Edward Said, "Reflections on Exile," in *Out There: Marginalization and Contemporary Cultures*, ed. Russell Ferguson et al. (Cambridge, Mass., 1992), 366; Bhabha, "The Other Question: Difference, Discrimination, and the Discourse of Colonialism," in *Out There: Marginalization and Contemporary Cultures*, ed. Russell Ferguson et al. (Cambridge, Mass., 1992), 81; Trinh T. Minh-Ha, *When the Moon Waxes Red: Representation, Gender, and Cultural Politics* (London, 1991), 74. Iain Chambers also underscores the "critical necessity" of thinking about the construction of colonial subjectivity in similar terms: "to navigate, sometimes to drift, between the seeming security of the shore and the hazy promise of the horizon, where narratives of identity and belonging are compounded and rendered composite, complex." Chambers, "Signs of Silence, Lines of Listening," 53.

43. Margaret Dickie, *Stein, Bishop, and Rich: Lyrics of Love, War, and Place* (Chapel Hill, 1997), 122, and further on 91 and in Travisano, *Elizabeth Bishop*, 3–4; Millier, *Elizabeth Bishop*, 304; Kwame Anthony Appiah, "Is the 'Post-' in 'Postcolonial' the 'Post-' in 'Postmodern'?" *Dangerous Liaisons: Gender, Nation, and Postcolonial Perspectives*, ed. Anne McClintock, Aamir Mufti, Ella Shohat (Minneapolis, 1997), 433; cf. Bhabha, *The Location of Culture*, 71, 125. The rhetoric of realism will thus

An exhilarating sense of homelessness seems key to this reversal as the River-man, answering the call of his Dolphin muse "from far outstream," takes leave "through the window naked" of his dwelling on land early in the poem, pausing only momentarily to look "back at my house, / white as a piece of washing / forgotten on the bank" (*BCP*, 105–106). Yet as he makes his way through "room after room . . . [for] miles, under the river" (*BCP*, 106), the Riverman has not actually left home, we realize, but instead has completely altered his conceptual relation towards it, in contrast, for example, to the correspondent "old dream" epistemology of the Christian soldiers noted back in "Brazil, January 1, 1502" (*BCP*, 92):

> I need a virgin mirror
> no one's ever looked at,
> that's never looked back at anyone,
> to flash up the spirit's eyes
> and help me recognize them.
> The storekeeper offered me
> a box of little mirrors,
> but each time I picked one up
> a neighbor looked over my shoulder
> and then that one was spoiled—
>
> (*BCP*, 107)

In this extraordinary passage, the Riverman searches beyond home (where "no one's ever looked") for self-knowledge in some homeless Other ("that's never looked back at anyone") only "spoiling" to discover that Other already in the Self ("look[ing] over my shoulder") and the Self already in the Other. Yet as Slavoj

---

die a long and painful death, according to Appiah, "For the 'post' in postcolonial, like the 'post' in postmodern, is the 'post' of the space-clearing gesture . . . and many areas of contemporary African cultural life (what has come to be theorized as popular culture, in particular) are not in this way concerned with transcending—with going beyond—coloniality." Appiah, "Is the 'Post-' in Postcolonial," 432. In summing up the rhetorical split on the issue of realism between two poems in the *same* "Brazil" section of Bishop's third collection, Bhabha's theoretical speculations are once again helpful: "Two contradictory and independent attitudes inhabit the *same place*, one takes account of reality, the other is under the influence of instincts which detach the ego from reality. This results in the production of multiple and contradictory belief. The enunciatory moment of multiple belief is both a defence against the anxiety of difference, and itself *productive* of differentiations . . . [as] a strategy for articulating contradictory and coeval statements of belief . . . [that is,] a strategy for the negotiation of the knowledges of differentiation." Bhabha, *The Location of Culture*, 132.

Žižek remarks in a related context, "one 'surpasses' Understanding the moment one becomes aware of how it is already Understanding itself which is the living movement of self-mediation one was looking for in vain in its Beyond."[44]

Hence, self-knowledge continues to be haunted by its "otherness": in Bhabha's terms, "the impossible object" coterminous with "the liminal problem of colonial identity," or in Žižek's, "the spectre of an Object persisting in its Beyond." In the "spectral" postcolonial poetics of Elizabeth Bishop, however, whose *language* in "The Riverman" effects to distance itself equally from home and homelessness in the space in-between, there is the sense in which the impossibility of such beyondness is to be positively cultivated. "I know some things already," as her protagonist states, "but it will take years of study, / it is all so difficult" (*BCP*, 107).[45]

In such terms, therefore, "[t]o be unhomed is not [necessarily] to be homeless" if to be unhomed, in its most radical projection, "is the shock of the recognition of the world-in-the-home, the home-in-the-world".

> The river breathes in salt
> and breathes it out again,
> and all is sweetness there
> in the deep, enchanted silt.
>
> . . . .
>
> I'll be there . . .
> travelling fast as a wish,
> with my magic cloak of fish
> swerving as I swerve,
> following the veins,
> the river's long, long veins,
> to find the pure elixirs.
>   (*BCP*, 108–109)

In the lyrical fluidity of these magical lines from the concluding stanza of the poem, the notion of an autonomous subject "'positing' [its] substance" liquefies into something quite spectral: namely, "the gap within substance"—the distance opened up between fact and fiction once again—whose "discontinuity . . . prevents us from conceiving the substance as a self-contained totality." "You can peer

44. Žižek, *For They Know Not What They Do*, 158.
45. Bhabha, *The Location of Culture*, 45; Žižek, *For They Know Not What They Do*, 158.

down and down / or dredge the river bottom," as Bishop's Riverman hauntingly frames the case, "but never, never catch me" (*BCP*, 109).[46]

For Homi Bhabha, black American theorists like Patricia Hill Collins, Patricia Williams, and Toni Morrison are perhaps models of Bishop's "never-catch-me" subjectivity in the academy today—dissident subjects, that is to say, who see "the possibility of deploying [their "outsider-within" status] to describe an ambivalent, transgressive, fluid positioning" that (in Patricia Williams' words) "moves back and forth across a boundary which acknowledges that I can be black and good and black and bad and that I can also be black and white."[47] This extraordinarily paradoxical positioning of identity at the crossroads between self and other, fiction and fact, home and world is, in the end, what Bishop's "Manuelzinho," the third and final of her longer poems, is likely intended most to convey.

"A friend of the writer" who speaks the poem (*BCP*, 96) is apparently supposed to be Bishop's beloved Lota, so we know Manuelzinho existed in actual life as "the endearingly unreliable gardener at Samambaia," Lota Soares' Brazilian estate.[48] But precisely the *extent* to which the gardener exists as a real person is deliberately kept vague by the poet: "as if you'd been a gardener / in a fairy tale all this time / and at the word 'potatoes' / had vanished to take up your work / of fairy prince somewhere" (*BCP*, 97). Bishop sets the tone for this kind of indeterminacy right from the poem's outset:

> Half squatter, half tenant (no rent)—
> a sort of inheritance; white,
> in your thirties now, and supposed

46. Bhabha, "The World and the Home," 445, for which Chambers provides a useful gloss on the difficult thought here: "For the recognition of other histories, of other people, languages and sounds, of other ways of dwelling in the same space . . . invokes the recognition of their place, however obscured and repressed, in the very constitution of our own histories and culture; in our national and individual identities, in our psychic and social selves." Chambers, "Signs of Silence, Lines of Listening," 49; Žižek, *For They Know Not What They Do*, 221.

47. Bhabha, "The World and the Home," 453. The "truth" of the dissident subject is thus highly problematic, as each of Bhabha's models demonstrates. Yet as Bhabha remarks elsewhere, "The 'true' is always marked and informed by the ambivalence of the process of emergence itself, the productivity of meanings that construct counter-knowledges *in medias res*, in the very act of agonism, within the terms of a negotiation (rather than a negation) of oppositional and antagonistic elements." Bhabha, *The Location of Culture*, 22. Through such dissident subjects, therefore, "we learn the ambivalence of cultural difference: [that is,] the articulation *through* incommensurability that structures all narratives of identification, and all acts of cultural translation." Bhabha, *The Location of Culture*, 169.

48. Millier, *Elizabeth Bishop*, 271.

> to supply me with vegetables,
> but you don't; or you won't; or you can't
> get the idea through your brain—
> the world's worst gardener since Cain.
> (*BCP*, 96)

And the indeterminacy continues to the very end: "You helpless, foolish man, / I love you all I can, / I think. Or do I?" (*BCP*, 99)

Bishop's love-hate relationship with Manuelzinho conveyed in the poem's conclusion, wittingly or not, takes us to the very heart of her construction of colonial subjectivity. For love-hate seems to be what so inevitably *should* arise from that subjectivity's "ambivalence of psychic identification—that space where love and hate can be projected or inverted, where the relation of 'object' to identity is always split and doubled." Appropriately enough, Bishop imbues the space of her subject's psychic ambivalence with "wisps of fog":

> —All just standing, staring
> off into fog and space.
> Or coming down at night,
> In silence . . .
>
> . . . .
> Between us float a few
> big, soft, pale-blue,
> sluggish fireflies,
> the jellyfish of the air . . .
> (*BCP*, 98–99)

The image of the pale-blue "sluggish fireflies," calling attention as it does to the space of a certain in-between reality separating yet at the same time joining the poem's twin persona in the spectral night—"In the kitchen we dream together / how the meek shall inherit the earth—" (*BCP*, 98)—this image is powerfully suggestive of how delicate the psychic spaces were that Bishop's Brazilian poetry attempted to convey, and therefore how important it was that they be carefully guarded. Speaking very much to the "silence" pervading this passage as a whole, Bhabha would turn this guarding of colonial space into "an ethical act," and the occasion for "a statement on the responsibility of the critic": "For the critic must attempt to fully realize, and take responsibility for, the unspoken, unrepresented pasts that haunt the historical present."[49]

---

49. Bhabha, "The World and the Home," 448, 450. Following Nadine Gordimer (in her novel *My Son's Story* [1990]), Bhabha, very much like Bishop in the passage cited here, locates in silence

But perhaps it is Theodor Adorno who suggests how Bishop's "spectral" post-colonial poetics gain a wider ethical berth in cultural criticism today. Since "it is part of morality not to be at home in one's home," Adorno was wont to say about his own itinerant displacement after the Second World War, "the only home truly available now, though fragile and vulnerable, is in writing." And since "geography must be more mysterious than we realize," Bishop was given to observe (*OA*, 249), one would be hard pressed to locate another poet whose writing on Third World subjects could endeavor to be more at home in the world.[50] Nor in their spectral mysteries, more at home with Bishop's lesbian self, "wherever that may be" (*BCP*, 94).

"an image of 'interstices,' the in-between hybridity of the history of sexuality and race." Bhabha, "The World and the Home," 452. Exemplary of "the liminal problem of colonial identity," then, Bishop's Manuelzinho, as "[t]he silent Other of gesture and failed speech[,] becomes what Freud calls that 'haphazard member of the herd,' the Stranger, whose languageless presence evokes an archaic anxiety and aggressivity by impeding the search for narcissistic love-objects in which the subject can redis-cover himself, and upon which the group's *amour propre* is based." Bhabha, *The Location of Culture*, 166. "In acknowledging silence," Iain Chambers further remarks in this context, "the interval of the unsaid (and the unsayable), the shadows of the subaltern are thrown across the transparency of words accustomed to ignoring the ontology of silence; a silence which they invariably colonise as pure ab-sence, absolute lack." Chambers, "Signs of Silence, Lines of Listening," 51.

50. Theodor Adorno, quoted in Said, "Reflections on Exile," 365. As Iain Chambers might sum up the case more generally: "When occidental sounds, images, icons and languages travel elsewhere what remains peculiar to the West . . . [is that] [i]n travelling elsewhere its languages return in other forms, following other rhythms, bearing other desires. They cannot go home again. They are home." Chambers, "Signs of Silence, Lines of Listening," 57.

"To Hell with It":
Dissident Subjectivity's Feminist Distances

> *In* An American Tragedy, *defective membership means not only having no world but also having no self. . . . [Clyde Griffiths] is caught halfway through the door and imprisoned on the threshold. Literally, death row is such a threshold since the men there are no longer legally alive but not yet dispatched.*
>
> —PHILIP FISHER, *HARD FACTS*

> Le regard de l'autre, c'est l'enfer.
>
> —JEAN-PAUL SARTRE, *LES MOTS*

> *Woman, in the political vocabulary, will be the name for whatever undoes the whole.*
>
> —DENIS HOLLIER, *AGAINST ARCHITECTURE*

IN William Faulkner's Modernist classic, *The Sound and the Fury* (1929), we're likely to pass very quickly over a curious vignette about halfway through the second section, occurring as it does at the height of Quentin Compson's suicidal deliberations. The scene concerns three boys with fishing poles, and we find them chatting about what they might do with a reward for catching an old trout that has eluded anglers for years. "They all talked at once," writes Faulkner, "their voices insistent and contradictory and impatient, making of unreality a possibility, then a probability, then an incontrovertible fact, as people will when their desires become words." This passage is extraordinary not the least for the wisdom it speaks beyond its rather quaint homeliness. But mainly it is extraordinary I think because it's a passage that carries us toward the central problematic of all the American poets dealt with in this study, indeed, if not of nearly all Modernist

American writing in general, a problematic largely having to do with the desire
to make or manufacture reality—contrive "incontrovertible fact"—rather than
discover or emulate or transcribe reality as a fait accompli. The discursive shift
from the theological and ontological to something more programmatically anthropological and epistemological that licenses the *possibility* of reality, of course,
is much older than Faulkner. A whole tradition of Humanism, as Gianni Vattimo
argues, conspires to place "man at the centre of the universe" as "the master of
Being," and "maintains [his] position as the 'centre' of reality."[1]

William James, as we have had several occasions to glimpse in previous chapters, provides the theoretical backdrop to this tradition in American thought and
culture at the dawn of the twentieth century. In "Pragmatism and Humanism,"
for instance, he writes: "We *add*, both to the subject and to the predicate, part of
reality. The world stands really malleable, waiting to receive its final touches at
our hands. Like the kingdom of heaven, it suffers human violence willingly. Man
engenders truths upon it" (*P*, 167, emphases retained). What therefore becomes
problematic for a Modernist like Faulkner is the deeply divided sense of a reality
that is both infinitely made and, at the same time, finitely controlled and mas-
tered, "each in its ordered place" so Faulkner's novel concludes, at the center of
the discursive project. And if the contradictory and impatient voices of Faulkner's
three little boys are any indication, it is possible to imagine this divisiveness attaching itself to what perhaps ought to seem *most* real to the deeply troubled
Quentin Compson: male subjectivity itself.[2]

That subjectivity is hell for the literary Modernist—and for the male Modernist in particular, as we shall see—renders the most important level of meaning
suggested by my Conclusion's title. For modern art that is "genuinely bourgeois,"

1. William Faulkner, *The Sound and the Fury* (New York, 1946), 145; Gianni Vattimo, *The End
of Modernity: Nihilism and Hermeneutics in Postmodern Culture,* trans. and intro. Jon R. Snyder (Baltimore, 1988), 32–33. Gregor Campbell, following the work of Hans Blumenberg, states the case similarly as follows: "The absolutism of the gods creates a situation of dependency for both man and
nature, while the Promethean revolt of man against this dependency liberates man to begin the task
of turning nature into technology and suggests the social construction of reality as the foundation
of infinite progress and self-making." Gregor Campbell, "Work on Reason," *Diacritics* 21 (winter
1991): 63.

2. Faulkner, *The Sound and the Fury,* 401. Much later in this century, as Cary Wolfe recently
remarks on the work of neo-Pragmatist Cornel West, "the essence of Jamesian pragmatism is its
revisability; its first principle, in West's words, is that 'the universe is incomplete, the world is still "in
the making" owing to the impact of *human powers* on the universe and the world.'" Cary Wolfe,
Critical Environments: Postmodern Theory and the Pragmatics of the "Outside" (Minneapolis, 1998), 10,
second emphasis added.

CONCLUSION   183

as Peter Bürger cogently observes, holds out the genuine possibility for "the objectification of the self-understanding of the bourgeois class" in its historical "detachment from the sacral tie [which] is a first step in the emancipation of art."
And in Modernist discourse that is now in a position to validate and celebrate all
manner of constructed things, what must surely coincide with that objectification
of self-understanding is a subjectivity open to an increasing number of authentic
positions, in addition to the customary masculine (and by presumptive implication, heterosexual) one. The particular version of the artistic work that so-called
High Modernism usually presents us with, one that is autonomous, autotelic, au-
tomotive—this version comes into its own, as Bürger further notes, only at the
end of a long historical process that witnesses the "relative dissociation of the
work of art from the praxis of life," to the point where it "becomes transformed
into the (erroneous) idea that the work of art is totally independent of society."
The foreclosing of a quite complex set of gender issues concurrent with this
whole historical evolution is at no point a direct part of Bürger's extended argument. But it's at least implied by his view that the various movements of the
European avant-garde come together "as an attack on the status of art in bourgeois society," and specifically, an attack directed at Modernism "as an institution
that is unassociated with the life praxis of men."[3]

    Andreas Huyssen, whose indebtedness to Frankfurt School theory consider-
ably refines the general argument for art's "withdrawal from the concern for social
change," comes closer to the position I'm attempting to elaborate when he speaks
about how Modernism "has increasingly hollowed out . . . subjectivity and rendered its articulation highly problematic." But I'm not at all convinced that as a
result of Modernism's "anxiety of contamination" and "reaction formation to
mass culture and commodification," that "the powerful masculinist and misogy-
nist current within the trajectory of modernism," particularly in its association of
women with mass culture, requires that we look to a time considerably more recent if we are to expect that "the political aesthetic of feminism could thrive" and
thus transcend its "formerly neglected or ostracized form . . . of cultural expression."[4]

    3. Peter Bürger, *Theory of the Avant-Garde*, trans. Michael Shaw (Minneapolis, 1984), 47, 46,
49, and further on 19, 22. For heterosexual presumption as noted, see Susan Rubin Suleiman, *Subversive Intent: Gender, Politics, and the Avant-garde* (Cambridge, Mass., 1990), 37, 127, and 230 n. 42.
    4. Andreas Huyssen, *After the Great Divide: Modernism, Mass Culture, Postmodernism*
(Bloomington, 1986), 218, 46, vi, 24, 49, 61; further on 11, 53–54, 150, 163, 190. If my argument
at this point seems to impart to Huyssen's position a certain untenableness derived from a rather
seamless and homogeneous view taken toward literary Modernism, in all fairness to Huyssen, he
does remark that "modernism was never a monolithic phenomenon," and that the "alternative cultural

Surely the validation of female subjectivity, if what we have seen previously in the early work of Stein and Bishop (if not of Williams and Hughes) holds—surely this validation lies right within the making of Modernism itself, in *possibility*, to recur to Faulkner once more. And if masculinity seems more probable, and later, an "incontrovertible fact," as I think it does in the mode of High Modernism of Faulkner's novel, it's certainly not something that Modernism itself is discursively or rhetorically principled to arrange. Indeed, by starting from the conservative incontrovertibility of High Modernism, and working back through a more liberal or "probable,"[5] and an even more radical or "possible" phase of Modernism—the exemplary genealogy of two modern British poets, A. E. Housman and Gerard Manley Hopkins, and one American, Ezra Pound, as I briefly hope to show—we are perhaps better able to understand how Modernism's infamous collision with feminism begins to take on the appearance of something framed more by collusion, and without necessarily having to attend upon a later post-Modernism to tell us why.

Before turning to the excavation of this Modernist triangulation of poetic discourse, however, it is necessary to render a second, darker and more hidden level of meaning implied by my title that opens up with the historical authentication of female subjectivity just outlined. This meaning has largely to do with the new discursive direction in which we suddenly begin to find ourselves traveling when, in the detachment from the sacral noted previously, it is at last possible to proclaim that "Beauty *is* Truth," rather than *like* Truth, which according to the epistemology of John Keats, "is all / [We] know on earth, and all [we] need to know." This valorization of "earth" that greets us so often in Modernist poetry, for instance, when Yeats' "Horses of Disaster plunge in the heavy clay," or when Lawrence's Kangaroo comes "flop to the center / of the earth," or, to take the American example alluded to earlier in this study, when Williams' Elsie makes "the earth under our feet / . . . an excrement of some sky"—this desacralization turns Modernism into another kind of living hell for the writer. Only this time, the prospect is extraordinarily liberating.[6]

---

traditions" that we therefore can expect to discover within Modernism ought to be "directed against the politics of a depoliticized version of modernism." Huyssen, *After the Great Divide*, 186, 190–91.

5. The introduction of "the concept of probability into the definition of objective knowledge," according to Carolyn Porter, carries us, once again, from a "found" or illustrated (factual) world to a "made" or posited (possible) world, that is to say, from a pre-Modern theological episteme to one more anthropological and Modernist, as noted at the outset. Carolyn Porter, *Seeing and Being: The Plight of the Participant Observer in Emerson, James, Adams, and Faulkner* (Middletown, Conn., 1981), 30–32.

6. See Matei Calinescu, *Five Faces of Modernity: Modernism, Avant-garde, Decadence, Kitsch, Postmodernism* (Durham, 1987), 36.

The sense of liberation in one sense, of course, is attributable to the positive coding that a whole (mostly male) tradition of Romanticism has labored to establish as a legitimate and legitimating response to nature in the preceding texts. But in a more far-reaching way, liberation experienced here is a response to the demarcation of an exhilarating feminine space perceived by early Modernism as an *expansion* of the human personality, rather than as a fearful curtailment, in the later phase of Modernism, that leads, for instance, to Eliot's famous call for "a continual self-sacrifice, [and] a continual extinction of personality." Thus, according to the late Irving Howe,

The modernist-writer . . . becomes entranced with depths—whichever you choose: the depths of the city, or the self, or the underground, or the slums, or the extremes of sensation induced by the interstices of society: *Lumpen*, criminals, hipsters; or the drives at the base of consciousness. . . . [Moreover,] [t]he search for meaning through extreme states of being reveals a yearning for the primal . . . the turning-in upon one's primary characteristics, the hatred of one's gifts, the contempt for intelligence, which cuts through the work of men so different as Rimbaud, Dostoevsky, and Hart Crane. . . . [Nonetheless,] [o]ne of the seemingly hopeful possibilities is a primitivism bringing a vision of new manliness, health, blood consciousness, a relief from enervating rationality.[7]

Like the American Irving Howe, E. M. Forster, too, captures this exhilarating sense of promise at a secondary level of discourse, towards which all the hopeful possibilities of Modernism seem happily to be headed, and is even prepared to attach a kind of renewed mystical significance to it, when he writes:

each human mind has two personalities, one on the surface, one deeper down. The upper personality . . . is conscious and alert, does things like dining out, answering letters, etc., and it differs vividly and amusingly from other personalities. The lower personality is a very queer affair. In many ways it is a perfect fool, but without it there is no literature, because unless a man dips a bucket down into it occasionally he cannot produce first-class work. . . . It has something in common with all other

7. T. S. Eliot, *Selected Prose of T. S. Eliot,* ed. Frank Kermode (New York, 1975), 40; Irving Howe, *The Decline of the New* (New York, 1970). "[F]or my meaning," Eliot records further, "is, that the poet has, not a 'personality' to express, but a particular medium, which is only a medium and not a personality, in which impressions and experiences combine in peculiar and unexpected ways. Impressions and experiences which are important for the man may take no place in the poetry, and those which become important in the poetry may play quite a negligible part in the man, the personality." Thus, "[p]oetry is not a turning loose of emotion, but an escape from emotion; it is not the expression of personality, but an escape from personality" Eliot, *Selected Prose,* 42–43.

deeper personalities, and the mystic will assert that the common quality is God, and that here, in the obscure recesses of our being, we near the gates of the Divine.

Forster's commentary within the context of American Modernism perhaps reminds us of the Emersonian "double consciousness" of Pragmatist discourse dealt with earlier, and its inevitable split between "a realistic, publicly articulable social text" on the one hand, and "a private, ineffable subtext of desire and imagination" on the other that ineluctably does tend to conjure up the mystical.[8]

But what is more, Forster's words read almost like a challenge to any Modernist writer: either he is prepared to enter into the rather "queer affair" of exploring the dissident potentialities of human subjectivity, and thereby legitimate the literature which is almost guaranteed to result, or he is not. Gates, doorways, walled thresholds, and the like, as we shall soon discover, become the frequent markers of the challenge in symbolic terms, both early (as in "the gold mosaic of a wall" in Yeats' "Sailing to Byzantium") and late (as in "the Mothers, / . . . who guard the Sacred Gates" in Auden's "A Lullaby"). And women writers would not appear to be immune to this challenge either. Luce Irigaray, for instance, follows Freud in noting "that one would have to dig down very deep indeed to discover beneath the traces of this civilization, of this history, the vestiges of a more archaic civilization that might give some clue to woman's sexuality." Accordingly, "I was talking casually / with friends in the other room," the American expatriate-writer H.D. (Hilda Doolittle) writes in *Tribute to the Angels,* "when we saw the outer hall / grow lighter—then we saw where the door was, / there was no door (this was a dream of course)"; and, in another place, in the persona of the archaeologist Helen, in Egypt, in *Palimpsest:* "She wanted to dive deep, deep, courageously down into some unexploited region of the consciousness, into some common deep sea of unrecorded knowledge and bring, triumphant, to the surface some treasure buried, lost, forgotten."[9] Before taking up the Modernist implications of

8. E. M. Forster, *Two Cheers for Democracy* (Harmondsworth, Eng., 1972), 91; Carney, *American Vision,* 424. Joyce Carol Oates, *(Woman) Writer: Occasions and Opportunities* (New York, 1988), 185, usefully explains what the word "mystical" might mean in the American context in contrast to the decidedly theological cast of Forster's commentary when she observes: "As the work of art most succeeds when a delicate balance is struck between that which is known, and conscious, and that which is not yet known, and unconscious, so the psyche seems to be at its fullest when contradictory forces are held in suspension. This mystical state is frequently the subject of lyric poetry because it is so notoriously difficult to describe except in the briefest of spaces. As a state of mind rather than an arid intellectual concept it is evanescent, though its power to transform the entire personality has been documented (by, among others, William James in his classic of American psychology, *The Varieties of Religious Experience*)."

9. Luce Irigaray, *This Sex Which Is Not One,* trans. Catherine Porter (Ithaca, 1985), 25; H.D.

the crisis betokened by such passageways into subterranean and psychic depths in my trio of male poets, three final observations with respect to the new highway to hell they open up might be useful.

First, it is quite likely that not only are some writers not up to the challenge of countenancing the multiplicity of subjectivity in Modernist terms, but in view of "the supposed impersonality of high modernist practice" that the previous reference to T. S. Eliot would appear to support, they are perhaps happily unaware that it even exists. For them, Modernism has solidified into an incontrovertible fact, projected, once again, in purely masculinist terms. And the High Modernists' foreshortening of a more expanded discursive space or distance coincident with the imaginative (re)construction of subjectivity latent within poetry's expressive power and signed by the female—such masculinist rejection and silence would provide all the more reason for going that distance, probing modern discourse further, as I suggested earlier, for the possibilities and probabilities that are *also* built into what Faulkner had called the "desire" of words. Faulkner himself, as John Irwin recounts, "realized that it is precisely because the novelist stands outside the dark door, wanting to enter the dark room but unable to, that he [considered himself] a novelist, that he must imagine what takes place beyond the door." What is more, observes Irwin, "it is just that tension toward the dark room that he cannot enter that makes that room the source of all his imaginings—the womb of art. He understood that a writer's relation to his material and to the work of art is always a loss, a separation, a cutting off, a self-castration that transforms the masculine artist into the feminine-masculine vase of the work." The gender-coding of Irwin's persuasive description, moreover, might suggest to some that a discourse of dark mystery and desiring possibility is essentially a feminist enterprise, making it perfectly obvious why so many male practitioners of Modernism are likely to be predisposed to foreclose upon these feminist distances, or to become "imprisoned on [their] threshold" rather like the figure of Clyde Griffiths in *An American Tragedy*.[10]

(Hilda Doolittle), *Collected Poems: 1912–1944*, ed. Louis Martz (New York, 1983), 562, 179. Nor is the challenge restricted merely to the Modernist writer. "In his Jena lecture," Renée Riese Hubert writes of Paul Klee, "the painter comments on the creative process as a journey into the recesses of his mind, where the image of the tree alludes to both the visible and the invisible, the conscious and the unconscious, and the slow maturation of the work of art." Renée Hubert, "Paul Klee: Modernism in Art and Literature," in *Modernism: Challenges and Perspectives*, eds. Monique Chefdor, Ricardo Quinones, and Albert Wachtel (Urbana, 1986), 217.

10. David Bergman, *Gaiety Transfigured: Gay Self-Representation in American Literature* (Madison, 1991), 52; John T. Irwin, *Doubling and Incest/Repetition and Revenge: A Speculative Reading of Faulkner* (Baltimore, 1977), 171; Philip Fisher, *Hard Facts: Setting and Form in the American Novel*

This second observation, in fact, calls to mind some fairly recent feminist readings of Modernism that are very much in line with the kind of critical archaeology that the comments of Howe, Forster, and Irigaray justifiably invite when "a persistent ambiguity in early modernism" is finally addressed; namely, "the desire for the autonomy of form" when in fact "the root source and justification for art is individual expression." Thus for Marianna Torgovnick, "An *other* stands at the gates of being, admitting and yet mocking the self," and the notion of suicide in the discourse of Georges Bataille may perhaps be one way Modernism invents in order to transcend "the intolerable uncertainty and limits of being." In more severely probing terms, Marianne DeKoven finds in Joseph Conrad the opportunity "to look through all of us into 'the very hell,' to make accessible the dark substratum (cave) from which the subversive material of modernism is erupting," and thus finds as well "the point of entry into a different order of gender relations" significantly marked by the guarding of a "door of Darkness." And in the terms of a more broad-ranging literary history, Sandra M. Gilbert and Susan Gubar can detect in Rider Haggard, even though he was "a professed antifeminist," a discursive entry-point that perhaps prefigures the whole revolution of desire that was to follow for literature generally when his own mother's writing "opened to [his] childish eyes that gate of ivory and pearl which leads to the blessed kingdom of Romance." In such a mounting tide of formidably expert feminist theorizing, it may hardly seem possible to think that literary Modernism even exists apart from the self-authorization it now lends to its readers, in addition to that which it has all along instilled in a wide variety of writers in the Modernist canons of American poetry attended to in previous chapters.[11]

On this third and final point, I think we can make a bridge to my three exemplary poets, for it is precisely within this issue of self-authorization that the whole problematic of subjectivity as a constructed reality for them resides. As we noticed at the start, it is the *desire* for words that Modernism primordially authorizes, so that the words themselves, words as the constitutive *effects* of desire mediating our relation to the real, and indeed, mediating reality itself, are what become such

---

(New York, 1987), 152. Further to the foreclosure of feminist distances, see Huyssen, *After the Great Divide*, 47–49, 55, 70, 72, 79.

11. Michael H. Levenson, *A Genealogy of Modernism: A Study of English Literary Doctrine, 1908–1922* (New York, 1984), 135, and further on 114, 116–20, 134; Marianna Torgovnick, *Gone Primitive: Savage Intellects, Modern Lives* (Chicago, 1991), 190; Marianne DeKoven, *Rich and Strange: Gender, History, Modernism* (Princeton, 1991), 70, 98; Sandra M. Gilbert and Susan Gubar, *Sexchanges*, vol. 2 of *No Man's Land: The Place of the Woman Writer in the Twentieth Century* (New Haven, 1989), 35, 385 n. 92.

a hellish prospect for writers in their words' radical sense of ungroundedness, and hence, contra-diction. Julia Kristeva puts the case precisely with her notion of the "rejection" (i.e., displacement) of "free energy" subtending modern discourse, that is to say, the constant movement or compulsive repetition of desire, when she writes:

> rejection *re*constitutes real objects, "creates" new ones, reinvents the real, and re-symbolizes it. Although in so doing rejection recalls a schizoid regressive process, it is more important to note that rejection positivizes that process, affirming it by introducing the process into the signifying sphere: the latter thus finds itself separate, divided, put in process/on trial. This symbolization of rejection is the place of an untenable contradiction which only a limited number of subjects can reach.

This passage thus foregrounds the three most salient aspects of Modernism already scanned: the positivizing of process (as in the manufacture of discourse), the bringing to trial of what is constructed or symbolized (as in the manufactured discourse's sense of challenge), and finally, the separation between those who are capable of tolerating the contra-dictions of subjectivity's multitudinous dissident fabrications, and those who are not.[12] Another aspect of this contradiction is, of course, Kristeva's own attempt to focus on the movement of desire rather than its constitutive effects, for "in reading the theory of drives, one begins to suspect . . . that *desire* cannot completely account for the mechanisms of the signifying process. In technology and politics but also in art, areas have been found in which desire is exceeded by a 'movement' that surpasses the stases of desiring structuration [i.e., comprehension, knowledge] and displaces the frameworks of intersubjective devices where phantasmatic identifications congeal." Hence, my own reading of Modernism in this Conclusion within a feminist "distance" argues not a little of a similar contradiction. Nonetheless, I would like to suggest even further that the figure of the female at the gate is frequently for Modernism a kind of rhetorical shorthand or frame for the three aspects of Modernism just outlined—the positing, probing, and proving of possibilities—but having said that, I scruple to make plain at the same time that the framing of such distance ought never to be axiomatically construed as *parti pris* merely to a platform or agenda of feminism itself. Rather, it is the sense of *alterity* suggested by this figure—"*le regard de l'autre*"—and not the figure itself

---

12. Julia Kristeva, *Revolution in Poetic Language*, trans. Margaret Waller (New York, 1984), 155, and further on 160–61.

for which Modernism expresses its greatest interest, though these can (and often will) amount to the same thing. Thus, Betsy Erkkila's ascription of Marianne Moore as "a kind of moral keeper at the gate of literary modernism" exemplifies the latter conflation of figure and frame, particularly when Erkkila further notes that not only did Moore fault "her fellow modernists for their ego, moral failings, and lack of a larger spiritual vision, she also vigorously sponsored the work of women writers who appeared to embody transforming, but nevertheless proper, notions of the feminine." But if "woman [stands] outside the gates of culture," as Rachel Blau Duplessis suggests, it should, in the former sense of "alterity," be possible to trope with this dissident figure at the gate that discursive distance or space so privileged in the work of all of the American poets in this study, hence in the words of neo-Pragmatist Cary Wolfe, "to think of the space of the outside as composed of 'points' or 'singularities' that are free and unstructured, that have not yet been brought into a 'plane' of consistency, and that thus generate maximum force because they exist in maximum potential connectivity."[13]

Dissident "points" or "singularities" so alternatively figured, however, risk discursive control and containment of the High Modernist variety—containment of a kind perhaps suggested traditionally by the male poet and his female "muse." By contrast, within a feminist frame rather than form, the distanciation of Modernism is indicative of "an intuition of consciousness about being" that, as Leo Bersani recently argues, "consists of mobile fusions and correspondences—or, in other terms, that being is not reducible to identities . . . [since] Each 'I' [lodges] an intrinsically universal 'non-I,' a 'non-I' that would 'be' nothing but its continuously shifting contacts, affinities, and positions."[14]

13. Kristeva, *Revolution in Poetic Language*, 144–45; Jean-Paul Sartre, *Les Mots* cited in Denis Hollier, *Against Architecture: The Writings of Georges Bataille* (Cambridge, Mass., 1992), 75; Betsy Erkkila, *The Wicked Sisters: Women Poets, Literary History, and Discord* (New York, 1992), 104; Rachel Blau Duplessis, *The Pink Guitar: Writing as Feminist Practice* (New York, 1990), 36; Wolfe, *Critical Environments*, 113. Going the distance even further in his Pragmatist commentary, Wolfe further observes (following Gilles Deleuze): "To submit discourse to the challenge of the outside, then, involves 'a listening less to what is articulated in language than to the void circulating between its words, to the murmur that is forever taking it apart,' to the 'non-discourse of all language' steadily, erosively at work in 'the invisible space in which it appears' . . . but *also* mobilizing [language] as a force of dissimulation and Deleuzian differentiation that opens up new possibilities for praxis and resistance." Wolfe, *Critical Environments*, 115.

14. Leo Bersani, *The Culture of Redemption* (Cambridge, Mass., 1990), 99. "What saves (or releases, redeems) consciousness from its inability to posit an identity for itself," Bersani goes on to conclude, "is not an identity *for consciousness* (which could perhaps only be a subjectivity) but rather a kind of visionary (necessarily nonperceptual) experience of traces, lines, demarcations . . . a Dionysian yearning for ever mobile fusions . . . a magnetic field of other figures." Bersani, *The Culture of Redemp-*

If, as Kristeva further notes, the "representation of the 'character' who becomes the place of [the discursive] process is one that normative consciousness
finds intolerable," it's not an allergic reaction to woman per se. It's instead a
pathological response to Modernism, or at any rate, a pathological response to its
"'character's' polymorphism [as] one that knows every perversion and adheres to
none, one that moves through every vice without taking up any of them. Un-
identical and in-authentic, [Modernism] is the wisdom of artifice which has no
interiority and is constant rejection . . . [and thus to] the social organism and its
paranoid reality . . . an unbearable monstrosity." To confuse Modernism with
Feminism, that is to say, to confuse distance with substance, therefore, is merely
to collapse the second meaning or level of hell described earlier into the first, and
in the end, by characterizing the first as "demonic," to "stop the galloping evolution of organic forms and their symbolizing capacity in order to return to a state
of inertia and constancy." High Modernism for so long has perhaps traditionally
inured us to such a state of "inertia and constancy." The signature of modern
discourse's gated females, however, ought at least to alert us to other forms and
other frames. Susan Rubin Suleiman, who uses the Avant-Garde interchangeably
with Modernism, is entirely correct, I think, when she remarks that there can be
"no such thing as *the* avant-garde." Like Kristeva's galloping forms—
Modernism(s) as I am arguing—"there are only specific avant-garde movements,
situated in a particular time and place," as we are now about to see.[15]

A. E. Housman's "Hell Gate" from 1922 is a poem in the mode of High
Modernism, I would argue, precisely because of its attempt to foundationalize
subjectivity, to discipline or regulate its sense of distance signed by the female,
and so return its personality to the state of inertia or constancy just observed, and
beyond that, reduce its positionality to the state earlier described of incontrovertible fact. Richard Graves' documentation of Housman's intense homosocial desire, particularly in relation to his lifelong passion for Moses Jackson, invites us
to attend very closely in this text to the narrator and his "dark conductor's" passing beyond a "wall and rampart risen to sight," only to confront a "gate of gloom"
(*HsCP*, 94) at a more mysterious, subterranean level. Recollection by the narrator
of past experiences ("Battle, and the loves of men," "Knowledge gained and virtue
lost," "Cureless folly done and said," etc. [*HsCP*, 94]) would all seem to suggest

---

tion, 99–100. Bersani's resistance to a determinate identity "for consciousness" here provides sufficient
warrant, once again, for maintaining a clear separation between the figure and frame of Modernism
in its feminist inflections.

15. Kristeva, *Revolution in Poetic Language*, 156, 160; Suleiman, *Subversive Intent*, 18, emphasis
retained, and further on 12, 50, and passim.

that the sentry policing the gate of gloom holds more than just a passing interest for the speaker, especially when we read:

> one saw the sentry go,
> Trim and burning, to and fro,
> One for women to admire,
> In his finery of fire.
> Something, as I watched him pace
> Minded me of time and place,
> Soldiers of another corps
> And a sentry known before.
>
> (*HsCP*, 95)

We are thus given to speculate whether *this* sentry, so "sunk into himself" and "the hell-fire of his heart" (*HsCP*, 95), is not a projection of the narrator, and a displacement of queer subjectivity for which the figures of Sin and Death are perhaps deployed, on either side of the gate, to constrain his dissident positionality. For it's at that point that a female "portress foul to see" lifts up her eyes to him, and joins him in a knowing gaze that is equally shared by the sentry, before the sentry in turn averts his head, and suddenly and inexplicably, takes his own life. After which the portress, along with Sin and Death, mysteriously disappears, leaving the narrator and his guide to experience further "the hollowness of hell" in their own abject silence, before returning whence they came (*HsCP*, 96–97). Backing away from what Kristeva would call the production of an innovative "social formation," then, Housman's discourse cannot help but demonize its feminist figuration for dissident subjectivity through the highly conservative gesture of exclusion, and with the image of the sentry's musket at his chin, ultimate effacement.[16]

Gerard Manley Hopkins' "The Wreck of the Deutschland" from 1918 offers us, once more, "the hurtle of hell" that, as in the previous text, positions its narrator "at the wall" (*HPP*, 13). However, the account of the extraordinary valor of

16. Richard Percival Graves, *A. E. Housman: The Scholar-Poet* (New York, 1979), 49–70, and passim; Kristeva, *Revolution in Poetic Language*, 162. At about this time, as Ed Cohen writes, "So long as sodomy continued to merit execution—even if only theoretically—its punishment still provided an occasion for the state to inscribe the offender's body with/as a hieroglyph that signified its power *to use death* in order to regulate the very basis of life, even while it was in the process of creating and organizing new technologies which (re)produced a more diffuse, yet more minute exercise of power over all aspects of that life." Ed Cohen, *Talk on the Wilde Side: Toward a Genealogy of a Discourse on Male Sexualities* (New York, 1993), 118, emphasis added.

five exiled nuns who drown when their ship sinks in the mouth of the Thames during a snowstorm in 1876 provides Hopkins, unlike Housman, with an unusual opportunity to approach the representation of the female on its own terms, particularly in view of the courageous leadership of the tallest of the Franciscan sisters:

> Till a lioness arose breasting the babble,
> A prophetess towered in the tumult, a virginal tongue told.
>
> Ah, touched in your bower of bone
> Are you! turned for an exquisite smart,
> Have you! *make words break from me* here all alone
>
> . . . .
>   . . . she rears herself to divine
> Ears, and the call of the tall nun
> To the men in the tops and the tackle rode over the storm's brawling.
>   (*HPP*, 18, emphasis added)

We sense that in descriptions like this, Hopkins' discourse is actually at the threshold of acceding to those obscure recesses of being—"Do you!—mother of being in me, heart, / O unteachably after evil, but uttering truth" (*HPP*, 18)— mystic depths that Forster talks about as we near the gates of the divine. Once again, we seem to be at the line of probability—"maximum potential connectivity" in Wolfe's terms just noted—separating possibility from fact, a point that Hopkins had reached in his own life several years previously when the love of another man and the call to Roman Catholic conversion both fell within a year of each other.[17]

Hopkins' ordination soon after the death of his beloved Digby Dolben, and his very curious later remark, "I am a eunuch, but it is for the kingdom of God's sake," indicate roughly the extent to which he might be prepared to explore further his own somewhat convoluted subjectivity, but it's clear that he was quite

17. Robert Bernard Martin, *Gerard Manley Hopkins: A Very Private Life* (New York, 1991), 80–97, 118–28. Hopkins was obviously torn between two quite discrete callings. His biographer comments further on the poet's plight: "We know from what he wrote when he was finally ordained that he thought the dedications of priest and poet were too much alike to exist easily in one person, since they derived from the same sources. And like Savonarola, he was aware that art, even when it was guiltless in itself, could be highly distracting. A vocation to the priesthood implied the renunciation of worldly pursuits, and since poetry was surely dearest of those to him, it was the logical activity to be given up." Robert Bernard Martin, *Gerard Manley Hopkins*, 165.

happy to allow a liberal kind of institutional co-optation to settle much of the rest. And we're given to wonder if a quite similar form of appropriation is not allowed to overtake the striking model of individual conduct in the female personage of Hopkins' Franciscan lioness, described elsewhere as an "Other, I gather, in measure [of] her mind's / Burden" (*HPP*, 21), and then miraculously transformed into perhaps a more canonically authentic and correct exemplum of what we may properly be expected to think is *really* going on in her imperilment:

> But how shall I . . . make me room there:
> Reach me a . . . Fancy, come faster—
> Strike you the sight of it? look at it loom there,
> Thing that she . . . there then! the Master,
> *Ipse*, the only one, Christ, King, Head . . .
>
> . . . .
>
> Let him ride, her pride, in his triumph, despatch and have done with his doom there.
>   (*HPP*, 21)

If ever there was a model instance of the "symbolization of rejection" noted previously in Kristeva's analysis of Modernist discourse, surely the leap over the third ellipsis here—from "she" to Master, Christ, King, Head—comes very close indeed.[18]

It is perhaps more accurate to view within the distance we descry within Hopkins' ellipsis in this crucial passage the incorporation of the force of the nun's mysterious example, rather than its exclusion or "rejection" in the narrow sense, as in the previous text by Housman. Thus, Kristeva would more likely prefer to speak of the nun as an instance of "instinctual heterogeneity" at this point in Hopkins' poem, as she puts it in her aptly distanciated critical formulation: "neither deferred nor delayed, not yet understood as a becoming-sign—is precisely that which *enters into contradiction with différance* and brings about leaps, intervals, abrupt changes, and breaks in its spacing [*espacement*]. Contradiction can only be the irruption of the heterogeneous which cuts short any *différance*." In other words, Hopkins' own inability to understand, or more likely, come to terms

---

18. Gerard Manley Hopkins, *Further Letters of Hopkins*, 2d ed., ed. C. C. Abbott (London, 1956), 30. Once again, Cohen writes: "if one of the ways that the stability and dominance of normative masculinity has been shored up over the last century is by (re)producing it in opposition to its antithetical '*other(s)*,' then the (violent) repudiation of those who are categorically defined as antagonistic to it can be imagined by those interpellated as 'manly men' to fix the vicissitudes of their own subjectivity." Ed Cohen, *Talk on the Wilde Side*, 212, emphasis added.

earlier in his life with the counter-normative subjectivity imaged here by the mas-
culated figure of the nun—such incapability could conceivably explain the distance of this particular ellipsis, and the others like it in the above passage. In any
case, while it is true that the incontestable fact of the nun's unsponsored heroism
receives considerable qualification through what Hopkins later in the poem calls
the "Grasp of God, throned behind," and "a sovereignty that heeds but hides,
bodes but abides" (*HPP*, 23), nonetheless it's at least *probable* to think that, in
contrast to Housman, "female," that is to say, a sense of dissident (non-masculi-
nist, non-heterosexist) subjectivity has gained a legitimate berth for itself within
some inarticulable stratum of Hopkins' verse, as signed by the image of the
"Dame, at our door" in the final stanza of "The Wreck of the Deutschland"
(*HPP*, 24). Historically speaking, we are perhaps given a somewhat inchoate subject position on the way to becoming a more fully formed queer construction. Yet
the construction is incipient merely. Unfortunately perhaps, as Luce Irigaray is
led to surmise in a related context that may also apply here, there can be "no
desire for a difference that would not be repeatedly and eternally co-opted and
trapped within an economy of sameness."[19]

I would like to conclude by briefly examining three short texts from the early
work of American Ezra Pound that actually begin to direct us to the level in
modern poetry upon which the female presence qua female actually begins to
manifest itself as a genuine possibility or "singularity" in the Pragmatist terms in
which we have had occasion to witness it earlier, and in the context of what Kristeva has previously alluded in the discourse as "the wisdom of artifice." To some,
this might seem a highly improbable claim to make for the Modernism of Pound,
given the generally repulsive misogyny of a text like *Hugh Selwyn Mauberley* from
1920, and given his even more repulsive collaborations with T. S. Eliot, especially
over the next two years after leaving England, and before settling down permanently in Italy to begin serious work on the High Modernism of his longer *Can-
tos*. But all of these poems (and there are many others like them) come from
Pound's early period, before the Great War and "Vorticism," that is to say, before
the time when women like H.D. and Harriet Monroe, but especially Amy Lowell, began to threaten "his place as the leader of the Imagist movement," and to
challenge his pride of artistic prominence "as the acknowledged legislator of the
world."[20]

19. Kristeva, *Revolution in Poetic Language*, 144; Irigaray, *This Sex Which Is Not One*, 130.

20. James Longenbach, *Stone Cottage: Pound, Yeats, and Modernism* (New York, 1988), 136–37,
and further on 139, 146, 153 and passim. "For Pound," Longenbach notes further, "the legislation of
the arts had to take the form of a dictatorship, not a democracy, and Imagism had to retain its status
as a secret society—not a 'democratic beer-garden'—if it were to continue to be the guide and lamp

Accordingly, in this earlier work, Pound evinces attitudes less like those of Housman's exclusion or Hopkins' co-optation, and instead, a general frame of mind running more to inclusionary openness and expansionary tolerance, with a somewhat heedless disregard for rhetorical control or constraint. In the much read "The Return," for example, from 1912, we're never really clear about what animal or human, man or god, is making its return with such thunderous movement and energy. Yeats' plunging Horses of Disaster are certainly not far away (cf. Pound's "Sub Mare" and "The Plunge" [*PSP*, 82–83]). But whatever it is, the poem's concluding broken line, "Slow on the leash, / pallid the leash-men" (*PSP*, 85) makes clear, like Nietzsche's "rider on a charging steed [letting] fall the reins before the infinite," that the surrender to or unleashing of force rather than regulation or containment by form is the privileged gesture, thus reversing Kristeva's own "return" to an inert constancy noted earlier, to allow more for her "galloping evolution of organic forms" that is generally consistent with the modernist revolution in poetic language.[21]

Astradur Eysteinsson's paraphrase of Kristeva exactly in that context is, "allowing the subject to slip out from under," so that when we turn to two final poems with the female as subject, we're not surprised to discover Pound at a loss for words, and what is more, actually celebrating that fact:

> Great minds have sought you—lacking someone else.
> You have been second always. Tragical?

---

of civilization." Longenbach, *Stone Cottage*, 137. For Longenbach's further expansion of Pound's troubling elitism that obviously here reveals women as one of its prime targets, see also 155, 168, 263, and 267. See Suleiman, *Subversive Intent*, further on 28, and Gilbert and Gubar's Chapter 7 of *Sexchanges* more generally.

21. Friedrich Nietzsche, *Beyond Good and Evil: Prelude to a Philosophy of the Future*, trans. R. J. Hollingdale (Harmondsworth, Eng., 1979), 135, and further on 69, 149. The passage cited from Nietzsche continues: "we modern men, like semi-barbarians . . . attain *our* state of bliss only when we are most—in *danger*" (emphases retained). Hence, in Kristeva: "Going through the experience [of modern poetry] exposes the subject to impossible dangers: relinquishing his identity in rhythm, dissolving the buffer of reality in a mobile discontinuity, leaving the shelter of family, the state, or religion. The commotion the practice creates spares nothing [*sic*]: it destroys all constancy to produce another and then destroys that one as well." Kristeva, *Revolution in Poetic Language*, 104. Moreover, such "constancy" in Nietzsche is linked, according to Mark Warren, to "psychic order, repose, and etiquette," whose preservation is maintained by a principle of "active forgetfulness" and "repression" in the figure, not unexpectedly, of "a doorkeeper." Warren notes further: "Nietzsche held, as did Freud, that ego-identity requires repression; that repression serves to exclude both internal and external threats to identity." Mark Warren, *Nietzsche and Political Thought* (Cambridge, Mass., 1991), 178, and further on 205.

> No. You preferred it to the usual thing:
> One dull man, dulling and uxorious,
> One average mind—with one thought less, each year.
>
> (*PSP*, 74)

In these lines from "Portrait d'une Femme," again from 1912, Hopkins and Housman seem to go floating by, as does Faulkner: "one comes to you / And takes strange gain away: Trophies fished up . . . *Fact* that leads nowhere" (*PSP*, 74, emphasis added). At some more primordial level than these, Pound would have us return to the radical of desire at back of "this sea-hoard" (*PSP*, 74) where we began this Conclusion, that is to say, to the linguistic processes at back of Modernism rather than to its products—"Strange spars of knowledge and dimmed wares of price" (*PSP*, 74), in other words (picking up on Pound's "You have been second always"), to "a 'second' return of instinctual functioning within the symbolic," to cite Kristeva terminally, "as a negativity introduced into the symbolic order, and as the transgression of that order." The lacking or desire that leads nowhere is certainly at the heart of this negativity. Which is precisely where Pound wishes to end his portrait: "In the slow float of differing light and deep, / No! there is nothing! In the whole and all, / Nothing that's quite your own. / Yet this is you" (*PSP*, 75). The "you," here, is also Modernism's last word on subject-hood, whose radical possibility is constituted and authorized through engagement with fecund process, but cannot be identified with or imposed on or privileged over linguistic process itself. Hence in Pound's "The Flame" from 1910, to conclude, it is only the voice of this feminine Other that the subject is allowed to experience, for as that voice states, "We who are wise beyond your dream of wisdom . . . have gone forth beyond your bonds and borders":

> If I have merged my soul, or utterly
> Am solved and bound in, through aught here on earth,
> There canst thou find me, O thou anxious thou,
> Who call'st about my gates for some lost me . . .
> If thou hast seen that mirror of all moments,
> That glass to all things that o'ershadow it,
> Call not that mirror me, for I have slipped
> Your grasp, I have eluded."
>
> (*PSP*, 67, 68)[22]

---

22. Astradur Eysteinsson, *The Concept of Modernism* (Ithaca, 1990), 48; Kristeva, *Revolution in Poetic Language*, 69.

In this final passage from the early Pound, we perhaps understand how rich the possibilities are when the gates of Modernism are at last *heard* to turn upon the self, thereby suggesting the multiplicity we are permitted to make of that self, if we could only find the courage and stamina to go on listening. In my argument focused briefly on male writers, woman is sign for such multiplicity in Modernism's "feminist" distances, and dissident subjectivity is perhaps its most unspoken radical. To that extent, as Duplessis (invoking H.D.) remarks, "Pound understood and . . . identified himself with [women] and their art"—at least for a time, at any rate. As a consequence, like other early Modernists, including the ones taken up in this study, Pound's was an effort "to practice listening to and interpreting the unconscious so that these pursuits no longer create hierarchical relations where sexual difference is concerned." But only for a time—hence, Pound's paradox. "A man of paradox, like any writer, I am indeed *behind the door,*" the secretly homosexual Roland Barthes once remarked, but he also ruminated that the danger for him was wanting "to pass through . . . to see what is being said," and so, ended up "constantly *listening to what I am excluded from.*" But much before Barthes, the even more ambivalently closeted Eliot, lingering in the chambers of the sea, thought he too saw mermaids singing, and thereafter, traumatically imagined that "human voices wake us, and we drown." "All great noise leads [man] to move happiness into some quiet distance," the Modernist philosopher (and proto-Pragmatist) Friedrich Nietzsche observes in *The Gay Science,* where "he is apt also to see quiet, magical beings gliding past him and to long for their happiness and seclusion: women," and concludes: "The magic and the most powerful effect of women is, in philosophical language, action at a distance, *actio in distans;* but this requires first of all and above all—*distance.*" Either the call of Modernism from its feminist distances, and the myriad subject-possibilities such a call enlists, is something we are emboldened to accept on faith, or to hell with it. With the separate projects of Stein, Williams, Hughes, Bishop, and O'Hara, it has been the burden of this study to reveal that "going the distance" can have more salutary and, what is hoped for the future of Modernist writing in America, more life-affirming and life-sustaining consequences.[23]

23. Duplessis, *The Pink Guitar,* 179 n. 24; Irigaray, *This Sex Which Is Not One,* 146; Roland Barthes, *Roland Barthes by Roland Barthes,* trans. Richard Howard (New York, 1977), 123, emphases retained; Friedrich Nietzsche, *The Gay Science,* trans. Walter Kaufmann (New York, 1974), 124.

Bibliography

Adorno, T. W. "The Actuality of Philosophy." *Telos* 31 (spring 1977): 120–31.

———. "Cultural Criticism and Society." In *Prisms*, trans. Samuel Weber and Shierry Weber, 17–34. Cambridge, Mass.: MIT Press, 1986.

———. "The Essay as Form." Translated by Bob Hullot-Kentor. *Telos* 32 (spring 1984): 151–71.

———. *Minima Moralia: Reflections from Damaged Life.* Trans. E. F. N. Jephcott. 1974. Reprint, London: NLB, Verso Editions, 1978.

———. *Negative Dialectics.* Trans. E. B. Ashton. New York: Seabury Press, Continuum, 1973.

———. "A Portrait of Walter Benjamin." In *Prisms*, trans. Samuel Weber and Shierry Weber, 224–41. Cambridge, Mass.: MIT Press, 1986.

———. *Prisms.* Trans. Samuel Weber and Shierry Weber. Cambridge, Mass.: MIT Press, 1986.

———. "Subject and Object." In *The Essential Frankfurt School Reader*, ed. Andrew Arato and Eike Gebhardt, 497–511. New York: Continuum, 1992.

Altieri, Charles. "'Varieties of Immanentist Expression.'" In *Frank O'Hara: To Be True to a City*, ed. Jim Elledge, 189–208. Ann Arbor: University of Michigan Press, 1993.

Appiah, Kwame Anthony. "Is the 'Post-' in 'Postcolonial' the 'Post-' in 'Postmodern'?" In *Dangerous Liaisons: Gender, Nation, and Postcolonial Perspectives*, ed. Anne McClintock, Aamir Mufti, and Ella Shohat, 420–44. Cultural Politics, vol. 11. Minneapolis: University of Minnesota Press, 1997.

Avi-Ram, Amitai. "The Unreadable Black Body: 'Conventional' Poetic Form in the Harlem Renaissance." *Genders* 7 (1990): 32–46.

Baker, Houston A., Jr. "Caliban's Triple Play." In *"Race," Writing, and Difference*, ed. Henry Louis Gates, Jr., 381–95. Chicago: University of Chicago Press, 1986.

———. *Modernism and the Harlem Renaissance.* Chicago: University of Chicago Press, 1987.

Barthes, Roland. *Image, Music, Text.* Ed. and trans. Stephen Heath. New York: Hill and Wang, 1977.

———. *The Pleasure of the Text.* Trans. Richard Miller. Intro. Richard Howard. New York: Hill and Wang, 1975.

———. *Roland Barthes by Roland Barthes.* Trans. Richard Howard. New York: Hill and Wang, 1977.

———. *S/Z.* Trans. Richard Miller. Preface by Richard Howard. New York: Hill and Wang, 1974.

Battaglia, Debbora. "Problematizing the Self: A Thematic Introduction." In *Rhetorics of Self-Making,* ed. Debbora Battaglia, 1–15. Berkeley: University of California Press, 1995.

Bell, Michael Davitt. *The Problem of American Realism: Studies in the Cultural History of a Literary Idea.* Chicago: University of Chicago Press, 1993.

Bennett, Paula. "The Pea That Duty Locks: Lesbian and Feminist-Heterosexual Readings of Emily Dickinson's Poetry." In *Lesbian Texts and Contexts: Radical Revisions,* ed. Karla Jay and Joanne Glasgow. New York: New York University Press, 1990.

Benston, Kimberly W. "I Yam What I Am: The Topos of (Un)naming in Afro-American Literature." In *Black Literature and Literary Theory,* ed. Henry Louis Gates, Jr., 155–72. New York: Routledge, 1990.

———. "Performing Blackness: Re/Placing Afro-American Poetry." In *Afro-American Literary Study in the 1990s,* ed. Houston A. Baker, Jr., and Patricia Redmond, 164–85. Chicago: University of Chicago Press, 1992.

Bergman, David. *Gaiety Transfigured: Gay Self-Representation in American Literature.* Madison: University of Wisconsin Press, 1991.

Berkson, Bill. "Frank O'Hara and His Poems." In *Frank O'Hara: To Be True to a City,* ed. Jim Elledge, 226–33. Ann Arbor: University of Michigan Press, 1993.

Berkson, Bill, and Joe LeSueur, eds. *Homage to Frank O'Hara.* Berkeley: Creative Arts, 1980.

Berlant, Lauren, and Michael Warner. "What Does Queer Theory Teach Us about *X*? *PMLA* 110 (summer 1995): 343–49.

Bernstein, Charles. *A Poetics.* Cambridge, Mass.: Harvard University Press, 1992.

Bersani, Leo. *The Culture of Redemption.* Cambridge, Mass.: Harvard University Press, 1990.

Bérubé, Allan. *Coming Out under Fire: The History of Gay Men and Women in World War Two.* New York: Plume, 1990.

Bhabha, Homi K. "The Commitment to Theory." *New Formations* 5 (1988): 5–22.

———. *The Location of Culture.* London: Routledge, 1994.

———. "The Other Question: Difference, Discrimination, and the Discourse of Colonialism." In *Out There: Marginalization and Contemporary Cultures,* ed. Russell Ferguson, Martha Gever, Trinh T. Minh-Ha, and Cornel West, 71–87. Cambridge, Mass.: MIT Press, 1990.

———. "The World and the Home." In *Dangerous Liaisons: Gender, Nation, and Postcolonial Perspectives,* ed. Anne McClintock, Aamir Mufti, and Ella Shohat, 445–55. Cultural Politics, vol. 11. Minneapolis: University of Minnesota Press, 1997.

Bishop, Elizabeth. *The Collected Prose.* Ed. and intro. Robert Giroux. New York: Noonday Press, 1991.

———. *The Complete Poems: 1927–1979.* New York: Farrar, Straus, Giroux, 1986.

———. *One Art: Selected Letters.* Ed. Robert Giroux. New York: Farrar, Straus, Giroux, 1994.

Blasing, Mutlu Konuk. *American Poetry: The Rhetoric of Its Forms.* New Haven: Yale University Press, 1987.

Boone, Bruce. "Gay Language as Political Praxis: The Poetry of Frank O'Hara." *Social Text* 1, no. 1 (1979): 59–92.

Bowers, Neal. "The City Limits: Frank O'Hara's Poetry." In *Frank O'Hara: To Be True to a City,* ed. Jim Elledge, 321–33. Ann Arbor: University of Michigan Press, 1993.

Bredbeck, Gregory W. "B/O—Barthes's Text/O'Hara's Trick." *PMLA* 108 (March 1993): 268–82.

Bremen, Brian A. *William Carlos Williams and the Diagnostics of Culture.* New York: Oxford University Press, 1993.

Breslin, James E. B. "Frank O'Hara." In *Frank O'Hara: To Be True to a City,* ed. Jim Elledge, 253–98. Ann Arbor: University of Michigan Press, 1993.

Brinnin, John Malcolm. *The Third Rose: Gertrude Stein and Her World.* Reading, Mass.: Addison-Wesley, 1987.

Brodhead, Richard. *The School of Hawthorne.* New York: Oxford University Press, 1986.

Brown, Ashley. "An Interview with Elizabeth Bishop." In *Elizabeth Bishop and Her Art,* ed. Lloyd Schwartz and Sybil P. Estess, 289–302. Ann Arbor: University of Michigan Press, 1983.

Buck-Morss, Susan. *The Origin of Negative Dialectics: Theodor W. Adorno, Walter Benjamin, and the Frankfurt Institute.* New York: Free Press, 1977.

Bürger, Peter. *Theory of the Avant-Garde.* Trans. Michael Shaw. Foreword by Jochen Schulte-Sasse. Theory and History of Literature, vol. 4. Minneapolis: University of Minnesota Press, 1984.

Butler, Judith. *Bodies That Matter: On the Discursive Limits of "Sex".* New York: Routledge, 1993.

———. "The Force of Fantasy: Feminism, Mapplethorpe, and Discursive Excess." *Differences* 2 (spring 1990): 105–25.

———. *Gender Trouble: Feminism and the Subversion of Identity.* New York: Routledge, 1990.

———. "Imitation and Gender Insubordination." In *Inside/out: Lesbian Theories, Gay Theories,* ed. Diana Fuss, 13–31. New York: Routledge, 1991.

———. "Lana's 'Imitation': Melodramatic Repetition and the Gender Performative." *Genders* 9 (fall 1990): 1–18.

Cadden, Michael. "Engendering F. O. M.: The Private Life of *American Renaissance.*" In *Engendering Men: The Question of Male Feminist Criticism,* ed. Joseph A. Boone and Michael Cadden, 26–35. New York: Routledge, 1990.

Calinescu, Matei. *Five Faces of Modernity: Modernism, Avant-garde, Decadence, Kitsch, Postmodernism.* Durham: Duke University Press, 1987.

Campbell, Gregor. "Work on Reason." *Diacritics* 21 (winter 1991):

Caputo, John. "On Not Knowing Who We Are: Madness, Hermeneutics, and the Night of Truth in Foucault." In *Foucault and the Critique of Institutions*, ed. John Caputo and Mark Yount, 233–62. University Park, Pa.: Pennsylvania State University Press, 1993.

Caramello, Charles. "Gertrude Stein as Exemplary Theorist." In *Gertrude Stein and the Making of Literature*, ed. Shirley Neuman and Ira B. Nadel, 1–7. Boston: Northeastern University Press, 1988.

Carney, Ray. *American Vision: The Films of Frank Capra.* Hanover: University Press of New England, 1996.

Case, Sue-Ellen. "Toward a Butch-Femme Aesthetic." In *The Lesbian and Gay Studies Reader*, ed. Henry Abelove, Michèle Aina Barale, and David M. Halperin, 294–306. New York: Routledge, 1993.

Chambers, Iain. *Border Dialogues: Journeys in Postmodernity.* New York: Routledge, 1990.

———. "Signs of Silence, Lines of Listening." In *The Post-Colonial Question: Common Skies, Divided Horizons*, ed. Iain Chambers and Lidia Curti, 47–62. London: Routledge, 1996.

Champagne, John. *The Ethics of Marginality: A New Approach to Gay Studies.* Foreword by Donald Pease. Minneapolis: University of Minnesota Press, 1995.

Chauncey, George. *Gay New York: Gender, Urban Culture, and the Making of the Gay Male World, 1890–1940.* New York: Basic Books, 1994.

Chessman, Harriet Scott. *The Public Is Invited to Dance: Representation, the Body, and Dialogue in Gertrude Stein.* Stanford: Stanford University Press, 1989.

Clarke, Stuart Alan. "Fear of a Black Planet." *Socialist Review* 21 (summer-fall 1991): 37–59.

Cohen, Ed. "Foucauldian Necrologies: 'Gay' 'Politics'? Politically Gay?" *Textual Practice* 2 (spring 1988): 87–101.

———. *Talk on the Wilde Side: Toward a Genealogy on Male Sexualities.* New York: Routledge, 1993.

Cope, Karin. "Painting after Gertrude Stein." In "Critical Crossings," special issue, ed. Judith Butler and Biddy Mayne. *Diacritics* 24 (summer-fall: 190–203).

Copjec, Joan. "Sex and the Euthanasia of Reason." In *Supposing the Subject*, ed. by Joan Copjec, 16–44. S₁. New York: Verso, 1994.

———. "The Unvermögender Other: Hysteria and Democracy in America." *New Formations* 14 (summer 1991): 27–41.

Cornell, Drucilla. "What Is Ethical Feminism?" In *Feminist Contentions: A Philosophical Exchange?* by Seyla Benhabib, Judith Butler, Drucilla Cornell, and Nancy Fraser, intro. Linda Nicholson, 75–106. New York: Routledge, 1995.

Costello, Bonnie. "One Art: The Poetry of Elizabeth Bishop, 1971–1976." In *Elizabeth Bishop and Her Art*, ed. Lloyd Schwartz and Sybil P. Estess, 109–32. Ann Arbor: University of Michigan Press, 1983.

Crane, Hart. *The Complete Poems and Selected Letters and Prose of Hart Crane.* Ed. Brom Weber. Garden City, N.Y.: Doubleday, 1966.

D'Emilio, John. "The Bonds of Oppression: Gay Life in the 1950s." In *Sexual Politics, Sexual Communities: The Making of a Homosexual Minority in the United States, 1940–1970*, 40–53. Chicago: University of Chicago Press, 1983.

———. "The Homosexual Menace: The Politics of Sexuality in Cold War America." In *Making Trouble: Essays on Gay History, Politics, and the University*, 57–73. New York: Routledge, 1992.

———. *Sexual Politics, Sexual Communities: The Making of a Homosexual Minority in the United States, 1940–1970*. Chicago: University of Chicago Press, 1983.

Damon, Maria. *The Dark End of the Street: Margins in American Vanguard Poetry*. Minneapolis: University of Minnesota Press, 1993.

de Lauretis, Teresa. *Alice Doesn't: Feminism, Semiotics, Cinema*. Bloomington: Indiana University Press, 1984.

———. *The Practice of Love: Lesbian Sexuality and Perverse Desire*. Bloomington: Indiana University Press, 1994.

DeKoven, Marianne. *A Different Language: Gertrude Stein's Experimental Writing*. Madison: University of Wisconsin Press, 1983.

———. *Rich and Strange: Gender, History, Modernism*. Princeton: Princeton University Press, 1991.

Derrida, Jacques. "'Eating Well,' or the Calculation of the Subject: An Interview with Jacques Derrida." In *Who Comes after the Subject?* ed. Eduardo Cadava and Peter Connor, trans. Peter Connor and Avital Ronell, 96–119. New York: Routledge, 1991.

———. *The Other Heading: Reflections on Today's Europe*. Trans. Bascale-Anne Brault and Michael B. Naas. Bloomington: Indiana University Press, 1992.

Dewey, John. *Experience and Nature*. Paul Carus Lectures: 1st Series, 1925; rev., 1929. La Salle, Ill.: Open Court, 1989.

———. *The Philosophy of John Dewey*. vol. 1: *The Structure of Experience*. Ed. & intro. John J. McDermott. New York: G. P. Putnam's Sons, 1973.

Dickie, Margaret. *Stein, Bishop, and Rich: Lyrics of Love, War, and Place*. Chapel Hill: University of North Carolina Press, 1997.

Dickinson, Emily. *The Complete Poems of Emily Dickinson*. Ed. Thomas H. Johnson. Boston: Little, Brown, 1960.

———. *The Letters of Emily Dickinson*. 3 vols. Ed. Thomas H. Johnson. Cambridge, Mass.: Belknap Press of Harvard University Press, 1960.

Diehl, Joanne Feit. *Women Poets and the American Sublime*. Bloomington: Indiana University Press, 1990.

Diggins, John Patrick. *The Promise of Pragmatism: Modernism and the Crisis of Knowledge and Authority*. Chicago: University of Chicago Press, 1994.

Dirlik, Arif. "The Postcolonial Aura: Third World Criticism in the Age of Global Capitalism." In *Dangerous Liaisons: Gender, Nation, and Postcolonial Perspectives*, ed. Anne McClintock, Aamir Mufti, and Ella Shohat, 501–28. Cultural Politics, vol. 11. Minneapolis: University of Minnesota Press, 1997.

Dolar, Mladen. "The Legacy of the Enlightenment: Foucault and Lacan." *New Formations* 14 (summer 1987): 43–56.

Dollimore, Jonathan. *Sexual Dissidence: Augustine to Wilde, Freud to Foucault.* New York: Oxford University Press, 1991.

Doty, Mark. "Ice and Salt: An Interview with Mark Doty." *Poetry Flash* 270 (November 1996): 1–6.

Dubnick, Randa. *The Structure of Obscurity: Gertrude Stein, Language, and Cubism.* Urbana: University of Illinois Press, 1984.

Duffey, Bernard. *A Poetry of Presence: The Writing of William Carlos Williams.* Madison: University of Wisconsin Press, 1986.

Duplessis, Rachel Blau. *The Pink Guitar: Writing as Feminist Practice.* New York: Routledge, 1990.

Dydo, Ulla E. "Gertrude Stein: Composition as Meditation." In *Gertrude Stein and the Making of Literature,* ed. Shirley Neuman and Ira B. Nadel, 42–60. Boston: Northeastern University Press, 1988.

Dyer, Richard. "White." *Screen* 29 (winter 1988): 44–64.

Easthope, Antony. *Poetry as Discourse.* New York: Methuen, 1983.

Edelman, Lee. "The Geography of Gender: Elizabeth Bishop's 'In the Waiting Room.'" In *Elizabeth Bishop: The Geography of Gender,* ed. Marilyn May Lombardi, 91–107. Charlottesville: University of Virginia Press, 1993.

Eliot, T. S. *Selected Prose of T. S. Eliot.* Ed. Frank Kermode. New York: Farrar, Straus, and Giroux, 1975.

Emerson, Ralph Waldo. *Essays and Lectures.* Ed. Joel Porte. New York: Literary Classics of the United States, 1983.

Eribon, Didier. *Michel Foucault.* Trans. Betsy Wing. Cambridge, Mass.: Harvard University Press, 1991.

Erkkila, Betsy. *The Wicked Sisters: Women Poets, Literary History, and Discord.* New York: Oxford University Press, 1992.

Escoffier, Jeffrey. "The Limits of Multiculturalism." *Socialist Review* 21, no. 3-4 (1991): 61–73.

Eysteinsson, Astradur. *The Concept of Modernism.* Ithaca: Cornell University Press, 1990.

Farwell, Marilyn R. "The Lesbian Narrative: 'The Pursuit of the Inedible by the Unspeakable.'" In *Professions of Desire: Lesbian and Gay Studies in Literature,* ed. George E. Haggerty and Bonnie Zimmerman, 156–68. New York: MLA, 1995.

Faulkner, William. *The Sound and the Fury.* New York: Random House, 1946.

Fisher, Philip. *Hard Facts: Setting and Form in the American Novel.* New York: Oxford University Press, 1987.

Ford, Karen Jackson. "Do Right to Write Right: Langston Hughes's Aesthetics of Simplicity." *Twentieth Century Literature* 38 (fall 1992): 436–56.

Forster, E. M. *Two Cheers for Democracy.* Harmondsworth, Middlesex, Eng.: Penguin Books, 1972.

Foucault, Michel. *The Archaeology of Knowledge.* Trans. A. M. Sheridan Smith. 1972. Reprint, London: Tavistock Publications, 1974.

———. *The History of Sexuality.* Vol. 1: *An Introduction.* Trans. Robert Hurley. New York: Random House, Vintage, 1980.

———. *Politics, Philosophy, Culture: Interviews and Other Writings, 1977–1984.* Trans. Alan Sheridan et al., ed. Lawrence D. Kritzman. New York: Routledge, 1988.

———. "What Is Enlightenment?" In *The Foucault Reader,* ed. Paul Rabinow, 32–50. New York: Pantheon Books, 1984.

Fountain, Gary, and Peter Brazeau. *Remembering Elizabeth Bishop: An Oral Biography.* Amherst: University of Massachusetts Press, 1994.

Fuss, Diana. "Pink Freud." *GLQ* 2, no. 1-2 (1995): 1–9.

Garber, Eric. "A Spectacle of Color: The Lesbian and Gay Subculture of Jazz Age Harlem." In *Hidden from History: Reclaiming the Gay and Lesbian Past,* ed. Martin Duberman, Martha Vicinus, and George Chauncey, Jr., 318–31. New York: New American Library, 1990.

Garber, Marjorie. *Vested Interests: Cross-dressing and Cultural Anxiety.* New York: Harper-Perennial, 1993.

Gates, Henry Louis, Jr. *Loose Canons: Notes on the Culture Wars.* New York: Oxford University Press, 1992.

———. *The Signifying Monkey: A Theory of African-American Literary Criticism.* New York: Oxford University Press, 1988.

———. "Talkin' That Talk." In *"Race," Writing, and Difference,* ed. Henry Louis Gates, Jr., 402–409. Chicago: University of Chicago Press, 1986.

Gilbert, Sandra M., and Susan Gubar. *Sexchanges.* Vol. 2 of *No Man's Land: The Place of the Woman Writer in the Twentieth Century,* 3 vols. projected. New Haven: Yale University Press, 1989.

Gilroy, Paul. "Route Work: The Black Atlantic and the Politics of Exile." In *The Post-Colonial Question: Common Skies, Divided Horizons,* Eds. Iain Chambers and Lidia Curti, 17–29. London: Routledge, 1996.

Giroux, Henry A. *Living Dangerously: Multiculturalism and the Politics of Difference.* New York: P. Lang, 1996.

Goldensohn, Lorrie. *Elizabeth Bishop: The Biography of a Poetry.* New York: Columbia University Press, 1992.

Gooch, Brad. *City Poet: The Life and Times of Frank O'Hara.* New York: Alfred A. Knopf, 1993.

Graves, Richard Perceval. *A. E. Housman: The Scholar-Poet.* New York: Charles Scribner's Sons, 1979.

Grey, Thomas C. *The Wallace Stevens Case: Law and the Practice of Poetry.* Cambridge, Mass.: Harvard University Press, 1991.

Grosz, Elizabeth. "Experimental Desire: Rethinking Queer Subjectivity." In *Supposing the Subject,* ed. Joan Copjec, 133–57. S_1. New York: Routledge, 1994.

Gunn, Giles. "Religion and the Recent Revival of Pragmatism." In *The Revival of Prag-matism: New Essays on Social Thought, Law, and Culture,* ed. Morris Dickstein, 404–17. Durham: Duke University Press, 1998.

———. *Thinking across the American Grain: Ideology, Intellect, and the New Pragmatism.* Chicago: University of Chicago Press, 1992.

H.D. [Hilda Doolittle]. *Collected Poems: 1912–1944.* Ed. Louis L. Martz. New York: New Directions, 1983.

Hall, Stuart. "Cultural Studies and Its Theoretical Legacies." In *Cultural Studies,* ed. Lawrence Grossberg, Cary Nelson, and Paula Treichler, 277–94. New York: Routledge, 1992.

———. "Ethnicity: Identity and Difference." *Radical America* 23 (fall 1989): 9–20.

———. "When Was 'The Post-Colonial'? Thinking at the Limit." In *The Post-Colonial Question: Common Skies, Divided Horizons,* ed. Iain Chambers and Lidia Curti, 242–60. London: Routledge, 1996.

Halperin, David. *Saint Foucault: Towards a Gay Hagiography.* New York: Oxford University Press, 1995.

Harpham, Geoffrey Galt. "So . . . What Is Enlightenment? An Inquisition into Modernity." *Critical Inquiry* 20 (spring 1994): 524–56.

Harrison, Victoria. *Elizabeth Bishop's Poetics of Intimacy.* New York: Cambridge University Press, 1993.

Hawkins, Susan E. "Sneak Previews: Gertrude Stein's Syntax in *Tender Buttons.*" In *Gertrude Stein and the Making of Literature,* ed. Shirley Neuman and Ira B. Nadel, 119–23. Boston: Northeastern University Press, 1988.

Hocquenghem, Guy. *Homosexual Desire.* Trans. Caniella Dangor. Durham: Duke University Press, 1993.

Hoffman, Daniel, ed. *Ezra Pound and William Carlos Williams: The University of Pennsylvania Conference Papers.* Philadelphia: University of Pennsylvania Press, 1983.

Hollier, Denis. *Against Architecture: The Writings of Georges Bataille.* Cambridge, Mass.: MIT Press, 1992.

Hopkins, Gerard Manley. *Further Letters of Hopkins.* 2d ed. Ed. C. C. Abbott. London: Oxford University Press, 1956.

———. *Poems and Prose of Gerard Manley Hopkins.* Ed. W. H. Gardner. New York: Penguin Books, 1990.

Horkheimer, Max, and Theodor W. Adorno. *Dialectic of Enlightenment.* Trans. John Cumming. New York: Seabury Press, Continuum, n.d.

Housman, A. E. *The Collected Poems.* London: Jonathan Cape, 1971.

Howard, Richard. "Frank O'Hara: 'Since Once We Are We Always Will Be in This Life Come What May.'" In *Frank O'Hara: To Be True to a City,* ed. Jim Elledge, 105–24. Ann Arbor: University of Michigan Press, 1993.

Howe, Irving. *The Decline of the New.* New York: Horizon Press, 1970.

Hubert, Renée Riese. "Paul Klee: Modernism in Art and Literature." In *Modernism: Chal-*

lenges and Perspectives, ed. Monique Chefdor, Ricardo Quinones, and Albert Wachtel. Urbana: University of Illinois Press, 1986.

Hudson, Theodore R. "Technical Aspects of the Poetry of Langston Hughes." *Black World* (1973): 24–45.

Hughes, Langston. *The Collected Poems of Langston Hughes.* Ed. Arnold Rampersad. New York: Vintage Books, 1994.

Hurston, Zora Neale. *Their Eyes Were Watching God.* New York: Harper and Row, 1990.

Hutcheon, Linda. *Irony's Edge: The Theory and Politics of Irony.* New York: Routledge, 1994.

Huyssen, Andreas. *After the Great Divide: Modernism, Mass Culture, Postmodernism.* Theories of Representation and Difference. Bloomington: Indiana University Press, 1986.

Imbriglio, Catherine. "'Our Days Put on Such Reticence': The Rhetoric of the Closet in John Ashbery's *Some Trees.*" *Contemporary Literature* 36, no. 2 (1995): 249–88.

Irigaray, Luce. *This Sex Which is not One.* Trans. Catherine Porter. Ithaca: Cornell University Press, 1985.

Irwin, John T. *Doubling and Incest/Repetition and Revenge: A Speculative Reading of Faulkner.* Baltimore: Johns Hopkins University Press, 1977.

James, William. "Philosophical Conceptions and Practical Results." In *William James, Writings, 1878–1899,* Comp. and ed. Gerald E. Myers, 1077–97. New York: Library of America, 1992.

———. *Pragmatism and Four Essays from "The Meaning of Truth."* New York: New American Library, 1974.

———. "What Pragmatism Means." In *Pragmatism, and Four Essays from "The Meaning of Truth",* 41–62. New York: New American Library, 1974.

Jameson, Fredric. "Cognitive Mapping." In *Marxism and the Interpretation of Culture,* ed. and intro. Cary Nelson and Lawrence Grossberg, 347–60. Urbana: University of Illinois Press, 1988.

Jarraway, David. "Review of *Elizabeth Bishop: Life and the Memory of It* by Brett C. Millier (1993)." *Journal of Canadian Poetry* 10 (1995): 140–46.

———. "Saint Elizabeth." Review of *Elizabeth Bishop One Art: Letters,* sel. and ed. Robert Giroux (1994), and *Remembering Elizabeth Bishop,* by Gary Fountain and Peter Brazeau (1994). *MLA Lesbian and Gay Studies Newsletter* 22 (summer 1995): 30–32.

Jarraway, David R. "Ammons Beside Himself: Poetics of 'The Bleak Periphery.'" *Arizona Quarterly* 49 (winter 1993): 99–116.

———. "The Novelty of Revolution/The Revolution of Novelty: Williams' First Fiction." *William Carlos Williams Review* 18 (spring 1992): 21–33.

———. *Wallace Stevens and the Question of Belief: "Metaphysician in the Dark."* Baton Rouge: Louisiana State University Press, 1993.

Jay, Martin. *Adorno.* Cambridge, Mass.: Harvard University Press, 1984.

Jeme, Onwucheka. *Langston Hughes: An Introduction to the Poetry.* New York: Columbia University Press, 1976.

Julien, Isaac. "Filling the Lack in Everybody Is Quite Hard Work, Really . . . : A Roundtable Discussion with Joy Chamberlain, Isaac Julien, Stuart Marshall, and Pratibha Parmer." In *Queer Looks: Perspectives on Lesbian and Gay Film and Video*, ed. Martha
Gever, Pratibha Parmer, and John Greyson, 41–60. New York: 1993.

Kalstone, David. *Becoming a Poet: Elizabeth Bishop with Marianne Moore and Robert Lowell.* Ed. and preface by Robert Hemenway, afterword by James Merrill. New York:
Noonday Press, 1989.

———. *Five Temperaments: Elizabeth Bishop, Robert Lowell, James Merrill, Adrienne Rich,
John Ashbery.* New York: Oxford University Press, 1977.

Kennedy, Elizabeth Lapovsky, and Madeline D. Davis. *Boots of Leather, Slippers of Gold:
The History of a Lesbian Community.* New York: Penguin Books, 1993.

Kikel, Rudy. "The Gay Frank O'Hara." In *Frank O'Hara: To Be True to a City*, ed. Jim
Elledge, 334–49. Ann Arbor: University of Michigan Press, 1993.

Kristeva, Julia. *Revolution in Poetic Language.* Trans. Margaret Waller, intro. Leon S. Roudiez. New York: Columbia University Press, 1984.

———. *Tales of Love.* Trans. Leon S. Roudiez. New York: Columbia University Press,
1987.

Laclau, Ernesto, and Chantal Mouffe. *Hegemony and Socialist Strategy: Towards a Radical
Democratic Politics.* 1985. Reprint, New York: Verso, 1989.

Langbauer, Laurie. "Cultural Studies and the Politics of the Everyday." *Diacritics* 20 (winter 1992): 47–65.

Lauter, Paul. "Race and Gender in the Shaping of the American Literary Canon: A Case
from the Twenties." In *Feminist Criticism and Social Change*, ed. Judith Newton and
Deborah Rosenfelt, 19–44. New York: Methuen, 1985.

Lawrence, D. H. *Studies in Classic American Literature.* Harmondsworth, Middlesex,
Eng.: Penguin Books, 1971.

Lehman, David. "'In Prison': A Paradox Regained." In *Elizabeth Bishop and Her Art*, ed.
Lloyd Schwartz and Sybil P. Estess, 61–74. Ann Arbor: University of Michigan Press,
1983.

Lensing, George S. "Wallace Stevens and Elizabeth Bishop: The Way a Poet Should See,
the Way a Poet Should Think." Special issue on Wallace Stevens and Elizabeth
Bishop. Guest-edited by Jacqueline Vaught Brogan. *Wallace Stevens Journal* 19 (fall
1995): 115–32.

Lentricchia, Frank. *Modernist Quartet.* New York: Cambridge University Press, 1994.

Levenson, Michael H. *A Genealogy of Modernism: A Study of English Literary Doctrine,
1908–1922.* New York: Cambridge University Press, 1984.

Leverich, Lyle. *TOM: The Unknown Tennessee Williams.* New York: Crown Publishers,
1995.

Lewis, David Levering. *When Harlem Was in Vogue.* New York: Oxford University Press,
1989.

Libby, Anthony. "O'Hara on the Silver Range." In *Frank O'Hara: To Be True to a City*,
ed. Jim Elledge, 131–55. Ann Arbor: University of Michigan Press, 1993.

Lombardi, Marilyn May, ed. *Elizabeth Bishop: The Geography of Gender*. Charlottesville: University of Virginia Press, 1993.

———. *The Body and the Song: Elizabeth Bishop's Poetics*. Carbondale: Southern Illinois University Press, 1995.

Longenbach, James. *Stone Cottage: Pound, Yeats, and Modernism*. New York: Oxford University Press, 1988.

Lowney, John. "Langston and the 'Nonsense' of Bop." *American Literature* 72 (spring 2000): 357–85.

McCabe, Susan. *Elizabeth Bishop: Her Poetics of Loss*. University Park: Pennsylvania State University Press, 1994.

McClintock, Anne, Aamir Mufti, and Ella Shohat. Introduction to *Dangerous Liaisons: Gender, Nation, and Postcolonial Perspectives*, ed. Anne McClintock, Aamir Mufti, and Ella Shohat, 1–12. Cultural Politics, vol. 11. Minneapolis: University of Minnesota Press, 1997.

Mariani, Paul. *William Carlos Williams: A New World Naked*. New York: McGraw-Hill, 1981.

Martin, Biddy. "Lesbian Identity and Autobiographical Difference[s]." In *The Lesbian and Gay Studies Reader*, ed. Henry Abelove, Michèle Aina Barale, and David M. Halperin, 274–93. New York: Routledge, 1993.

Martin, Robert Bernard. *Gerard Manley Hopkins: A Very Private Life*. New York: G. P. Putnam's Sons, 1991.

Martin, Robert K. "*The Mother of Us All* and American History." In *Gertrude Stein and the Making of Literature*, ed. Shirley Neuman and Ira B. Nadel, 210–22. Boston: Northeastern University Press, 1988.

———. "Roland Barthes: Toward an '*Ecriture Gaie*.'" In *Camp Grounds: Style and Homosexuality*, ed. David Bergman, 282–98. Amherst: University of Massachusetts Press, 1993.

Martin, Ronald E. *American Literature and the Destruction of Knowledge: Innovative Writing in the Age of Epistemology*. Durham: Duke University Press, 1991.

Mellow, James R. *Charmed Circle: Gertrude Stein and Company*. New York: Avon Books, 1974.

Melville, Stephen. "Oblique and Ordinary: Stanley Cavell's Engagements of Emerson." *American Literary History* 5 (spring 1993): 172–92.

Merck, Mandy. *Perversions: Deviant Readings*. New York: Routledge, 1993.

Miller, Baxter. *The Art and Imagination of Langston Hughes*. Lexington: University of Kentucky Press, 1989.

Miller, J. Hillis. "Williams." In *The Linguistic Moment: From Wordsworth to Stevens*, 349–89. Princeton, Princeton University Press, 1985.

Millier, Brett C. *Elizabeth Bishop: Life and the Memory of It*. Los Angeles: University of California Press, 1993.

Minh-Ha, Trinh T. "Documentary Is/Not a Name." *October* 52 (1990): 76–100.

———. *When the Moon Waxes Red: Representation, Gender, and Cultural Politics.* London: Routledge, 1991.

Molesworth, Charles. "'The Clear Architecture of the Nerves': The Poetry of Frank O'Hara." In *Frank O'Hara: To Be True to a City,* ed. Jim Elledge, 209–25. Ann Arbor: University of Michigan Press, 1993.

Montag, Warren. "The Emptiness of a Distance Taken: Freud, Althusser, Lacan." *Rethinking MARXISM* 4 (spring 1991):31–38.

Morrison, Toni. *Nobel Lecture: 1993.* Ottawa, Canada: Nobel Foundation, Courtesy of the Swedish Embassy, 1993.

———. *Playing in the Dark: Whiteness and the Literary Imagination.* Cambridge, Mass.: Harvard University Press, 1992.

Mouffe, Chantal. "The Civics Lesson." *New Statesman and Society* 7 (October 1988): 28–31.

Nadel, Alan. "God's Law and the Wide Screen: *The Ten Commandments* as Cold War 'Epic.'" *PMLA* 108 (May 1993): 415–30.

Nadel, Ira B. "Gertrude Stein and Henry James." In *Gertrude Stein and the Making of Literature,* ed. Shirley Neuman and Ira B. Nadel, 81–97. Boston: Northeastern University Press, 1988.

Nelson, Cary. *Repression and Recovery: Modern American Poetry and the Politics of Cultural Memory, 1910–1945.* Madison: University of Wisconsin Press, 1989.

Neuman, Shirley. "'Would a Viper Have Stung Her If She Had Only One Name?' *Doctor Faustus Lights the Lights.*" In *Gertrude Stein and the Making of Literature,* ed. Shirley Neuman and Ira B. Nadel, 168–93. Boston: Northeastern University Press, 1988.

Newton, Esther. *Cherry Grove, Fire Island: Sixty Years in America's First Gay and Lesbian Town.* Boston: Beacon Press, 1993.

Nietzsche, Friedrich. *Beyond Good and Evil: Prelude to a Philosophy of the Future.* Trans. R. J. Hollingdale. Harmondsworth, Eng.: Penguin, 1979.

———. *The Gay Science.* Trans. and commentary by Walter Kaufmann. New York: Random House, Vintage Books, 1974.

O'Hara, Frank. *Art Chronicles: 1954–1966.* New York: George Braziller, 1975.

———. *The Collected Poems of Frank O'Hara.* Ed. Donald Allen, intro. John Ashbery. New York: Alfred A. Knopf, 1972.

———. *Standing Still and Walking in New York.* Ed. Donald Allen. San Francisco: Grey Fox Press, 1983.

Oates, Joyce Carol. *(Woman) Writer: Occasions and Opportunities.* New York: E. P. Dutton, 1988.

Omi, Michael, and Howard Winant. "By the Rivers of Babylon: Race in the United States (Part 1)." *Socialist Review* 71 (September-October 1983):50–65.

———. "On the Theoretical Concept of Race." In *Race, Identity, and Representation in Education,* ed. Cameron McCarthy and Warren Crichlow, 3–10. New York: Routledge, 1993.

Ostriker, Alicia. "I Am (Not) This: Erotic Discourse in Bishop, Olds, and Stevens." Special issue on Wallace Stevens and Elizabeth Bishop. Guest-edited by Jacqueline Vaught Brogan. *Wallace Stevens Journal* 19 (fall 1995): 234–54.

Page, Barbara. "Elizabeth Bishop and Postmodernism." Special issue on Wallace Stevens and Elizabeth Bishop. Guest-edited by Jacqueline Vaught Brogan. *Wallace Stevens Journal* 19 (fall 1995): 166–79.

Parker, Robert Dale. *The Unbeliever: The Poetry of Elizabeth Bishop.* Urbana: University of Illinois Press, 1988.

Pease, Donald. *Visionary Compacts: American Renaissance Writings in Cultural Context.* Madison: University of Wisconsin Press, 1987.

Perloff, Marjorie. "Frank O'Hara and the Aesthetics of Attention." In *Frank O'Hara: To Be True to a City,* ed. Jim Elledge, 156–88. Ann Arbor: University of Michigan Press, 1993.

——. *Frank O'Hara: Poet among Painters.* New York: George Braziller, 1977.

——. "(Im)personating Gertrude Stein." In *Gertrude Stein and the Making of Literature,* ed. Shirley Neuman and Ira Nadel, 61–80. Boston: Northeastern University Press, 1988.

——. *The Poetics of Indeterminacy: Rimbaud to Cage.* Evanston, Ill.: Northwestern University Press, 1983.

Philipson, Ilene. "What's the Big I.D.? The Politics of the Authentic Self." *Tikkun* 6 (1991): 51–55.

Poirier, Richard. *Poetry and Pragmatism.* Cambridge, Mass.: Harvard University Press, 1992.

——. "Why Do Pragmatists Want to Be Like Poets?" In *The Revival of Pragmatism: New Essays on Social Thought, Law, and Culture,* ed. Morris Dickstein, 347–61. Durham: Duke University Press, 1998.

Porter, Carolyn. *Seeing and Being: The Plight of the Participant Observer in Emerson, James, Adams, and Faulkner.* Middletown, Conn.: Wesleyan University Press, 1981.

Posnock, Ross. *Color and Culture: Black Writers and the Making of the Modern Intellectual.* Cambridge, Mass.: Harvard University Press, 1998.

——. "The Politics of Nonidentity: A Genealogy." In "New Americanists 2: National Identities and Postnational Narratives," special issue, ed. Donald Pease. *Boundary 2* 19 (spring 1992): 34–68.

——. *The Trial of Curiosity: Henry James, William James, and the Challenge of Modernity.* New York: Oxford University Press, 1991.

Pound, Ezra. *Selected Poems.* Ed. and intro. T. S. Eliot. London: Faber and Faber, 1973.

Probyn, Elspeth. *Sexing the Self: Gendered Positions in Cultural Studies.* New York: Routledge, 1993.

Rambuss, Richard. "Homodevotion." In *Cruising the Performative: Interventions into the Representation of Ethnicity, Nationality, and Sexuality,* ed. Sue-Ellen Case, Philip Brett, and Susan Leigh Foster, 71–89. Bloomington: Indiana University Press, 1995.

Rampersad, Arnold. *The Life of Langston Hughes.* Vol. 2, *1941–1967, I Dream a World.* New York: Oxford University Press, 1988.

———. *The Life of Langston Hughes.* Vol. 1, *1902–1941, I, Too, Sing America.* New York: Oxford University Press, 1986.

Reimonenq, Alden. "Countee Cullen's Uranian 'Soul Windows.'" *Journal of Homosexuality* 24 (spring-summer 1993): 143–65.

Reynolds, David S. *Walt Whitman's America: A Cultural Biography.* New York: Alfred A. Knopf, 1995.

Rich, Adrienne. "Compulsory Heterosexuality and Lesbian Existence." In *The Lesbian and Gay Studies Reader,* ed. Henry Abelove, Michèle Aina Barale, and David M. Halperin, 227–54. New York: Routledge, 1993.

Riddel, Joseph N. *The Inverted Bell: Modernism and the Counterpoetics of William Carlos Williams.* Baton Rouge: Louisiana State University Press, 1991.

Rogin, Michael Paul. *Subversive Genealogy: The Politics and Art of Herman Melville.* Berkeley: University of California Press, 1985.

Rorty, Richard. *Consequences of Pragmatism: Essays, 1972–1980.* Minneapolis: University of Minnesota Press, 1982.

———. "Pragmatism as Romantic Polytheism." In *The Revival of Pragmatism: New Essays on Social Thought, Law, and Culture,* ed. Morris Dickstein, 21–36. Durham: Duke University Press, 1998.

Rose, Jaqueline. *Sexuality in the Field of Vision.* New York: Verso, 1986.

Rubin, Gayle. "Thinking Sex: Notes for a Radical Theory of the Politics of Sexuality." In *Pleasure and Danger: Exploring Female Sexuality,* ed. Carole S. Vance, 267–319. London: Pandora, 1989.

Runzo, Sandra. "Dickinson, Performance, and the Homoerotic Lyric." *American Literature* 68 (June 1996): 347–63.

Said, Edward. "An Ideology of Difference." In *"Race," Writing, and Difference,* ed. Henry Louis Gates, Jr., 38–58. Chicago: University of Chicago Press, 1986.

———. "Reflections on Exile." In *Out There: Marginalization and Contemporary Cultures,* ed. Russell Ferguson, Martha Gever, Trinh T. Minh-ha, and Cornel West, 357–62. Cambridge, Mass.: MIT Press, 1992.

Sanger, Peter. "Elizabeth Bishop and Nova Scotia." *Antigonish Review* 60 (1985): 15–27.

Savran, David. *Communists, Cowboys, and Queers: The Politics of Masculinity in the Work of Arthur Miller and Tennessee Williams.* Minneapolis: University of Minnesota Press, 1992.

Sayre, Henry M. "The Artist's Model: American Art and the Question of Looking like Gertrude Stein." In *Gertrude Stein and the Making of Literature,* ed. Shirley Neuman and Ira B. Nadel, 21–41. Boston: Northeastern University Press, 1988.

Schmidt, Peter. *William Carlos Williams, the Arts, and Literary Tradition.* Baton Rouge: Louisiana State University Press, 1988.

Schmitz, Neil. "The Difference of Her Likeness: Gertrude Stein's *Stanzas in Meditation.*" In *Gertrude Stein and the Making of Literature,* ed. Shirley Neuman and Ira B. Nadel, 124–49. Boston: Northeastern University Press, 1988.

Schor, Naomi. *Reading in Detail: Aesthetics and the Feminine.* New York: Routledge, 1987.

Schwartz, Lloyd, and Sybil P. Estess, eds. *Elizabeth Bishop and Her Art.* Ann Arbor: University of Michigan Press, 1983.

Schwartzwald, Robert. "'Symbolic' Homosexuality, 'False Feminine,' and the Problematics of Identity in Quebec." In *Fear of a Queer Planet: Queer Politics and Social Theory,* ed. Michael Warner, 264–99. Minneapolis: University of Minnesota Press, 1993.

Scobie, Stephen. "The Allure of Multiplicity: Metaphor and Metonymy in Cubism and Gertrude Stein." In *Gertrude Stein and the Making of Literature,* ed. Shirley Neuman and Ira B. Nadel, 98–118. Boston: Northeastern University Press, 1988.

Sedgwick, Eve Kosofsky. *Epistemology of the Closet.* Los Angeles: University of California Press, 1990.

———. "How to Bring Your Kids Up Gay." In *Fear of a Queer Planet: Queer Politics and Social Theory,* ed. Michael Warner, 69–81. Minneapolis: University of Minnesota Press, 1993.

Shaviro, Steven. *Passion and Excess: Blanchot, Bataille, and Literary Theory.* Tallahassee: Florida State University Press, 1990.

Silverman, Kaja. *The Threshold of the Visible World.* New York: Routledge, 1996.

Souhami, Diana. *Gertrude and Alice.* London: Pandora Press, 1991.

Spillers, Hortense. "'All the Things You Could Be by Now, If Sigmund Freud's Wife Was Your Mother': Psychoanalysis and Race." *Boundary 2* 23 (summer 1996): 75–141.

Spraggs, Gillian. "Hell and the Mirror: A Reading of Desert of the Heart." In *New Lesbian Criticism: Literary and Cultural Readings,* ed. and intro. Sally Munt, 115–31. New York: Columbia University Press, 1992.

Stein, Edward, ed. *Forms of Desire: Sexual Orientation and the Social Constructionist Controversy.* New York: Routledge, 1992.

Stein, Gertrude. *The Geographical History of America, or the Relation of Human Nature to Human Mind.* Intro. William H. Gass. New York: Vintage Books, 1973.

———. *Geography and Plays.* Intro. Cyrena N. Pondrom. Madison: University of Wisconsin Press, 1993.

———. *Lectures in America.* New York, Random House.

———. "Poetry and Grammar." In *Lectures in America,* intro. Wendy Steiner. New York: Random House, 1935; Boston: Beacon Press, 1985.

———. *Selected Writings of Gertrude Stein.* Ed. and intro. Carl Van Vechten. New York: Vintage Books, 1972.

Stein, Kevin. "'Everything the Opposite': A Literary Basis for the Anti-Literary in Frank O'Hara's *Lunch Poems.*" In *Frank O'Hara: To Be True to a City,* ed. Jim Elledge, 358–72. Ann Arbor: University of Michigan Press, 1993.

Steinman, Lisa. "Once More with Feeling: Teaching *Spring and All.*" *William Carlos Williams Review* 10 (spring 1984): 7–12.

Stendhal, Renate. "Stein's Style: A Passion for Sentences." *Harvard Gay and Lesbian Review* 2 (spring 1995): 18–20.

Stevens, Wallace. *The Collected Poems of Wallace Stevens.* New York: Random House, 1954.

Stimpson, Catharine R. "Afterword: Lesbian Studies in the 1990s." In *Lesbian Texts and Contexts: Radical Revisions,* ed. Karla Jay and Joanne Glasgow, 377–82. New York: New York University Press, 1990.

———. "The Somograms of Gertrude Stein." In *The Lesbian and Gay Studies Reader,* ed. Henry Abelove, Michèle Aina Barale, and David M. Halperin, 642–52. New York: Routledge, 1993.

Suleiman, Susan Rubin. *Subversive Intent: Gender, Politics, and the Avant-garde.* Cambridge, Mass.: Harvard University Press, 1990.

Taylor, Charles. *Sources of the Self: The Making of the Modern Identity.* Cambridge, Mass.: Harvard University Press, 1989.

Torgovnick, Marianna. *Gone Primitive: Savage Intellects, Modern Lives.* Chicago: University of Chicago Press, 1991.

Travisano, Thomas J. *Elizabeth Bishop: Her Artistic Development.* Charlottesville: University of Virginia Press, 1989.

Twichell, Chase. "Everything Only Connected by 'And' and 'And': The Skewed Narrative of Elizabeth Bishop." *NER/BLQ* 8, no. 1 (1985): 130–37.

Vance, Carole S. "Pleasure and Danger: Toward a Politics of Sexuality." In *Pleasure and Danger: Exploring Female Sexuality,* ed. Carole S. Vance, 1–27. London: Pandora, 1989.

Vattimo, Gianni. *The End of Modernity: Nihilism and Hermeneutics in Postmodern Culture.* Trans. and intro. Jon R. Snyder. Baltimore: Johns Hopkins University Press, 1988.

Vendler, Helen. "Domestication, Domesticity, and the Otherworldly." In *Elizabeth Bishop and Her Art,* ed. Lloyd Schwartz and Sybil P. Estess, 32–48. Ann Arbor: University of Michigan Press, 1983.

———. "Frank O'Hara: The Virtue of the Alterable." In *Frank O'Hara: To Be True to a City,* ed. Jim Elledge, 234–52. Ann Arbor: University of Michigan Press, 1993.

Walker, Jayne L. *The Making of a Modernist: Gertrude Stein, from "Three Lives" to "Tender Buttons."* Amherst: University of Massachusetts Press, 1984.

Warren, Mark. *Nietzsche and Political Thought.* Cambridge, Mass.: MIT Press, 1991.

Weaver, Mike. *William Carlos Williams: The American Background.* Cambridge, Eng.: Cambridge University Press, 1977.

West, Cornel. *The American Evasion of Philosophy.* Madison: University of Wisconsin Press, 1989.

———. "The New Cultural Politics of Difference." In *Beyond a Dream Deferred: Multicultural Education and the Politics of Excellence,* ed. Becky W. Thompson and Sangeeta Tyagi, 18–40. Minneapolis: University of Minnesota Press, 1993.

Westbrook, Robert B. *John Dewey and American Democracy.* Ithaca: Cornell University Press, 1991.

Wheeler, Kathleen. *Romanticism, Pragmatism, and Deconstruction.* Oxford: Blackwell Publishers, 1993.

Williams, Patricia J. *The Alchemy of Race and Rights: Diary of a Law Professor.* Cambridge, Mass.: Harvard University Press, 1991.

Williams, Raymond. *Marxism and Literature.* Oxford: Oxford University Press, 1977.

Williams, William Carlos. *The Autobiography of William Carlos Williams.* New York: New Directions, 1967.

———. *The Collected Poems of William Carlos Williams.* vol. 1: *1909–1939.* Ed. A. Walton Litz and Christopher MacGowan. New Directions, 1986.

———. *Selected Essays of William Carlos Williams.* New York: New Directions, 1969.

———. *The Selected Letters of William Carlos Williams.* Ed. John C. Thirlwall. New York: New Directions, 1984.

Winant, Howard. "Postmodern Racial Politics in the United States: Difference and Inequality." *Socialist Review* 20 (January 1990): 121–47.

Wolfe, Cary. *Critical Environments: Postmodern Theory and the Pragmatics of the "Outside".* Theory Out of Bounds, vol. 13. Minneapolis: University of Minnesota Press, 1998.

Wolfe, Cary, and Jonathan Elmer. "Subject to Sacrifice: Ideology, Psychoanalysis, and the Discourse of Species in Jonathan Demme's *Silence of the Lambs.*" *Boundary 2* 22 (fall 1995): 141–70.

Wonham, Henry B. "Writing Realism, Policing Consciousness: Howells and the Black Body." *American Literature* 67 (fall 1995): 701–24.

Woolf, Virginia. *The Death of the Moth, and Other Essays.* 9–11. London: Hogarth Press, 1981.

Yocum, Demetrio. "Some Troubled Homecomings." In *The Post-Colonial Question: Common Skies, Divided Horizons,* ed. Iain Chambers and Lidia Curti, 221–27. London: Routledge, 1996.

Young, Robert. *White Mythologies: Writing History and the West.* New York: Routledge, 1990.

Zimmerman, Bonnie. "Lesbians Like This and That: Some Notes on Lesbian Criticism for the Nineties." In *New Lesbian Criticism: Literary and Cultural Readings,* ed. and intro. Sally Munt, 1–15. New York: Columbia University Press, 1992.

Žižek, Slavoj. *Enjoy Your Symptom! Jacques Lacan in Hollywood and Out.* New York: Routledge, 1992.

———. *For They Know Not What They Do: Enjoyment as a Political Factor.* New York: Verso, 1991.

———. " 'In His Bold Gaze My Ruin Is Writ Large' " In *Everything You Always Wanted to Know about Lacan (But Were Afraid to Ask Hitchcock),* ed. Slavoj Žižek, 211–72. New York: Verso, 1992.

———. *The Metastases of Enjoyment: Six Essays on Women and Causality.* New York: Verso, 1994.

———. *The Sublime Object of Ideology.* New York: Verso, 1989.

———. *Tarrying with the Negative: Kant, Hegel, and the Critique of Ideology.* Durham: Duke University Press, 1993.

Index

24, 136. *See also* Homosexuality; Lesbianism;
Sexual identity

Homosexuality: of Barthes, 198; black and white
middle class attacks on, 91–92; camp discourse of gay writers, 114–18; and "closeted
openness," 92, 92*n*29; Foucault on, 40*n*29;
gay subjectivity and O'Hara, 121–34; Grosz
on, 157, 159; Hocquenghem on, 35; and ho-
mophobia of Cold War era, 103–5, 103–
5*nn*4–6, 107, 123–24; and Hughes, 88–96,
90–92*nn*27–29; identities of gay men, 128,
128*n*38, 134; and law, 107–8, 192*n*16; of Mathiessen, 104*n*5; middle-class gay men, 92–
93*n*29, 93–94; of O'Hara, 103, 104,
107–8*n*10, 121–22; and queer theory, 15–17,
99–102, 100–101*n*2, 134–38; Steiner on, 35;
and Stonewall riot (1969), 104, 136; and uncontrollability, 39; of writers of Harlem Renaissance, 91, 92–94, 92*n*29. *See also*
Lesbianism; Queer theory; Sexual identity

Hopkins, Gerard Manley, 184, 192–95, 193*n*17,
196, 197

Hopper, Edward, 64

Horney, Karen, 147*n*11

"House in Taos" (Hughes), 96

Housman, A. E., 184, 191–92, 193, 195, 196,
197

Howard, Richard, 114–15*n*20

Howe, Irving, 185

Hubert, Renée Riese, 187*n*9

Huckleberry Finn (Twain), 86–87

Hugh Selwyn Mauberley (Pound), 195

Hughes, Langston: and Africa, 73, 74, 76, 77,
78; and circularity of deferred subjectivity,
82–85; critical response to poetry by, 70*n*2,
71, 88*n*24; darkness in poetry by, 73–74, 76–
78, 95–96; and Harlem ghetto, 76–80, 87;
Jews in poetry by, 76–77, 80; on Negro culture
in America, 71, 71*n*4, 73; and Pragmatism,
72, 83; publisher's response to, 70; referred
versus deferred subjectivity in poetry by,
81–88; sexuality of, 88–96, 90–92*nn*27–29;
subjectivity in poetry by, 80–97; video on,
92*n*29; on Whitman, 84; women in poetry by,
78–80, 81–83, 96

—works: "Afro-American Fragment," 72, 73;
"As I Grew Older," 74; "Ballad of the Girl
Whose Name Is Mud," 79; "Boogie 1 a.m.,"
78; "Border Line," 75; "Café: 3 a.m.," 88–89;
"Ceaseless Rings of Walt Whitman," 84;
"Consider Me," 74; "Cross," 85; "Crossing,"
85; "Deferred," 78; "Desire," 96; "Dime," 78;
"Dream Boogie," 78; "Fantasy in Purple," 75;
"Final Curve," 83–84; "Havana Dreams," 75;
"House in Taos," 96; "Island," 96–97; "Juke
Box Love Song," 79, 81, 83; "Kids in the
Park," 96; "Lament over Love," 79; "Madam
and the Census Man," 80, 83; *Madam to You*,
80, 81; "Merry-Go-Round," 84–85, 88; "Misery," 78–79; *Montage of a Dream Deferred*, 69,
76–77, 87, 96–97; "Mother to Son," 82; "Mulatto," 85; "Negro," 74; "Negro Artist and the
Racial Mountain," 71, 71*n*4; "Negro Mother,"
74, 82; "Neighbor," 95–96; "Projection,"
77–78; "Same in Blues," 78; "Snail," 75;
"Strange Hurt," 96; "Tell Me," 78; "Theme
for English B," 87–88, 88*n*24, 93; *Weary
Blues*, 91

Humanism, 182

Hurston, Zora Neale, 1–4, 5, 73, 76*n*9

Hutcheon, Linda, 132

Huyssen, Andreas, 183, 183–84*n*4

Idealism, 52*n*6

Identity: Adorno on, 14, 49, 86; Butler on,
39*n*27, 87*n*23, 98, 112–13, 113*n*18, 122–
23*n*31, 126; constructed identities in American Modernism, 2–3, 50–51; Costello on
amorphous self, 155; Dewey on, 50–51,
121*n*29; Escoffier on, 86*n*22; evolution of,
through time, 3; Foucault on, 9, 122*n*30;
Freud on, 196*n*21; gay men's identities, 128,
128*n*38, 134; and infinity of selves, 11, 13;
William James on social selves, 122*n*30; Lawrence on, 15; Nietzsche on, 196*n*21; non-
static notion of, 3*n*5; O'Hara's self-characterization and identities, 121–22, 122–23*n*31;
Posnock on American identity, 74; as process
of identification, 3, 7, 8; reconstruction and
reinvention of the self, 9, 9–10*n*14; Schopen-

Laplanche, Jean, 34n20
Lauter, Paul, 70
Law: and sexuality, 107–8, 192n16; Žižek on, 113
Lawrence, D. H., 1, 15, 184
Lectures in America (Stein), 34n20
Lefebvre, Henri, 66, 66n22
Lehman, David, 165n32
Lesbianism: of Bishop, 139–41, 140–41nn1–2, 145, 146–47, 149–50, 154–55, 168, 170–71, 175; and butch role, 132; Cold War scapegoating of, 103–4, 103–4nn4–5; differences in, 89, 89n25; Grosz on, 157, 159; in Hughes' poetry, 88–89; of Miss Breen, 170–71; of Stein, 20–21, 20n3, 35–36, 40–41, 42, 44, 90n27. *See also* Homosexuality; Queer theory; Sexual identity
Lewis, David Levering, 91n28
Lewis, Theophilus, 90n27
Libby, Anthony, 109n12
Lincoln, Abraham, 17n24
Locke, Alain, 71, 73, 89, 91
Lombardi, Marilyn May, 139, 141n2, 162n29
Longenbach, James, 195–96n20
Looking for Langston, 92n29
Lowell, Amy, 195
Lowell, Robert, 115, 116, 141, 152, 167, 175
"Lullaby" (Auden), 186
Lundberg, Ferdinand, 112n16

"Madam and the Census Man" (Hughes), 80, 83
Madam to You (Hughes), 80, 81, 83
Madness and Civilization (Foucault), 105
Mallarmé, Stéphane, 162
"Man and Bottle" (Stevens), 11–13
"Man-Moth" (Bishop), 157–61, 162, 165
"Manuelzinho" (Bishop), 178–79, 180n49
Mapplethorpe, Robert, 16
Mariani, Paul, 56n11
Martin, Robert Bernard, 193n17
Martin, Robert K., 39n27
Mathiessen, F. O., 104n5
McCabe, Susan, 154–55, 159n24
McCarthy, Mary, 109, 109n13
McClintock, Anne, 168n34

McKay, Claude, 91, 92n29, 94
Me, Vashya (Tennessee Williams), 117
"Mechanics of Pretence" (Bishop), 160n26
"Meditations in an Emergency" (O'Hara), 103, 110–11, 115, 122
Meigs, Mary, 140–41n2
Mellow, James R., 21, 43n32
Melville, Herman, 23
Melville, Stephen, 84
"Merry-Go-Round" (Hughes), 84–85, 88
Meyerowitz, Jan, 90
"Milk" (from Stein's *Tender Buttons*), 28–29, 31
Miller, J. Hillis, 58, 58n13, 61
Miller, Jacques-Alain, 43n34
Millier, Brett C., 168
Minh-Ha, Trinh T., 3, 69, 86
Minima Moralia (Adorno), 45, 49, 54, 63–64, 66, 86
"Misery" (Hughes), 78–79
Modernism: Barthes on, 161; and black literature, 70, 79; and cultural criticism, 52; Diggins on, 23; feminist distances of, 183–98; Foucault on, 10–11; High Modernism, 183, 184, 187, 190, 191–92, 195; Huyssen on, 183–84n4; and in-between space, 12, 12–13n17; Jolas on, 24; and male subjectivity, 182–84; Stein on dead modern writers, 34–35; and stream of consciousness, 41–42; and subjectivity generally, 2, 10n14, 182–83; summary on salient aspects of, 189; Taylor on subjectivism, 161–63. *See also* specific authors
Molesworth, Charles, 122
Mondrian, Piet, 115
Monroe, Harriet, 195
Montag, Warren, 5
Montage of a Dream Deferred (Hughes), 69, 76–77, 87, 96–97
Moore, Marianne, 147n11, 154n17, 190
Morrison, Toni, 4, 5, 86–87, 87n23, 167, 178
"Mother to Son" (Hughes), 82
Motherwell, Robert, 102n3
"Motive for Metaphor" (Stevens), 11
Mouffe, Chantal, 17n24, 131, 131n40
"Mrs. Alfred Uruguay" (Stevens), 14n19